International Political Economy Series

General Editor: **Timothy M. Shaw**, Professor and Director, Institute of International Relations, The University of the West Indies, Trinidad & Tobago

Titles include:

Morten Bøås, Marianne H. Marchand and Timothy Shaw (*editors*)
THE POLITICAL ECONOMY OF REGIONS AND REGIONALISM

Paul Bowles and John Harriss (*editors*)
GLOBALIZATION AND LABOUR IN CHINA AND INDIA
Impacts and Responses

James Busumtwi-Sam and Laurent Dobuzinskis
TURBULENCE AND NEW DIRECTION IN GLOBAL POLITICAL ECONOMY

Bill Dunn
GLOBAL RESTRUCTURING AND THE POWER OF LABOUR

Myron J. Frankman
WORLD DEMOCRATIC FEDERALISM
Peace and Justice Indivisible

Fred Gale and Marcus Haward
GLOBAL COMMODITY GOVERNANCE
State Responses to Sustainable Forest and Fisheries Certification

Richard Grant and John Rennie Short (*editors*)
GLOBALIZATION AND THE MARGINS

Graham Harrison (*editor*)
GLOBAL ENCOUNTERS
International Political Economy, Development and Globalization

Adrian Kay and Owain David Williams (*editors*)
GLOBAL HEALTH GOVERNANCE
Crisis, Institutions and Political Economy

Dominic Kelly and Wyn Grant (*editors*)
THE POLITICS OF INTERNATIONAL TRADE IN THE 21st CENTURY
Actors, Issues and Regional Dynamics

Sandra J. MacLean, Sherri A. Brown and Pieter Fourie (*editors*)
HEALTH FOR SOME
The Political Economy of Global Health Governance

Craig N. Murphy (*editor*)
EGALITARIAN POLITICS IN THE AGE OF GLOBALIZATION

Morten Ougaard
THE GLOBALIZATION OF POLITICS
Power, Social Forces and Governance

Jörgen Dige Pedersen
GLOBALIZATION, DEVELOPMENT AND THE STATE
The Performance of India and Brazil Since 1990

K. Ravi Raman and Ronnie D. Lipschutz (*editors*)
CORPORATE SOCIAL RESPONSIBILITY
Comparative Critiques

International Political Economy Series
Series Standing Order ISBN 978–0–333–71708–0 hardcover
Series Standing Order ISBN 978–0–333–71110–1 paperback

You can receive future titles in this series as they are published by placing a standing order. Please contact your bookseller or, in case of difficulty, write to us at the address below with your name and address, the title of the series and one of the ISBNs quoted above.

Customer Services Department, Macmillan Distribution Ltd, Houndmills, Basingstoke, Hampshire RG21 6XS, England

Critical International Political Economy

Dialogue, Debate and Dissensus

Edited by

Stuart Shields

Ian Bruff

Huw Macartney

First published 2011 by
PALGRAVE MACMILLAN

Palgrave Macmillan in the UK is an imprint of Macmillan Publishers Limited, registered in England, company number 785998, of Houndmills, Basingstoke, Hampshire RG21 6XS.

Palgrave Macmillan in the US is a division of St Martin's Press LLC, 175 Fifth Avenue, New York, NY 10010.

Palgrave Macmillan is the global academic imprint of the above companies and has companies and representatives throughout the world.

Palgrave® and Macmillan® are registered trademarks in the United States, the United Kingdom, Europe and other countries.

ISBN 978–0–230–28030–4 hardback

This book is printed on paper suitable for recycling and made from fully managed and sustained forest sources. Logging, pulping and manufacturing processes are expected to conform to the environmental regulations of the country of origin.

A catalogue record for this book is available from the British Library.

A catalog record for this book is available from the Library of Congress.

10   9   8   7   6   5   4   3   2   1
20   19   18   17   16   15   14   13   12   11

Printed and bound in the United States of America

To Jola, Laura and Raquel

Contents

Acknowledgements

As with all such collective endeavours we are indebted to many people. Audiences at three events provided the main sources of inspiration for this volume in the way that they encouraged us to talk and think beyond our theoretical comfort zones. First, the participants at a panel on reconnecting theory and practice at the 2008 annual conference of the British International Studies Association at the University of Exeter. Second, a workshop devoted to the theme 'Critical International Political Economy' at the University of Birmingham in May 2009; many thanks to Jill Steans for organizing the event and the participants in Birmingham for continuing the conversation started in Exeter. Finally, in March 2010 we organized a workshop in Manchester where many of the contributors presented first drafts of their chapters. Thanks to Nicola Entwhistle whose organizational skills ensured the smooth running of the event.

At Palgrave Macmillan, we are grateful to Steven Kennedy, Timothy Shaw and Alexandra Webster for their enthusiastic support for the volume. Thanks to Renée Takken for all her help and to Christina Brian who came on board late in the day to help see the project through to the end. We are also grateful to Fabiola Mieres for her hard work compiling the index.

We would like to extend our appreciation to the International Political Economy working group of the British International Studies Association, and the Manchester Historical Materialism Research Group, as well as the Global Political Economy cluster and the Political Economy Institute at the University of Manchester for their generous support of the project.

Finally, we would like to thank our friends and families for their continued support, tolerance of unorthodox working hours and practices, and ability to force us to talk about topics unrelated to our work. This book is dedicated to them.

Stuart Shields
Ian Bruff
Huw Macartney

Notes on the Contributors

Lucian M. Ashworth is Senior Lecturer in Politics at the University of Limerick, Ireland. His main area of research interest is the history of International Relations theory, with a particular focus on the interwar period. His publications on this subject include three books, of which the most recent, *International Relations Theory and the Labour Party: Intellectuals and Policy Making 1918–1945*, was published by IB Tauris in 2007. He is currently writing a history of international thought for Pearson.

Ian Bruff is Lecturer in European and International Politics in the School of Social Sciences at the University of Manchester, UK. He is the Coordinator of the Critical Political Economy Research Network of the European Sociological Association. He has published widely on European varieties of capitalism, globalization, and social (especially historical materialist) theory. His book *Culture and Consensus in European Varieties of Capitalism: A 'Common Sense' Analysis*, published by Palgrave Macmillan, was shortlisted for the 2008 Book Prize awarded by the International Political Economy working group (IPEG) of the British International Studies Association (BISA) and was IPEG's 2009 nomination for the BISA Susan Strange Book Prize.

Paul Cammack teaches at Manchester Metropolitan University, UK, where he is Head of the Department of Politics and Philosophy. His recent work is on the governance of global capitalism (http://www.politicsofglobalcompetitiveness.net).

Juanita Elias is Research Fellow at the Griffith Asia Institute at Griffith University, Australia. Her research has mainly focused on issues concerning the gendered nature of work and employment in the global economy, with a specific focus on South-East Asia. Her book *Fashioning Inequality: The Multinational Corporation and Gendered Employment in a Globalising World* was published by Ashgate in 2004. Recent research has appeared in the journals *Economy and Society, Third World Quarterly, Men and Masculinities, Review of International Studies* and *Globalizations*. She is also the co-author of the textbook *International Relations: The Basics* (Routledge, 2007), and in 2009 was awarded a four-year Australian

Research Council Future Fellowship for the project 'The gender politics of economic competitiveness in South-East Asia'.

Anita Fischer is a doctoral candidate at the Goethe University Frankfurt, Germany, funded by the Hans-Böckler-Stiftung. Her doctoral thesis analyses the relationship between gender, European anti-discrimination law and the transformation of the nation state. She recently published an article about the interrelation of state, gender and division of labour in an edited volume on Nicos Poulantzas's work (*Staatstheorie vor neuen Herausforderungen: Analyse und Kritik*, edited by Jens Wissel and Stefanie Wöhl, published by Westfälisches Dampfboot).

Randall Germain is Professor of Political Science at Carleton University, Canada. His publications include *The International Organization of Credit: States and Global Finance in the World-Economy* (Cambridge University Press, 1997) and *Global Politics and Financial Governance* (Palgrave Macmillan, 2010). He is the editor of *Globalization and Its Critics: Perspectives from Political Economy* (Palgrave Macmillan, 2000), and co-editor with Michael Kenny of *The Idea of Global Civil Society: Politics and Ethics in a Globalizing Era* (Routledge, 2005). His scholarship has also been published in journals such as the *European Journal of International Relations*, *Global Governance*, *Review of International Studies*, *International Affairs* and *Review of International Political Economy*.

Penny Griffin is Senior Lecturer in International Relations at the University of New South Wales (Sydney, Australia). Her research explores the creation and reproduction of human identity, particularly forms of and assumptions about gendered identity, in the global political economy and includes publications with Palgrave Macmillan (*Gendering the World Bank: Neoliberalism and the Gendered Foundations of Global Governance*) and in the journals *New Political Economy*, the *Review of International Political Economy*, the *British Journal of Politics and International Relations*, the *Australian Journal of International Affairs*, the *International Studies Encyclopedia* and *Globalizations*.

Huw Macartney is Lecturer in International Political Economy at the University of Manchester, UK. His research interests include financial market integration within the EU and Gramscian historical materialism. He is particularly interested in the production and reproduction of neoliberalism in and through contemporary crises. Huw's work has appeared in the *British Journal of Politics & International Relations*, *Review* *of International Studies* and *Politics*, and his book *Variegated Neoliberalism: Convergent Divergence in European Varieties of Capitalism* was recently published by Routledge.

Stuart Shields teaches International Political Economy at the University of Manchester, UK. His research is concerned with critical approaches to international relations/international political economy and post-communist transition. He is the current convenor of the BISA International Political Economy working group (IPEG) and is on the editorial board of the journal *Capital & Class*. His book *The International Political Economy of Transition: Transnational Social Forces and Eastern Central Europe's Transformation* will be published in 2011 by Routledge. Recent work has been published in *Global Society* (2009), *Competition & Change* (2007) and *International Politics* (2006).

Daniela Tepe is Lecturer in European Studies and German at King's College London, UK. Her research is concerned with the absence of a theorizing of the (gendered) state in International Relations and International Political Economy. She is particularly interested in the ways in which historically specific societal discourses and interest constellations are translated into policy. Furthermore, she is interested in the organization of the relationship between social reproduction and reproduction in the global political economy. Her recent publications have appeared in *Review of International Political Economy* (2010) and *Public Administration* (2009).

Owen Worth is Lecturer in International Relations at the University of Limerick, Ireland. He is the Managing Editor of *Capital & Class*, the author of *Hegemony, International Political Economy and Post-Communist Russia* (Ashgate, 2005), and his most recent work was published in *Third World Quarterly*, *Review of International Studies* and *International Politics*.

Introduction: 'Critical' and 'International Political Economy'

Stuart Shields, Ian Bruff and Huw Macartney

Since the late 1970s, International Political Economy (IPE) has tended to be divided into those scholars who focus primarily upon empirical research questions in order to understand the dynamics of actors within the international system, and those who prefer to focus upon an ontological enquiry into its historical evolution. In recent developments this division has been extended into the 'British' and 'American' schools, or more vividly into the division of the 'orthodox/heterodox' or the 'positivist' and the 'critical' (Murphy and Nelson, 2001, 2002; Cohen, 2008a), which in turn has led to concerns that such divisions might be overplayed (Higgott and Watson, 2008). The development of critical perspectives in IPE has brought with it interpretations that have drawn from Marx, Gramsci, Polanyi, Schumpeter and from poststructuralism (especially Foucault), and have been applied to a wide variety of cases. Yet, for all the work done in developing this critical ontology, precisely what binds the diversity of approaches remains confusing, as core analytical categories are too often assumed to be self-evident (for example, the critical method, methodological eclecticism, and a multidisciplinary approach).

Indeed, this could be the reason why, for example, Geoffrey Underhill (2009) views critical IPE as engaged in 'template theorizing' which embodies a selective approach to the real world in order to preserve the purity of the conceptual construct. At the same time, however, it would seem that critical perspectives do, as argued forcefully by Palan (2009) in the same issue of *New Political Economy* on the 'British' school, have something to say – not least because more mainstream scholars did not anticipate the current economic crisis, even in the minimal sense that trouble was brewing through the 2000s. Indeed, the intense self-scrutiny engendered by debates on the state of the discipline is a curious phenomenon given that they are – Palan's contribution excepted – only weakly connected to the economic crisis that so few in IPE anticipated. As such, the timing – in terms of academic debates and empirical events – for a volume dedicated to critical IPE perspectives is more than appropriate.

The challenge posed by and to contributors to this volume is to assess the development of so-called critical IPE and interrogate whether the theoretical innovations that its foundations have been built upon have reached their potential. The most important contribution to the genesis of such an approach was undoubtedly Robert Cox's seminal articles in the early 1980s (Cox, 1981, 1983) and his subsequent monograph (Cox, 1987), and 'Coxians' have sought to develop such an ontology through engaging with 'world order' theory via Gramsci, Polanyi and others (for example, Gill, 2008). In addition, this work has reminded us that the purpose of critical theory differs from that of 'problem-solving theory' inherent within orthodoxy, in that its main aim is to stand back and look at how social interactions have formed historically. However, despite this significant contribution there is a tendency to accept the universality of many of these earlier openings as self-evident, and a reluctance to expand the capacity of ontological enquiries in the manner that other social sciences have often done (including International Relations itself, despite its continued state-centrism: see Jackson, 2008; Lawson and Shilliam, 2010).

The contributions to this book take up these challenges in a number of different ways, but all share a concern that critical IPE has often been less eager when looking to move beyond, for example, Coxian models of analysis, especially when faced with questions such as globalization, hegemony, gender, class and the role of the state. In addition, they are keen to stress that critical IPE remains contested. In discussing the current state of 'critical approaches' to IPE, the contributors aim to bring a number of points to wider discussion, reassessing the purpose of critical approaches and seeking to make a number of contributions to these debates in IPE. Moreover, we follow questions already noted concerning the nature of 'critique', and whether adopting a critical position places certain normative commitments towards the analysis of knowledge and emancipatory research that is all too often underplayed within IPE (Farrands and Worth, 2005).

Such debates also bring us to question why certain theorists (Gramsci, Polanyi, etc.) have been favoured as a point of departure, while others – particularly the Frankfurt School, feminists and geographers (and, of course, there are more) – have largely been ignored. This is not to imply a complete dearth of wider theoretical innovation, but that critical IPE risks closing down opportunities for dialogue, or, as Mark Blyth might frame it, reproducing unquestioned answers that build upon existing bodies of work as opposed to opening up new avenues. Finally, and in light of recent debates on the validity of the 'transnational divide' within the wider IPE community (Ravenhill, 2008), we aim to demonstrate through these contributions that the distinction between the 'critical' and the 'orthodox' is only significant if the 'critical' is geared towards a larger, more substantial body of critical social enquiry and engages with what it means to conduct such enquiry. That is, disputes about methodology presuppose ontological reflection, and to neglect this utterly essential aspect of research – as the *Review of International Political Economy (RIPE)* and *New Political Economy (NPE)* debates on the 'American' and 'British' schools tended to do – makes volumes such as this not just desirable but necessary.

Therefore, an attempt should be made to revisit the notion of the 'critical'. The contributors here all self-consciously situate themselves within critical 'traditions' – note the emphasis on the plural – and approach these studies as scholars outside what is often perceived as orthodox IPE. Indeed, the contributions to this edited volume seek to address the suspicion that the 'transatlantic' debate is serving to prevent dissensus and to put critical thinking in its place – in a closed black box – since it has thus far excluded (intentionally or not) a range of perspectives that offer a more holistic framework than questions of academic nationalism can address (cf. Leander, 2009). For these reasons, the book will provoke further debate on the nature of critical enquiry in IPE and the nature of IPE itself.

In summary, this volume seeks to:

- provide an overview of the contributions made by 'critical' IPE and also its shortcomings;
- suggest a variety of theoretical openings for critical enquiries to develop;
- place the development of the meaning of critique in IPE within the wider context of social science enquiry.

The structure of the book

One of the key aims of the book is to capture the different elements of critique that are, arguably, present in any self-consciously critical work. In the first part on 'Dialogue', the chapters aim to open up IPE's remit – critical or otherwise – in order to (1) consider issues that increase our conceptual reflexivity and thus (2) enrich our understanding of the world. Ashworth begins with the argument that IPE is not a new discipline, even if the label 'IPE' is a recent 'invention'. In particular, he argues that the recovery of a largely forgotten IPE, which was often critical of the western liberal global order at a time when that order was emerging from the ideological conflicts of the early twentieth century, was actually central to the study of international politics at this time. In turn, this is instructive for how we view IPE as a discipline, for it destabilizes some of the assumptions inherent to recent debates. Next, Macartney and Shields provide a contemporary example of how such disciplining processes have hindered a potentially rich dialogue with geographers on the politics and production of space. This suggests an alternative to disputes so often associated with notions of globalization, which in effect leads us to an either/or stance with regard to the continued relevance of the national state. A scalar-relational perspective helps us attain a more sophisticated understanding of these processes. Finally, Griffin's chapter addresses the criticisms often levelled at poststructuralist IPE via an interrogation of the current crisis, arguing that this is an indispensable approach which can make a theoretically and empirically valuable contribution to dialogues on critical IPE. In particular, she focuses on how, in its postcolonial and gendered forms, poststructuralism gives us a historicity to relations of exploitation, domination and force.

The rest of the book progresses to more pointed arguments, thus revealing other aspects of critical scholarship which have, intentionally or not, been excluded or marginalized. The second part on 'Debate' therefore contains chapters whose authors call attention to what they see as unwarranted silences within IPE. Germain argues that IPE falls short because of the way in which it has neglected the issue of subjectivity. This entails taking much more seriously two cardinal aspects of political economy that have been largely absent from discussion: law, or legal frameworks, and culture. However, it goes beyond this, for it also necessitates, as Germain shows through a critical discussion of what he terms the 'new Marxism', an engagement with the eclectic sources of inspiration for Cox's work – particularly Collingwood and Vico – which have not been present elsewhere in critical IPE. Through a focus on another silence, the implicit acceptance across IPE – critical or otherwise – of the state/market dichotomy, Bruff makes a similar argument with recourse to some of Gramsci's writings which are considerably more prevalent in other disciplines. Bruff argues that a truly holistic approach to the international political economy (not IPE – see below for more) would entail a rejection of frameworks that separate out different aspects of the world in which we live into isolated parts, with their own autonomous, intrinsic properties. Consequently, the ability of International Political Economy to study effectively the international political economy is an open question. Finally, Elias reminds us that much IPE, including self-professed critical works, frequently adheres to a gender-neutral approach to world order and the inequalities that pervade it. Therefore, discussions in critical IPE of hegemony are too restrictive, ignoring as they do both the irreducibly masculine nature of hegemony within the global political economy and the inherently multidisciplinary nature of feminist political economy.

The final part, 'Dissensus', moves to the most critical chapters, for – in contrast to the first two sections' emphases on dialogue and unwarranted silences – they assert that a transformed means of understanding the world in which we live is necessary. Otherwise, the notion of 'critical' scholarship will wax and wane in accordance with how it is received elsewhere, rather than through its own dynamics and development. First, Worth claims that the radical impulses of Cox's 1981 *Millennium* article have dissipated through the gradual construction of an 'orthodox' heterodoxy. In particular, the construction of a 'British' school – which places Cox alongside the undoubtedly less critical Susan Strange – sanitizes matters to such an extent that the notion of critique is lost. As stated earlier, this is a foundational aspect of critical theory, for it places normative commitments at the centre of our research. Through this discussion Worth invokes the Frankfurt School, which is at the core of Fischer and Tepe's chapter on critical IPE and feminism. They argue that critical theory has tended to adhere to a 'public' notion of production which privatizes the crucial issues of social reproduction and systemic gender inequalities. This requires us to be much more assertive about the constitutive and non-supplementary role played by profoundly unequal gender relations through a consideration of social reproduction, in order to make the case for a more holistic mode of enquiry. The final chapter goes further, for Cammack seeks to undermine the notion of 'critical IPE' itself, arguing that if one is to be critical then a complete break with IPE is necessary. This is accomplished through a thorough and detailed interrogation of Cohen's (2008a) monograph on IPE, which Cammack argues is built on sand, intellectually speaking, but is a powerful text in terms of institutional power and gatekeeping within the discipline. This means that IPE cannot identify, let alone address, the questions posed by global economic interdependence. Moreover, although IPE proposes 'international political economy' as its object of enquiry, it shies away from what would be required were that to be the case – an analysis of global capitalism at a systemic level.

It may seem odd that a book about 'critical IPE' ends with such a chapter, but critical scholarship is nothing if it is not reflexive, seeking as it does to engage with an irreducibly complex, ever-evolving world (cf. van Apeldoorn et al., 2010), and Cammack's chapter reminds us of the importance of the need to never rest on our laurels. Therefore, this volume will not only serve as an important reminder of the narrower, more mainstream approaches of the scholarship that are neglected in journals and curricula, but it will also destabilize some of the 'orthodox' heterodoxies that have developed over recent years. By giving each section a particular spirit and mode of engagement – dialogue, debate, dissensus – we hope the volume will make a significant contribution to the evolution of International Political Economy and the study of the international political economy.

Part I
Dialogue

1
Missing Voices: Critical IPE, Disciplinary History and H.N. Brailsford's Analysis of the Capitalist International Anarchy

Lucian M. Ashworth

Historical narratives: disciplining disciplines

One of the most effective ways of disciplining a discipline is to control the historical narratives that lay out the nature and origins of a field of study. IPE is no different. The recent disciplinary history of IPE by Benjamin Cohen (2008a) provides a coherent account of the origins of IPE that validates the division of IPE into 'American' and 'British' schools, represents the core question in IPE as the relation between economics and political science, and also tends to marginalize critical IPE. This chapter questions some of the assumptions in Cohen's narrative by looking at the critical IPE of H.N. Brailsford. Brailsford's work not only reveals the deep roots of critical IPE, but also questions Cohen's assumptions about the origins of IPE and IPE's relationship with International Relations (IR).

For Cohen 'IPE was born just a few decades ago. Prior to the 1970s in the English-speaking world economics and political science were treated as entirely different disciplines, each with its own view of international affairs' (ibid., p. 1). IPE for Cohen emerges as a recent attempt to merge economics with political science. Yet, in order to justify his image of IPE after 1970, Cohen also sets the scene with a short 'pre-history' of the field. While only brief, Cohen's presentation of the prehistory of IPE (whether intentionally or not) distances IPE from the broader history of IR and marginalizes critical IPE. For Cohen there is little or no IPE before 1970 because of the later nineteenth-century split between economics and political science, a split that he argues was 'complete' by the early twentieth century: 'By the mid-twentieth century the relation-ship between the two disciplines could best be described as non-existent' (ibid., pp. 18–19). Despite this, Cohen does concede that there was one place where the split had not taken effect, and this was in 'the radical perspectives', exemplified by the work of J.A. Hobson amongst others (ibid., p. 19). A defining feature of the 'radical tradition' is its roots in a fully political economy approach.

Although Cohen accepts that the split between politics and eco-nomics is not manifest in the 'radical tradition', the implication of Cohen's text is that this critical group are a small and marginalized constituency. This chapter argues that Cohen's account of the early twentieth century is flawed. What is more, it succeeds in marginalizing both the role of IR in the IPE story and the prominence of the critical tradition of IPE in the early twentieth century. The implications of this are: (1) to justify Cohen's view that IPE is largely a merger of politics and economics, and (2) to interpret critical IPE as a later 'add-on' to a more orthodox IPE, rather than as a parallel tradition to the more con-servative and liberal approaches. By 'critical tradition' in IPE I mean the use of a thoroughly political economy approach to unmask the struc-tural causes of both inequality and instability within the international system under capitalism. IPE *in general* thus becomes more than just Cohen's integration of market studies with political analysis, and grows to include the use of political economy to understand the structure of the international.

In contrast to Cohen, this chapter argues that there was a recogniz-able IPE prior to 1950, that a major part of this IPE was made up of a critical socialist tradition, and that, far from being a fringe group, this critical IPE was an important part of British intellectual currents in the first half of the twentieth century. Rather than being isolated, this critical tradition was part of a wider canon that included more liberal approaches, and I will analyse this through the work of H.N. Brailsford. Two issues stand out in my analysis of this period that put my account firmly at odds with that of Cohen. First, I argue that those writers, like Brailsford, who were producing a political economy account of interna-tional affairs, were not trying to combine economics and politics in the way that Cohen lays out. Rather, as Cohen implies in his adumbration of the radical tradition, they were taking a rich late nineteenth-century political economy tradition and applying it to the study of international affairs. In this sense writers like Brailsford were creating IPE by merging IR with political economy. Second, I argue that the labels used when we look back at early twentieth-century international thought have blinded us to the fact that there was a recognizable IPE before 1950. The central problem is that Cohen has not taken into account developments in IR. Basically, in interwar Britain the study of international affairs *was* IPE. We now tend to regard the likes of Brailsford, Angell and Woolf (and even Bowman in the US) as early IR scholars, which they are. But they also took a political economy approach to international problems. Put another way, early twentieth-century IR in Britain covered issues and approaches that we would now class as IPE.

Thus, a disciplinary history of IPE has to understand the peculiar nature of IR before 1950, especially in Britain. Basically, major figures in British IR before 1950 – including Norman Angell, J.M. Keynes, Leonard Woolf, J.A. Hobson, Konni Zilliacus and H.N. Brailsford – wrote from an IPE perspective. A number of key texts in IR, including Angell's (1911) *The Great Illusion*, Keynes's (1920) *The Economic Consequences of the Peace* and Woolf's (1928) *Imperialism and Civilization*, used a political economy approach to understand the workings of the international system. At the time, these works were all included under the heading of 'international affairs', and there was no clear separation between this kind of work and analyses that were blatantly less concerned with political economy. It was only gradually that the political economy aspect of IR was eroded between the mid-1930s and early 1940s. Part of this was due partially to the strategic and structural crises associated with the Second World War, and partially to major changes in the make-up of IR that saw it become a far more conservative university-based subject. Thus it was IR, which up until the late 1940s included a wider political economy approach to international questions, that gradually withdrew from dealing with IPE topics. Therefore, the emergence of IPE after 1970 was not the development of a new field, but a reactivation of a political economy approach that IR had largely abandoned by the 1950s. In this sense, Brailsford's international theory was a manifestation of the rich critical political economy tradition that existed in pre-1950s' IR. Brailsford's contemporary popularity and radical credentials invalidate Cohen's claim that politics and economics were almost completely detached, and that the radical tradition of political economy was largely marginalized.

Cohen's disciplinary history of IPE places the origins of the field in a short period during the 1970s. Recent disciplinary histories of international thought have tended to be more open-ended about origins, and increasingly unwilling to fix clear start dates (see Schmidt, 1998; Ashworth, 1999; Williams, 2007; Sylvest, 2009). Instead, they have tended to stress the complex and intertwining continuities and discontinuities that go to forging an academic field and validating its agenda. Cohen has set up a sharp discontinuity of about eight decades in his narrative. Disciplinary histories are never that simple, and a study of Brailsford's critical IPE stands as a case study of a wider set of trends, ignored by Cohen, that point to a greater degree of disciplinary continuity in the study of the emergent global system.

I have divided this chapter into four sections. The first explores the background to Brailsford's work, stressing particularly the influence of both J.A. Hobson and Norman Angell, as well as how his work as a journalist in Macedonia influenced his analysis of the problems that underlay twentieth-century politics. The second section explores the construction of his world view in his best-known work, *The War of Steel and Gold*. It is here that Brailsford showed the strong connections that existed between the state system and capitalism. The third section discusses how he took these ideas and applied them first to his analysis of international organization, and second to his criticisms of western policy towards the fascist powers. Out of this also came Brailsford's analysis and criticism of the emergent American-led western hegemony. The final section assesses the strengths and weaknesses of Brailsford's world view, and discusses the lessons of his story for critical IPE. The value of exploring Brailsford's IPE is twofold. First, it presents a radically different narrative of the history of IPE to the one presented by Cohen; and second, it reveals a largely forgotten critical IPE that developed a criticism of the western liberal global order at a time when that order was emerging from the ideological conflicts of the early twentieth century.

'The knight errant of socialism.' The making of a political economist

In 1958 Labour Party MP and leader Michael Foot wrote a moving tribute to the then recently deceased Brailsford in *Tribune*. For Foot, Brailsford 'must be accounted the greatest Socialist journalist of the century'. Rather than seeing this as hyperbole, Foot regarded his estimation as 'an inadequate tribute to so fine a man'.[1] Born in 1873, Brailsford first worked as a lecturer at Glasgow University (where he had been a student of Gilbert Murray), before going to Greece to fight as a volunteer against the Turks. His experience in the Balkans led him to rethink his attitude towards nationalism. Turning to journalism, he became editor of the Independent Labour Party's periodical *The New Leader*, and later *Reynolds News*. In addition to his articles in *The Manchester Guardian*, *The Nation* and the *New Statesman*, Brailsford wrote many books on a range of topics that included historical and political biography and decolonization, plus works on the Balkans and international affairs. Brailsford once told Michael Foot that it was Shelley who had made him a socialist, and his attitude to the state seems to have been coloured by an appreciation of William Godwin's anarchism; although, unusual amongst his generation of British socialist writers, he was also interested in Marx (Foot, 1958). He had been a friend of Lenin, and had even raised funds for the Bolsheviks in 1902 (Martin, 1958, p. 403), although his belief in the importance of freedom to socialism led him towards democratic socialism and the Labour Party rather than to communism. A member of the Labour Party's influential Advisory Committee on International Questions, he was also active in the Fabian Society.

Brailsford's work in IR was at the confluence of three aspects of his thought: his socialism, which led him to condemn the inequities and inefficiencies of global capitalist interests; his belief in democratic freedoms as an essential element of all political discourse and practice; and his internationalism, which drove him to condemn both nationalism and the international anarchy of states. Through his IR he remained a lifelong advocate of the establishment of a just and democratic system of global governance. In terms of the development of his approach to IR, three influences stand out. The first was the political economy of J.A. Hobson that would form the backbone of his criticism of capitalism, while the second was the work of Norman Angell. Although critical of Angell's less-than-robust attitude to the problems of capitalism, Brailsford was a great admirer of Angell's *The Great Illusion*, and his subsequent *The War of Steel and Gold* was a friendly attempt to take Angell's analysis of the failings of great power foreign policy and give it a more aggressively socialist flavour. The third influence on Brailsford was his work in the Balkans, especially in Turkish Macedonia. Many of Brailsford's ideas on international order were already evident in his 1906 work on the Macedonian question, eight years before he published *The War of Steel and Gold*.

Basically, Brailsford's intellectual debts to Hobson and Angell gave him the tools to develop his radical political economy. From Hobson he took the argument that the capitalist policies of the great powers were a cause of instability. Hobson had argued that the fundamental cause of the new imperialism was domestic policies that served the interests of a rentier elite. In order to keep profits high it was necessary to keep wages low. However, this had the unintended consequence of depressing the home market, and leading to domestic overproduction of both goods and finance. As a result, major capitalist states were forced to seek new markets for their goods and financial surplus through the control of overseas markets. This led to an imperialism that was fundamentally different from the earlier waves of imperial acquisition, and which accounted for the expansion by the major powers into areas that otherwise did not serve the interests of those powers as a whole, but did serve the interests of the owners of financial capital (Hobson, 1902). It was this notion of a national booty capitalism causing instability due to its interests in profit that was further developed by Brailsford, and became the basis of his interpretation of how capitalism had become a cause of modern war. From Angell, Brailsford took the importance of a more international approach to political economy. Angell's examination of the structure of the international system in 1910 had demonstrated how old-fashioned concepts of conquest were now obsolete (1911, ch. 4). Brailsford agreed, but through his reading of Hobson he argued that the great capitalist powers had found a way to dominate others without resort to conquest. Thus, Hobson had given Brailsford the intellectual tools to criticize capitalism, while Angell had demonstrated the extent to which the old forms of international relations were now obsolete.

While Hobson and Angell were scholarly sources of Brailsford's IPE, his intellectual development was also a product of what he had seen during his many trips to the Balkans. Initially going to the Balkans as a classically educated Hellenophile, he soon lost his faith in nationalism. Brailsford still maintained a dislike for what he regarded as Ottoman despotism (1906, p. xi), but his experiences led him to realize that it was not ethnic identities that were the central issue, but rather it was the many local mini-tyrannies and kleptocratic structures using ethnicity that prevented the region from reaching its full potential (ibid., pp. x–xi). Thus, two problems emerged from the Balkan crisis: the chimera of national identity, which solved nothing and made matters worse by separating peoples; and the interests of local elites, which led to social and economic inequalities, and in so doing made war and conflict more likely. In his *Macedonia* Brailsford accepts that the self-interest of elites will prevent the emergence of sensible and equitable structures of government (ibid., p. 332). Yet, the sheer strength of these elite interests was neither a cause for despair nor was it a reason for seeking compromise with these elites. Rather, an understanding of the nature of elite interests was necessary to realize the full strength of the forces ranged against an equitable solution, while compromises with self-interested elites were no road to a fairer and peaceful society. In his later writings Brailsford would doubt capitalism's ability to reform itself, although he remained committed to change via parliamentary politics.

These three strands – the nature of modern capitalism, the nature of the international system, and the problems of nationalism and the tyrannies of elite interests – were welded together into a single view of the international political economy in Brailsford's *The War of Steel and Gold*.

The new wars of the new imperialism

The War of Steel and Gold was wrong in its conclusion, but the source of its error was being ahead of its time. Brailsford agreed with Angell that war for conquest on the European continent now made no sense, but whereas Angell thought that European leaders still suffered under the delusion that war paid, Brailsford argued that the problem was not the use of arms in war between the great powers, but their use to intimidate in an armed peace (1917a, p. 163). As a result of this Brailsford was sceptical of the idea that the European great powers would allow themselves to go to war with each other, while Angell was more worried that they would out of self-delusion. While Angell proved more correct in the immediate prediction of the course of events in Europe, Brailsford's analysis of the armed peace provided an interesting explanation for the emerging shape of the capitalist-dominated world order and its new use for armaments. Brailsford was only wrong about immediate events because the trends he observed were living uncomfortably alongside the earlier ideas of conquest that Angell regarded as outdated but dangerously persistent.

Fundamental to Brailsford's analysis was that the balance of power in 1914 was different from the balance in earlier centuries. He rejected the concept of the balance of power as a 'self-sufficing ideal' that, on its own, could explain state behaviour. Thus, before this concept of a balance of power for power's sake was adopted by a realist IR as the basis of a power-political interpretation of world politics, Brailsford had rejected it as politically naive. Instead, 'Power is sought for certain ends' (1917a, p. 29; see also 1928, p. 29). The nature of the ends of power affects the way that the balance of power is manifest. Since power now lay in finance, rather than land, the struggles between states were now over the control of investment opportunities and market share (1917a, pp. 31–2). This, for Brailsford, explains the shift of conflict from Europe to control of the extra-European world. States had thus become the means by which their elites pushed their own sectional interests. The goal of the new balance of power was not direct control of territories, but rather indirect control through the structures of capitalism and the threat of force through the build-up of armaments (hence the subtitle *A Study of the Armed Peace*). Consequently, a weaker state in the system maintained its independence, but was kept under the economic control of the great powers 'as a human cattle farm' (ibid., p. 72).

Thus, for Brailsford there was an important connection between the international anarchy on the one hand, and capitalist exploitation on the other. The balance of power under the international anarchy served those specific interests that controlled the state: 'it is not national necessities but class interests which condemn us to the armed peace' (ibid., p. 308). The competition over informal control of states and territories had led to the use of armaments as a means of great power intimidation, rather than of conquest. In other words, the overlaying of an industrial capitalist system on top of the nation-state system had fundamentally altered the nature of the international anarchy. Since states did not seek power as an end in itself, but rather as a means towards the ends of the most powerful elements in the state, capitalist interests now directed state power and military force towards indirect economic control rather than towards expensive direct control.

This concept of the changing nature of state power, and its role in developing new forms of imperialism, was not restricted to radical British circles. Indeed, Isaiah Bowman, one of the architects of the US-led global order that took hold after 1945, agreed that the new national economies, with their hunger for vital raw materials, naturally tended towards imperial control of the societies that possessed those raw materials. This, for Bowman, was a radical change from the days of the agrarian balance of power at the start of the nineteenth century (1928, pp. 12–14; 1930, pp. 18–20). Where Bowman and Brailsford parted company was on the nature of the solution. Bowman saw a system of free trade in goods and finance as the answer to state conflict over resources. Brailsford saw this as imperialism by different means. Bowman, in this sense, was an advocate of the very state-based capitalist world that Brailsford was starting to describe and attack.

During the First World War, Brailsford began to work on solutions to the problems that he had identified in 1914. These solutions flowed from his argument that the flaw in the current global order was the melding of a capitalist economic and social order with a system dominated by sovereign nation-states to create an order that had a propensity to solve problems by war. Here he altered his original 1914 argument that it was in the interests of the great powers to maintain an unstable armed peace. Instead, he conceded that the inflexible international anarchy created by sovereign states left no alternative for those seeking change than the outbreak of war (1917b, p. 70). While blaming the inflexible nature of the sovereign state for making war the only means of change, Brailsford also conceded that there was a psychological angle to the problem whereby states resorted to war, notably a conservative idea of a balance of power inherited from the eighteenth century that fetishized statecraft while denying the need for change (1917a, pp. 310–32). This denial of change led those seeking change, especially amongst oppressed minorities, to see war as the only means of achieving their ends.

While this psychological conservatism of the state was important, it did not take away the role played by capitalism in creating an armed peace based on the injustice of inequalities in wealth. Rather, any solution to the problem of war had to take into account how the causes of war were rooted in both modern (bourgeois) capitalism and atavistic (aristocratic) statecraft. Although modern capitalists used the state as a means towards their ends, capitalism itself made a nonsense of the idea of a self-sufficient sovereign state upon which the eighteenth-century statecraft of a balance of power had been based: 'unlimited independence of sovereign states is as impossible and as undesirable as the anarchical freedom of individual citizens' (ibid., p. 324). As a result the two chief causes of war were issues of nationality arising from the boundaries of sovereign states and economic expansion brought about by capitalism (1917b, p. 287).

The answer for Brailsford rested with the development of a new system that aimed not at the prevention of war per se, but one that provided for an 'international change without war' (1917a, p. 318). The resulting 'League of Nations' needed to tackle the issues of justice and 'commercial freedom' that the current system of capitalist states had failed to tackle, and this was only possible by substituting a system of sovereign states with 'some conception of a worldwide human society' based on tolerance of minorities and the removal of the state's ability to control trade for the benefit of its capitalists (1917b, pp. 266–7). The solution for Brailsford lay in the form of representation chosen for the new League. If the League remained a 'league of cabinets' in which states and state interests alone were represented, then the new order would be nothing more than a continuation of the diplomacy of international anarchy that merely aimed at a precarious armed peace between states. If, instead, representation was via delegates from parliaments, who would then sit in the League assembly alongside members of affiliated parties from other states, the League would be run by representatives of the many interests found in the world, while at the same time these interests would cut across lines of nationality (1917b, p. 313; see also 1944, pp. 137–8). For the socialist it would mean that 'the class line of cleavage' would be internationalized, and workers would be emancipated 'from the obsessions of a narrow nationalism' (1919, p. 2). In short, a League parliament would expose the class nature of global politics, and remove the chimera of national conflict.

In the end, though, the peacemakers at Paris chose to develop a League based upon cabinets, with a structure aimed at dealing with war as merely a security question between states. Brailsford thought a great opportunity had been missed. By concentrating only on the problem of international anarchy between states, Brailsford argued, the authors of the Covenant had failed to grasp that global inequality and the capitalist domination of state interests remained as unchecked global irritants (see Brailsford, 1920).

Problems of world government and capitalist domination

One of the problems we face when trying to integrate critical IPE into the broader history of IR is that the historical narratives of IR's founding are written in such a way that the objects of criticism by people like Brailsford are marginalized or absent from the narrative. Nowhere is this clearer than in the strange exclusion of the main architects of the American-led liberal order. Few in IR today have heard of Isaiah Bowman, but, perhaps more than any IR expert of the early twentieth century, he was the intellectual inspiration behind the global order that pervades the world today. Much as theorists of the new IPE in the 1970s had to rewrite the priorities of the study of IR in order to be taken seriously, so in order to understand the place of early critical IPE scholars such as Brailsford we need to tell a different story about the founding of IR as a field of study. The emergence of a realist-dominated IR in the United States was a relatively late post-Second World War development, and the writings of Morgenthau, Thompson, Spykman and others were directed at what they saw as a dominant liberal approach (see Guilhot, 2008). While realism was to become dominant in IR during the Cold War, it was a form of liberalism (not realism) that underpinned the emergence of the informal 'American Empire'. First mooted as the basis of a new global order during the Paris peace conference of 1919, it emerged from the crises of the 1930s and early 1940s as the stronger of two alternatives to fascism, becoming the basis of the western liberal order during the Cold War and Détente. After the 1980s it finally became the sole global order (see, for example, Williams, 2007).

The stories told by a realist-dominated IR have focused on the discontinuities of international order, with a heavy emphasis on the global security crisis of 1931–45. This often results in a Mackinderesque abstraction of IR that substitutes power and territory for an understanding of industrial capacity and politico-economic structures (see Mackinder, 1942; Spykman, 1944, pp. 3–4; Ashworth, 2010). What this narrative has hidden is the extent to which the twentieth century is also the story of the rise of a capitalist-friendly liberal global order. While many people contributed to this liberal 'new world', the key player in the field of IR was Isaiah Bowman, who was a significant player in the US delegation to Paris in 1919, a co-founder of the Council on Foreign Relations, a member of Roosevelt's inner circle during the Second World War, and present at Dumbarton Oaks and the San Francisco conference. Bowman's answer to the problem of global conflict was a state-based structure of international organizations that guaranteed free trade in both goods and finances. Seeing imperialism as a natural response by societies keen to guarantee the supply of necessary raw materials to their industries, Bowman suggested that this imperialism could be replaced by an open economy that would allow states to purchase what they needed without recourse to formal imperialism. This, of course, was the new form of political control that Brailsford had criticized earlier in his *War of Steel and Gold*. While both Brailsford and Bowman were supporters of stronger international organizations, there were fundamental differences in their conceptions. From 1919 onwards, Brailsford would reserve some of his sharpest invective for the new international organizations that singly failed to deal with the problems of global inequality.

Yet, it was not just the liberal internationalists that Brailsford criticized. He was also disturbed by the growth of a deeply cowardly national capitalism which he saw as being behind the 1930s' policy of appeasement. This second group, the national capitalists, were, like Brailsford, critics of the League structure, but, from Brailsford's point of view, they were critical of that part of the League system that was at least doing some good. Thus, Brailsford found himself confronting what he saw as two wrong paths: a liberal internationalism that did nothing to deal with the capitalist roots of global instability, and a more old-fashioned nationalist conservatism that sacrificed long-term global order for shorter-term capitalist interests. Interestingly, Brailsford sometimes presented these two wrong paths as a conflict between 'liberal idealism' and a conservative 'realism', and his own preferred path of a socialism that transcended both of these errors (1923, p. 4). Underlying all of this was Brailsford's growing belief that capitalist interests were incompatible with democracy, and that capitalist elites would be willing to sacrifice both security and western liberties for the narrower interests of capital. Brailsford's analysis of the post-1919 world can be broken down into two related strands: his criticism of the trajectory of international organizations, and the capitalist roots of both war and appeasement. Throughout both of these strands the problem remained the dominance, but ultimate frailty, of both the sovereign state and capitalism.

From Brailsford's point of view, the peacemakers in Paris had failed irredeemably to build a sustainable order out of the ashes of the old. The competitions of sovereign states in the international anarchy, alongside the injustices of capitalist economics, were the major causes of the instability that had led to war in 1914. The new League of Nations structure, for Brailsford, failed to deal with both of these major problems. First, the League was constructed as a 'league of cabinets', where the very people who ran the various sovereign states that had caused the war were now in control of the course that the League took. The peacemakers had caved in to conservative interests and created a League that was nothing more than a new venue for playing out the games of international anarchy. Second, the League lacked the machinery to deal with the root causes of war. Injustices in the form of capitalist exploitation, new forms of imperialism, and domination of narrow state interests over the formation of the peace treaties all remained outside of the League's abilities to rectify or reform.

Thus the League remained inadequate because it ignored the 'economic factor' and accepted 'the myth of the sovereign national state' (Brailsford, 1928, p. 48). This failure of the League to bring about a new order was, for Brailsford, not just a matter of leaving the world without justice or stability. The instabilities of capitalism were a symptom of a deeper malaise. Capitalism was on the brink of collapse, but if it buckled without the structures of an alternative system in place that dealt directly with the problems of capitalism, then the alternative would be a new form of barbarism (1920, p. 29). As it turned out, capitalism proved more resilient than Brailsford had thought in 1920, yet he saw in the emergence of fascism just such a product of the failings of capitalism and the absence of a more humane socialist alternative (1944, p. 9, pp. 19–23).

Despite his criticisms of the League as it emerged from the peace negotiations in 1919, Brailsford remained committed to the idea of the League. At several points in the interwar period his support for the idea led him to show guarded praise for it. Brailsford was particularly pleased with the successful negotiations in 1924 carried out by the new centre-left governments in Britain and France that aimed to give more legal teeth to the League's system of pooled security (1924a). Yet, even when he praised the League, he continued to point out that so long as it failed to deal with economic imperialism then the issues of arbitration and disarmament would not solve the problem of war (1924a, p. 4; 1924b, p. 11).

This set the pattern for Brailsford's future assessment of the League. Over the next decade he would praise it both as an idea and as a practical alternative to the self-destructive world of capitalism and the nation-state, singling out the excellent work of the specialized agencies and the provision of a forum where statesmen could meet in the full glare of the public gaze. Yet, at the same time, its failure to deal with the problems of sovereign state rivalry, economic interdependence and imperialism left the League weak and only tangentially dealing with the causes of war (1928, pp. 48ff.; 1933, pp. 82–3; 1936, p. 60). Often exasperated with the League's inaction, Brailsford once likened it to 'a functionless fifth wheel on the chariot of history that spun ineffective in the air' (1936, p. 49). Particularly glaring here was how the concept of sovereignty prevented the League from dealing with 'the political or economic maladjustment that drives nations to war' (1933, p. 278). Returning to his Hobsonian roots, Brailsford still saw the drive to war amongst modern states as a product of the capitalist structure of national societies (1938a, pp. 60–2).

Underlying this, however, was an issue that Brailsford had not yet resolved. Was it enough just to change the government of states to democratic socialism, or were more profound changes needed at the international level? The answer to this depended on whether it was capitalism alone that made states war-prone, or whether it simply exacerbated and encouraged already-existing problems inherent in a world of sovereign states. On the face of it, Brailsford's arguments on capitalism and war seem to point in the direction of domestic reform alone, but he was also aware that domestic capitalism was not the only problem standing in the way of peace. His discussions with David Mitrany during the Second had helped reinforce his internationalism (Ashworth, 2007, p. 47). Independent of the problem of capitalism, the issue of non-interference that underpinned the concept of state sovereignty allowed 'the erection of any regime which is, by the reason it embodies, necessarily aggressive'. The idea of the sovereign state system had to be replaced with the idea of the 'general good' of humanity (Brailsford, 1944, p. 14).

While Brailsford never explored the issue of the potential war-proneness of a non-capitalist socialist state, the implications of his discussions of the need to abolish sovereignty are that socialist states with their planned economies would come into conflict with other states over resources. This was an argument made by Hugh Dalton in 1928, and was central to David Mitrany's rejection of national planning (Dalton, 1928, p. 20; Mitrany, 1947, pp. 18–31). Yet, at the same time, Brailsford suggests that socialist states were naturally more peaceful, positing at one point that socialist states would be more likely to federate in a league of peace because they would have no need to attack each other (Brailsford, 1934, pp. 284–5). Similarly, in his discussions with Mitrany in the winter of 1942–3 he suggests that national planning could be a preamble to international planning – a point of major disagreement between Brailsford and Mitrany. Thus, Brailsford leaves unresolved what remains a central question within socialist political thought: is it enough to achieve socialism in individual states, or does a socialist alternative order require a global alternative to the (capitalist) sovereign state system? Behind this lies the question of whether the state is necessary for the survival of capitalism, or whether capitalism is a necessary condition of the sovereign state. While remaining anticapitalist and anti-sovereign state, Brailsford tends to flit between these two positions.

Ironically, Brailsford's deepest criticism of capitalism's influence on foreign policy during the late 1930s was not that it encouraged belligerence, but rather that it failed to be belligerent when it needed to be. At first glance this appears to be a contradiction, but there was in fact a strong link to his capitalism and war thesis, as well as to the wider argument found in *The War of Steel and Gold*. From 1935 onwards Brailsford was critical of the lacklustre response of Britain and its allies to fascist aggression. For Brailsford, the interests of capitalists lay in avoiding conflict with the fascist powers in order to safeguard the interests of British capitalism. Specifically, the National Government of Neville Chamberlain in Britain was willing to allow fascist gains in Manchuria, Abyssinia and Spain if that enabled the continuation of secure control over the British Empire and of the safety of Britain's interests in France, Belgium, Portugal, Iraq and Egypt.

This reflected class interests both at home and abroad: 'The Tory selection [on what to defend] ... appears to be based on the indispensable, but limited principle of self-preservation ... Class, indeed, talks audibly in any attempt to define this policy' (Brailsford, 1938b, pp. 332–3). Underlying this argument was a return to the 'armed peace' theory of *The War of Steel and Gold*. Britain and its allies were reserving their armaments for control of their own (economic) sphere, but were studiously avoiding a major war among the great powers which would be against the interests of the dominant capitalist classes. This policy meant making concessions to fascist powers in order to maintain the peace. Where Brailsford's argument differed from that in 1914 was in his additional concern that fascism represented a challenge to this capitalist peace in the form of older ideas of conquest. Although remaining critical of the idea of collective security under the League, which he saw as being too reliant on Anglo-French military power and the old-style threat of force (1938a, pp. 53–7), by the late 1930s Brailsford was arguing for the use of collective security (especially as part of a British–French–Soviet anti-fascist front) as the only serious alternative to the greater barbarism of fascism (1936, Part IV).

Brailsford and the origins of IPE

Brailsford's international thought is, at its base, a theory of imperialism which presents capitalist accumulation and the system of the sovereign state as the causes of an inherently violent and unjust global system. The balance of power under capitalism is different because power is never sought as an end in itself, but as a means towards the ends of the ruling class in the state. As financial and commercial interests replaced agrarian ones the aims of national policy under the balance of power shifted from control of territory towards control of markets for goods and investment. Armaments were used increasingly to gain economic advantage in an unstable armed peace, instead of as part of great power competition. As early as 1914, therefore, Brailsford had outlined the basis of neocolonial control.

Although his predictions of 1914 proved wrong in one respect – the great powers did end up fighting a classic war of conquest – he had foreseen the shift from formal to informal imperialism in the second half of the twentieth century. Indeed, this neocolonial armed peace was to be one of the key elements of the American-led western hegemony that gathered force during the century. If Angell had underplayed the global forces of production, Brailsford had underestimated the survival of earlier ideas of conquest. Spinning off from his theory of imperialism, Brailsford singled out the League's failure to be more than merely a 'League of cabinets', and as a result its inability to deal with the material injustices at the root of global politics, as being the main cause of its lack of success. Capitalist interests were also at the root of the failure of western states to properly confront fascism.

Brailsford's international theory was an unabashedly materialist one, and until after the Second World War he was dismissive of attempts to explain global politics via more psychological or idealistic arguments. In 1947 he admitted that he and Hobson had underestimated the power of 'psychological and moral' factors, and the main influence on his change of attitude had been fascism and the rise of the Nazis. Although the economic conditions had given fascism its opportunity, its roots were 'psychological rather than economic' and valued power 'for its own sake and not for economic fruits' (Brailsford, 1948, p. 27). After 1945 other socialists in Britain were coming to similar conclusions, leading G.D.H. Cole, in 1958, to lament the way that the idea of capitalism as the prime cause of war had come to dominate the left, and how there were many other causes that should have been addressed (1958, pp. 359–61). Yet, for both Brailsford and Cole, this did not mean that the materialist explanation for war was wrong, merely that it was not sufficient on its own.

Perhaps the problem here was that, in fitting in with the Zeitgeist of finding causes for war, Brailsford had been distracted from what his international theory was better at revealing: how the nature of capitalism was leading to a global neocolonial order dominated by an armed peace. Brailsford's work might be able to explain the dislocations that caused developments like fascism, but it could not explain the continued presence of old-fashioned ideas of conquest, nor the 'power for power's sake' politics of fascism. What his international theory did reveal, though, was the development of a new western imperial order based on the use of state power to gain informal control over weaker societies. This is the world that people like Isaiah Bowman were building from the Paris peace conference onwards, and it is the world that became truly global after 1989. Here power did serve a purpose, and the system of freeing up trade and finance, using international organizations to further western ideas of global governance, and maintaining a strong military capable of intervening to protect western interests, looks remarkably similar to what Brailsford predicted for the world in 1914. It was not war that was the problem, but the peace.

What Brailsford never managed to resolve was the question of the interaction between capitalism and the role of the sovereign national state. He was sure that both were wrong, but the question of how they interacted remained unsettled in his international theory. Perhaps the problem here was one that Leonard Woolf had tried to grapple with, and which Brailsford was moving towards in 1947: that while their interaction was central to understanding global politics, both capitalism and the state were incommensurate structures. The emerging capitalist 'American Empire' could be seen as a product of specific financial and commercial interests linked to ideas of using power to serve specific interests, yet the parallel concept of the national state obeyed a Nietzschean logic of power for its own sake (a concept that Morgenthau adopted for his own international theory), and relied on psychological attachments that were distinct from material class interests. These national sentiments could be mobilized by class interests, but were also capable of being the source of a non-socialist conservative resistance.

An understanding of these twin structures is, of course, the reason for the development of IPE in the first place, and it is worth pointing out that the question of the relation between economic structures and the sovereign state had been a matter of hot debate throughout the first part of the twentieth century, and that Brailsford had been at the centre of these debates in Britain. Although he never successfully dealt with the problem of the interaction between capitalism and the sovereign state, this was addressed in different ways by two of his friends during the war years: Harold Laski and David Mitrany (Laski, 1943, ch. 6; Mitrany, 1943). An analysis of Brailsford's IPE can both underscore the importance of studying these two logics, and lay out the continuing problem of making sense of what are two incompatible (yet constantly interacting) aspects of the international. This is what critical IPE is constantly grappling with: the reconciliation of a world in which instrumental class power predominates, with a world in which power is an end in itself. Brailsford came to recognize this, yet at the end of the day a solution eluded him. The central problem of finding a resolution rests with the starkly different forms of power – one a means and the other an end – that operate here. Yet they do not work in isolation, but, rather, within a global set of structures that are dependent on each other and need to be studied as a politico-economic whole.

In his intellectual biography of Brailsford, F.M. Leventhal (1985, p. 1) concludes that Brailsford's work was mainly written in response to particular events, and that once 'his articles ceased to appear in print his name was forgotten'. Leventhal is partially right here. Brailsford's articles on specific issues were certainly forgotten, and his name largely disappears from the IR literature during the 1960s. Yet, the intellectual conditions that Brailsford helped lay down, especially in Britain, were the academic seedbed for the critical IPE that emerged from the late 1970s onwards. Brailsford's ideas were used and quoted by people like Harold Laski, Konni Zilliacus and Michael Foot, while for the mercurial A.J.P. Taylor (1957) he was the archetypal modern version of the perennial British dissenter tradition. Although by the late 1970s he was rarely quoted, Brailsford had helped to form the intellectual environment on the British left that fostered a revolt against the narrowly state security-based English School realism of Manning, Wight, Bull and Northedge.

There is one other contribution that a study of Brailsford can provide to current IR in general and critical IPE in particular. History is one of many sites in which current ideological positions compete. Control of the commonly accepted historical narrative is a gatekeeping device that allows a dominant discourse to claim legitimacy in the here and now; what Herbert Butterfield called the Whig interpretation of history (1931). The narrative reproduced in Cohen's history of IPE is no different from any other Whig history. It tells a story that benefits particular groups at particular times. To paraphrase Robert Cox, history is always *for* someone and *for* some purpose. Cohen's history of IPE privileges the relationship between politics and economics, and marginalizes critical IPE as a parvenu paradigm. In fact, a critical international political economy has been central to IR ever since its formulation as a distinct field in the early twentieth century. Even before the First World War there were self-conscious works concerned with political economy questions in the international sphere. Some, like Angell's *Great Illusion* of 1910, are liberal in their approach, while others, like Brailsford's 1914 *War of Steel and Gold*, present a socialist viewpoint.

That the question of the role of capitalism in the causes of war was so important in the decades following the First World War, and that the issue of the role of the League of Nations in economic matters was seen as a topic of public debate, amply demonstrates that there was a lively IPE (combining international relations with political economy) in existence long before a realist IR was codified and established within political science during the late 1940s and early 1950s. Critical IPE has a history that goes back to the founding of IR as a field of study, and writing it back into disciplinary histories destabilizes cosy assumptions about what is and what is not orthodox IPE or IR.

Note

1. Michael Foot, 'The Knight Errant of Socialism', *Tribune*, 28 March 1958.

2
Space, the Latest Frontier? A Scalar-Relational Approach to Critical IPE

Huw Macartney and Stuart Shields

Finding space in IPE

This chapter focuses predominantly on the treatment of the *international* as a space within International Political Economy (IPE). This edited volume highlights, albeit often implicitly, two areas of concern within IPE. Many of the chapters tend to focus on the relationship between the political and the economic, for example in addressing the relationship between IPE and International Relations (IR). We argue that where the relationship between the political and economic has been the primary focus of debate within the discipline, the analogous question of the relationship between different spaces has been anything but clear. We further argue that in spite of numerous attempts to overcome it, the national–international dichotomy continues to permeate too much of contemporary IPE. We see this as somewhat ironic, given that critical IPE has deliberately positioned itself in opposition to orthodox IPE precisely because of the orthodoxy's failure to capture the social content or underlying power structures of global capitalism. This is most obvious in those attempts that analyse the historical and social but only include space as a nodal point for analysis of the political agency of capital (compare Morton, 2007b; Underhill, 2003). In contrast we argue that a more nuanced understanding of space as one constitutive element of capitalism is central to the notions of emancipation and resistance which are at the heart of a critical IPE project. We achieve this by exploring a scalar-relational approach to critical IPE that develops a more differentiated view of spatialization in the global economy.

To substantiate this we draw on work within political geography and the notion of scale as a relational approach to the question of space. Rather than reifying particular spatial forms at a specific scale, our analysis focuses on the process of scaling, that is, 'the production, reconfiguration or contestation of particular differentiations, orderings and hierarchies among [different] scales' (Brenner, 2001, p. 600). The chapter unfolds in three substantive sections. First, we examine so-called orthodox IPE and the question of space. Here we claim that the state-centric assumptions inherent to such accounts provide limitations which culminate in a move from an ostensibly Westphalian form of nationalism to internationalization and an overtly stratified conception of a levels-of-analysis approach. Second, the chapter examines critical IPE and extant notions of space. Here, many initial accounts bear striking similarities to the laminated internationalization evidenced in the orthodoxy. More recent accounts suggest the transnational as a potentially fruitful alternative. This concept is frequently invoked, yet remains problematically deployed, often giving way to a nodal conception of the transnational as simply another platform, another laminate, for social relations. Finally, we move to contend that the production of space and scale itself, rather than just the scales between spaces, is both constituent and outcome of these social relations. Put differently, space and scale are internal to capitalism rather than epiphenomenal. In the concluding section we propound an alternative reading of the transnational and suggest that this might be a useful contribution to the counter-hegemonic project at the heart of critical IPE.

Orthodox IPE: from the national to the international to the global

Realism to neoliberalism

As we begin to outline the problem of space, we explore how IPE has tended to 'add-space-and-mix' to its analytical focus on the political and the economic. The myth is maintained that IPE emerged because of its focus on global phenomena, the spread of financial and production networks, the rise of international and intergovernmental institutions, the proliferation of technologies and communications, and social movements transcending national boundaries, engendering both quantitative and qualitative change in world history. This particular myth supports and reinforces the notion that IPE is a sub-discipline of IR that emerged as a response to the global restructuring of capitalism in the 1970s (Murphy and Tooze, 1991; Strange, 1996).[1] Orthodox IPE originates in realist and liberal categories of analysis constituted around the idea of hegemonic stability and associated theory.

Where neo-realism provides by far the clearest and most self-conscious example of rationalist assumptions that the international system is determined by the coagulation of national economies and nationally based preferences, neo-liberalism articulates a structurally similar approach. The key difference is over the content of preferences referring to, for example, economic versus military power, and absolute versus relative gains. States-as-actors and the *inter*-national system are self-evidently axiomatic. These earliest accounts struggled, however, to conceptualize the interrelationship between the national and the so-called international.

To assert the international simply as the *overflow* of the national ignored important effects that the international had on shaping state preferences in an interdependent world. Robert Putnam's two-level game metaphor was an attempt within liberal theory to explain how political entrepreneurs bring the influence of the international to their national–domestic politics whilst, simultaneously, the politics emerging domestically, in turn, shape international positions (1988). Throughout this period in the development of IPE, there was an effort to theorize the changes taking place in the international system, while the key unitary actors, with determinant decision-making capabilities, remained nation-states (Keohane. 1988, pp. 379–96). In spite of their interconnectedness, the domestic and international were relatively independently constituted, with the latter overdetermined by the former (ibid., p. 242).

From here, orthodox accounts began to develop the notion of internationalization as the product of the increasing openness of national economies. This reproduced a separately constituted yet interconnected approach, meaning that to understand politics within countries an analysis of the nature of the linkages was required (Keohane and Milner, 1996, p. 3). Internationalization created both opportunities and constraints upon actors, which affected the policy preferences of states since it equated to the growth of international economic flows relative to domestic ones (ibid., p. 4). Not only are the underlying assumptions firmly rooted within the state-centric notion of national geographic territories as the key units of analysis, but the *international* – at least in so far as the focus of their analysis suggests – equates to the flows of investment, trade and actors that originate in and therefore emerge *out of* the domestic; the nation state remains the container out of which the international emerges.

Global governance

More recently, a useful example of the ongoing difficulties in addressing the question of the international as a space is highlighted by the burgeoning literature on global governance. It is ironic, though, how the global governance literature acknowledges the heterogeneity of knowledge, organizations and institutions in the global political economy but produces a generic image of the global governance scale-related qualities. These accounts are significant not simply because of their conception of space, but because in many ways they provide a point of departure for the critique provided by critical IPE. Competing conceptions of space are important to the development of IPE but remain a secondary concern to the emphasis on the political and economic relations of most accounts. We suggest an alternative starting point which sees the political, economic and spatial as initially and continually mutually constitutive to the production and reproduction of social relations.

Two broad perspectives to theorizing global governance have emerged to dominate the IPE literature: a complexity approach and a form of descriptive institutionalism. The defining feature of the former is its emphasis on the *complexity* of globalized processes. This presents an account that aims to provide the most epistemologically parsimonious analysis of the world in the pursuit of prediction and generalizable propositions. For James Rosenau, the complexity of emerging processes under globalization pre-empts an emphasis on technology as the determining factor (Rosenau, 1995) behind social change in keeping with the contemporary liberal IPE (Strange, 1996; Cerny, 1997). In addition, it is worth noting Cerny's journey which traverses the terrain of 'globalization' from a procumbent competition state to a labyrinthine transnational neopluralism (2010). The concentration on a series of connected but bounded spaces responding to the imperatives of competitiveness articulates a binary worldview that replicates a perspective driven by an 'in here' as distinct from a global 'out there'. From such foundations, complexity approaches proceed to examine the implications of the emergence of diverse actors such as the World Economic Forum, the European and World Social Forum, private groups like the International Chamber of Commerce and Non-Governmental Organizations (NGOs) in the micromanagement of political economic and social problems at competing and/or overlapping levels.

The crucial step, however, lies in the reproduction of the myth of a Westphalian topography in an *international* political economy, characterized by sovereign order (governance) imposed by the nation state (Rosenau, 1995, p. 48). On this reading the globalization era evokes a 'relocation of authority in a shrinking world' (Rosenau, 1992). Two key difficulties can be discerned: one relates to the not unproblematic assumption of the parallelism and coincidence of sovereignty and distinct nation states; the other relates to the social struggles and antagonisms concealed by positing the locus of change in a technological determinacy. Put differently, it is our contention that such complexity explanations obfuscate the continuities between so-called post-war and globalization periods.

For critical IPE, these criticisms have been equated with an absence of an underlying social content. In effect, complexity theory adequately highlights the formal transformations without embedding them within an analysis of the causal social and spatial relations (van Apeldoorn, 2002, p. 12). As a result, complexity approaches highlight the 'powerful tensions, profound contradictions and perplexing paradoxes' that refer to little more than the

> formal institutions and organisations through which the management of international affairs is or is not sustained; this includes systems of rule at all levels of human activity... [encompassing] the activities of governments, [and] many other channels through which commands flow in the form of goals framed, directives issued, and policy pursued.
>
> (Rosenau, 1995, pp. 45–6)

To (re-)emphasize, the complexity and interdependence of contemporary social reality mystifies as much as it reveals, providing a misleading account of *what* has changed and then failing to address the social relations that explain *why* these spatial transformations take place.

A second series of accounts of global governance has emerged which implicitly rejects the insights of the complexity approach. Here, the focus is on a microanalysis of key agents within the institutions of global governance. In spite of the rich empirical detail, by avoiding the simplifying assumptions and regularities of an overtly rationalist institutionalism, what we term descriptive institutionalism fails to critically reflect on unacknowledged theoretical assumptions concerning, *inter alia*, the function of prevailing institutions in the production and reproduction of capitalist social relations on a global scale. In particular, we are concerned with the distinct lack of theorization of the social and political context within which the emergent forms of global governance occur. This creates a different, yet equally serious, problem from that of complexity approaches, namely that it obscures the political through a presentation of 'extra'-national processes as objective phenomena. Descriptive institutionalism is therefore based on an uncritical institutionalist account of the events, processes and, in particular, the institutions of global governance. As a result, whilst 'multilateral agreements on investment, government procurement, trade facilitation, and competition policy' (Wilkinson, 2004, p. 149) do not occur within a vacuum, historical, social and spatial conditions are treated as merely inputs and/or outputs to the political process under scrutiny.

There is an unhealthy predilection for seeing the international realm, especially in terms of its spatial dimension, as unchanging; in other words, as somehow existing outside of history (Lawson, 2007). By fixating on a particular starting period, more often than not post-1945 institutional development and policy process, descriptive institutionalism effectively freezes history, relegating its explanatory power to that of epiphenomenon. A more convincing account might be developed from a perspective that shifts the focus from the institutions of global governance as a set of bounded spaces to a scalar-relational perspective. This would contrast with the static picture of the structure of world politics wherein sovereign states exist axiomatically; unit level differences between international organizations are accepted unproblematically; encompassing forces such as global capitalism are omitted; and agency is reduced to the musings of statesmen, financiers, generals and international bureaucrats. By failing explicitly and reflexively to examine these elements, such descriptive institutionalism, despite claims to the contrary, assumes these musings to be timeless and constitutive of ahistorical structures.

This reduces global governance to the politics of novelty whereby a purportedly critical approach becomes a variation on the common themes developed by orthodox scholars, albeit with the extrinsic addition of an emancipatory rhetoric aimed at fostering the illusion of progressive social change (Bonefeld, 1998). The descriptive institutionalist literature remains inspired, directly or indirectly, by a set of basic notions germane to identifying the most effective management of economic performance in a global economy. Should our loftiest ambition really be the amelioration of the worst excesses of capitalism? The theoretical and political priority, therefore, never resides in a particular space or scale, but 'in the processes through which particular scales become (re)constituted' as unproblematic, neutral, objective and natural parts of the global political economy (Swyngedouw, 2004, p. 6). Our goal in briefly exploring these orthodox accounts is simply to highlight the immanence of what we call the problem of space, which, as we shall see, has also plagued critical IPE.

Critical IPE: from the international to the transnational

Cox and internationalization

As other contributors to this volume have noted (see chapters by Worth and Ashworth), critical IPE owes an intellectual debt to the work of Robert Cox in at least two respects: first, in his characterization of critical theory as emancipatory theory predicated on the deconstruction of existing institutions and power configurations (1981), and second, because of his re-engagement with the work of Antonio Gramsci. Both of these interventions have meant that the criteria of assessment for critical IPE have been an attempt to disclose the underlying and reified social relations and to embed them within a particular theory of historical change (Bieler and Morton, 2001; van Apeldoorn, 2004, p. 145). Ironically, then, we argue that the intended goal of critical IPE in its normative and emancipatory agenda is hindered by the secondary and epiphenomenal status accorded to the production and reproduction of space within its accounts.

As noted above, there are certain similarities between the starting premises of Cox's analysis and those of more orthodox liberal institutionalism. For Cox, globalization was an elite-driven process, with states once again shaped in their preferences and outlooks by their particular position within these wider global processes. As a result, particular state apparatuses acted as mediators between the global restructuring of capitalism and the spheres of finance and production most closely linked to these exogenous changes. The interests of national social forces were therefore subordinated to the demands of the global economy. The *nébuleuse* of both formal and informal international institutions emerges to connect major capitalist states, with particular neoliberal ideology and discourse acting as a political rationalization of these nascent configurations (Cox, 1995, p. 30).

Stephen Gill sought to explain the liberalized and commodified historical structures driven by the restructuring of capital which characterizes contemporary world order. Central to his account is the 'spatial expansion and social deepening' of particular definitions of social enterprise and individualistic politics (1995, p. 399). Put differently, Gill notes that accumulation, legitimation, consumption and work carry with them expansionary tendencies, important to these wider transformations and, in particular, contributing to the emergence of a historical bloc. This bloc comprises local political structures as well as constituting a global political and civil society (ibid., p. 400). As a result, it is a neoliberal/transnational historical bloc existing within and across nations and forms the analytical core of his work.

This conception of space is perhaps most apparent though in Gill's discussions of the structural power of transnational capital, operating within this bloc (ibid., pp. 430, 407). By transnational capital Gill means transnational firms, operating across multiple jurisdictions. The structural power of capital is dependent upon the reduction in barriers to the international mobility of capital, and the constraints and incentive structures that this imposes upon national states (Gill and Law, 1989, p. 478). So the analysis targets the power of those fractions of capital that are both large in scope and internationally mobile. Further, the global character of these power relations is taken as self-evident, given the rise of transnational corporations and degree of international capital mobility (ibid., p. 482).[2] Again, despite protestations to the contrary, the social and the historical are privileged, whilst space is stratified as a platform for these relations.

Already, we begin to perceive the difficulties this raises for the normative project of critical IPE. The tendency here is to present a relatively homogenous transnational elite as the key agent of 'globalization'. This is only reinforced by the relatively autonomous partitioning of the transnational from the local or national (Gill, 1995, p. 411; see also Gill, 2008, p. 59). Precisely in seeking to avoid this tendency embedded within a state-centric approach, Gill and Law (1989) proffer social forces as new and alternative agents. This only reinforces the difficulty however, given the repeated recourse to other defunct remnants of orthodox IPE; remnants such as the 'global level' (ibid., p. 476). Put differently, space is unproblematically assumed to exist *a priori*, such that – as national governments remove barriers – this pre-existing space is available for newly liberated capital (ibid., pp. 479–81). Capital relocates from one country to another, depending on legal freedoms, production costs, labour relations, political stability and financial concessions, so that transnational capital is defined as internationally mobile capital, subsequently imposing structural power over states themselves (ibid., p. 484). The circularity of the argument can be appreciated through an understanding of the spatial.

The difficulty with this conception is also apparent at times in the work of the Amsterdam School. The central objective of these accounts has been to develop a more nuanced understanding of the relationship between the dynamics of capital accumulation and the formation of hegemonic ideas (Overbeek, 2000). Once again there has been a specific attempt to engage with the IR concepts employed by orthodox IPE (see above). Significantly, these accounts depart from the more straightforward Gramscian reading, which usually starts with Cox's work as the key interlocutor. Instead, the Amsterdam School begins most emphatically with Marx and Poulantzas rather than Cox or Gramsci (Overbeek, 2004). In contrast to the liberal and actor-centred perspectives of orthodox IPE, this emphasizes the importance of transnational (economic) structures, whilst reasserting the centrality of class agency. IR is perceived as being *inter*-national, whereas transnational historical materialism argues that these particular relations are inextricably bound up within an expanding capitalist world economy and transnational social relations (van Apeldoorn, 2004, p. 143). The key contribution of this position is the process of transnational class formation and, in our view, it is here that the underlying difficulty of this spatial characterization has significant political implications for critical IPE.

To understand transnational relations – a central prerogative of the Amsterdam project – 'the transnational' itself is depicted as a phenomenon as opposed to a level (ibid., p. 144). Though this conceptualization avoids the difficulties, on the one hand, of a levels of analysis approach comprised of national, international and/or global, and, on the other hand, a notion of the transnational as completely distinct and separate from national spaces (whatever this might mean), it infers, however, that these actors operate within *several* national contexts simultaneously (ibid., p. 145). Defining the transnational relies on recourse to the national as the determining frame of reference. From this point of inception, an analysis that privileges the agency of particular social forces unfolds, albeit within the context of economic relations characterized as *global* capitalism. The idea of space *itself* is not constituted in and through, *inter alia*, class struggle, only the ability to operate *within* it. A predetermined space already exists; social forces struggle over access to it. For the Amsterdam project, these social relations were therefore always at least partially transnational in nature; it is simply that they have become more extensive and deeply embedded in the contemporary world order. As Overbeek and van der Pijl note, one of the crucial dimensions of change in the historical process of capitalist development is capital's paradigmatic scale of operation, referring to the spatial dimensions of the process, in particular the widening scale of operation of productive capital, from local in the early capitalist period to national in the nineteenth century, to Atlantic in the mid-twentieth century, and to global in the early twenty-first century (Overbeek and van der Pijl, 1993; Arrighi, 2005a, 2005b).

Similar concerns also emerge within neo-Gramscian perspectives and their focus on the political agency of capital (Morton, 2007b). These approaches have, in many ways, been central to the reinvigoration of historical materialist analysis within IPE. Their dominant characteristics are the critical normative position and analysis of class struggle as a heuristic device for understanding the global restructuring of capitalism; in this respect they are the logical descendants of Cox's analysis outlined above. Their core contribution has been an examination of forms of cultural and moral leadership mediated through an extensive range of social institutions and organizations in understanding class hegemony in the contemporary world order.

With this particular focus in mind, there has been a growing appreciation of the complexity of the spatial relations of global capitalism which simply cannot be captured by a levels of analysis approach. In its initial instantiation, transnationalization was referred to as the 'material' reorganization of production and finance within and across nation states (Bieler and Morton, 2001, p. 4; Cox, 1993, pp. 259–260). More recently, there have been attempts to conceptualize the multiscalarity of capitalism, such that it does not simply supplant one spatial scale for another but instead works across spatial scales located within state forms and geopolitics (Morton, 2007a). Thus the transnational does not replace the national, nor do social forces operating on one scale lose touch with other scales, since capitalism operates at nodal rather than dominant points. In substantive terms however, the agency question that drives neo-Gramscian perspectives gives rise to a similar risk as encountered within the Amsterdam project: capitalism is multiscalar, but its key actors operate across and within these particular nodal points, thereby vying for access to pre-constituted social space. As a result, hegemony can operate at two levels, *within* a form of state as well as by expanding a mode of production *internationally* projecting through the level of world order (Bieler and Morton, 2004, p. 93). Though this avoids the zero-sum games of orthodox accounts, it continues to imply a binary logic that provides a problematic conceptualization of the relations between particular scales and the constitution of space. Instead, this essentializes the meaning of spatial relations in IPE as almost reducible to the national/international, with these spaces somehow bearing certain autonomous effects.

To recap, we began with the premise that an accurate understanding of the historical and social characteristics of the international political economy requires a conceptualization of space. Three key criticisms have therefore been raised. First, that within orthodox accounts of IPE a levels of analysis approach continues to reside, building upon the assumptions of IPE as a sub-discipline to IR; elsewhere, less explicit but equally unsatisfactory alternatives are provided by accounts of technological determinacy and thick descriptive institutionalism. Second, historical materialist-inspired readings within critical IPE offer a more nuanced account in their rendering of social space as a site for class struggle. Yet it is precisely through starting with the social – be it in the form of relations of production and/or hegemony – that the spatial becomes a platform for the all-important object of analysis. Third, therefore, we suggest that to examine the historical and the social, the mutually constitutive internal relations of the spatial are also required from the outset. The following section therefore addresses this concern, before focusing more explicitly on the politics of scale and its implications for critical IPE.

Towards a scalar-relational account of critical IPE

The above sections ought to have revealed the preoccupation of critical IPE with questions of resistance and emancipation, rooted in a critical normative position. Our concern in the following section is therefore twofold: we argue that an appreciation of the social content and relations of (historical) processes of change requires a nuanced conception of scale and space. To de-reify asymmetrical power relations, different spaces and scales of capitalism either lend themselves to the coherence and unity of dominant agents or suggest potential political openings for reform and change. There are different levels of 'where' capital can operate most efficiently and the transnational indicates the relationship between scales, not a zero-sum game but relational processes that can as easily be in contradiction and competition with one another, as they are complementary. We return to this below.

For now, our focus remains on the structures and agents at work within the processes of neoliberalization, as a particular example of how spatial matters concern us (Peck and Tickell, 2002, p. 993). We understand neoliberalism as an attempt to restore stable patterns of accumulation through the reconfiguration of political-economic institutions on multiple, competing and yet overlapping scales (Peck and Tickell, 2002). First, however, to contextualize our discussion of the IPE of scale it is necessary to understand the spatial. Rejecting an encompassing determinism we nonetheless argue that the production, reproduction and reconstitution of space are inherent to the material and ideological representations of class struggle and contradiction central to the global restructuring of capitalism. This requires a move from separate, independently constituted and therefore *externally* related components, to mutually constitutive, *internally* related units of a dialectical totality comprised of the social, the historical and the spatial.

At an abstract level, historical materialism has long noted the internal propensity of capitalism to engender the creative destruction of space and spatial configurations. On the one hand, capital, in its insatiable drive to secure new investment opportunities and realize greater profits, is inherently oriented towards the elimination of barriers to the circulation process (Marx, 1973[1857], p. 539). On the other hand, the continued temporal acceleration of capital circulation is predicated upon the production of space and spatial configurations (Harvey, 1985, p. 145). Complex matrices of transport, communications and regulatory institutional infrastructures therefore emerge to facilitate a reduction in the socially average turnover time of capital (Brenner, 1998, p. 433). The production, destruction and reconstruction of these spatial configurations are therefore immanent to capitalism itself and the reproduction of capitalist social relations.

This departs from the add-space-and-mix conception of critical IPE. As Brenner notes (1999b, p. 40), '[u]nder these circumstances, space no longer appears as a static platform of social relations, but rather as one of their constitutive dimensions, itself historically produced, reconfigured and transformed'. Much as critical IPE has been at pains to emphasize the internal relations of the political and economic, such that the state can be seen as an alternative form of the same social relations as the market, the spatial element captured by the '*international*' of the acronym IPE cannot be reduced to a platform or container of social relations and class struggle. Instead, space is bound within political-economic relations and, simultaneously, a product thereof. Space and scale are neither ontologically given nor politically and discursively neutral; space and scale embody power relations. The social constitution of space is therefore already imbricated in assumptions of class and gender which themselves must be elucidated as part of the project of critical IPE. Without precluding a particular entry point, this understanding of space requires a departure from the tendency towards a zero-sum analysis of the national and/or international. Swyngedouw suggests that 'starting analysis from a given geographical scale, such as the local, regional, national, or global, seems...to be deeply antagonistic to apprehending the world' (2004, p. 26). We would argue that such an entry point is inevitable and necessary in order for anything meaningful to be said about the power relations and the distribution of wealth in the global economy, but that closer attention needs to be paid to the relations between these various scales in a way that avoids the nodal points of critical IPE. Put differently, actors and processes do not simply pass in and out of focus at the national and then reappear at the international (or indeed transnational) scale, since the two remain not just connected but mutually constitutive and codependent (Shields, 2008, 2011; Macartney, 2010). The relationship is not of discrete scales and spaces, a series of boxes with neatly regularized attributes and processes. Territorial dependencies remain, but such dependencies are neither absolute nor deterministic.

For example then, though the foundational principles of neoliberal ideology posit economic and developmental beneficence in open, competitive markets via utility maximizing individual citizens, the application of such neoliberal strategies produces not simply markets – as organizational forms of collective rationality – but new institutional and regulatory landscapes with their own functional logics and political imperatives (Peck and Tickell, 2002). To freeze and therefore marginalize, or to separate as distinct, particular components of this complex and dynamic totality, overlooks how these processes are coterminous and codependent rather than autonomous (see, for example, McMichael, 1990). These processes cannot be understood in the singular since 'interrelated instances are integral to, and define, the general historical process' (ibid., p. 389). To fail to do so is tantamount to focusing on diverse historical processes through which a *particular* spatial form is established as a 'differentiated unit of socio-spatial organization, activity, conflict, struggle, discourse and/or imagination' (Brenner, 2001, p. 599).

To put it more bluntly, if we assume there to be national and transnational spaces then we risk homogenizing actors and processes that are not strictly contained within particular geographical parameters. Spatial forms are thus endowed with scale-specific qualities that define their position against other spatial forms. For example, social forces without links beyond their particular nation state are national, whilst social forces with operations in several national territories are transnational. The important idiosyncrasies of these agents are lost in the attempt to determine collective forms of agency. Instead, these historical, spatial and scalar social relations simultaneously encompass different territorial levels in a multilevel conception which can also accommodate non-territorial phenomena (Anderson, 2002, p. 16). In what follows we briefly outline an alternative approach which, in our view, overcomes these difficulties.

This alternative approach can be seen within the literature on the political economies of scale, where changes in the scale of state regulation typically characterized as globalization are integral to processes of neoliberalization (Gough, 2004, p. 432; for an IPE engagement see Charnock, 2010). This is the result of multiple competing, contradictory, cooperative scales ranging from

> the bodies of working people to the urban centres that concentrate and accumulate finance capital, to the space of the nation with its borders and laws and regulatory apparatuses. Difference and equalization, or at least some dialectic between these, is endemic in every cell, pore, and social body that capitalism produces.
>
> (Mitchell, 2001, p. 58)

Our proposed scalar-relational approach therefore captures the ubiquity of space in analysis of every aspect of social existence, whilst permitting interrogation of the sites and loci of power and – importantly – the relationship between these different scales.

The utility of this scalar-relational approach for critical IPE is most apparent when attempting to demystify the agents of the inherently asymmetrical processes of globalization. We argue, however, that the difficulty which, *inter alia*, neo-Gramscian perspectives have in conceptualizing the social constitution of space is manifest in attempts to analyse the struggles between dominant social forces within the global restructuring of capitalism. We argue that there is an overestimation of the coherence and unity of these elites precisely because their embedded relationship with the national–domestic remains undertheorized.

This notion resonates when Robinson and Harris posit a disembedded transnational capitalist class operating at the 'transnational level', whose interests and identity are no longer contingent upon national-domestic politics (2000, pp. 11–13). Conversely, we argue that so-called 'transnational' social forces remain simultaneously transnationally oriented and nationally embedded.[3] This is because the socio-institutional configurations, and circuits of capital upon which their accumulation strategies depend, are necessarily rooted in established conditions in specific 'national' and local contexts, in spite of the 'transnational' scale of operations (Macartney, 2009). Accounts of transnational capitalist classes in critical IPE tend to privilege the transnational at the expense of the national, precisely because of the methodological focus on political-economic agency. As we noted above, analysis therefore centres on *either* national *or* transnational forms of agency in a way that invariably marginalizes the significance of the other. As we explain, transnationalization concerns the reorganization and the reconstitution of capitalist social relations. Yet despite the mobility of capital, experienced most acutely in particular circuits and by particular fractions, no matter how footloose finance capital might be, it must 'land' in production somewhere. Capital remains embedded in territorially located institutional arrangements and infrastructures, as well as in particular social configurations such as class alliances and localized labour markets (Harvey, 1985, pp. 146–157) that are not solely reducible to the national (Charnock, 2010; Macartney, 2009; Shields, 2008; Wilson, forthcoming).

Our scalar-relational approach to the transnational contends that to speak of a transnational capitalist class and transnational hegemonic project, *pace* van Apeldoorn (2002) risks reifying their agency. This move also risks obfuscating political spaces for counter-hegemonic resistance by reproducing myths of the ubiquity and salience of both these agents and their associated ideological apparatuses. Instead, the concept of transnationally *oriented* fractions of capital emphasizes – at once – their emergence from particular national–domestic conditions and yet their continued embeddedness therein. As the crisis of 2007–09 has revealed, national forms of resistance remain fruitful given the revelation that transnationally oriented finance does not simply exist externally to the nation state, with an elusive exogenous power over domestic politics, but across a variety of scales simultaneously. Whilst this is no doubt also the argument of critical IPE, it is precluded by an analysis of *P*olitical and *E*conomic relations to which *S*patial relations are added only before the final stir.

Conclusions and beginnings?

This chapter has argued that both orthodox IPE and critical IPE have a problem with space. In effect, both sets of accounts have tended to focus on the relationship of the political to the economic, typified by the national/international trope, with space added to the mix later as the *internationalization* of the political economy became increasingly apparent. Paradoxically, in its critique of the orthodoxy, critical IPE has primarily addressed the internal relations of the state and the market through an emphasis on historicizing the emergence of social forces, yet it remains wedded – albeit implicitly – to the assumptions of the orthodoxy in relation to space. Just as Susan Strange (1970) highlighted the mutual neglect of the study of international politics to the study of international economics, critical IPE needs to reconsider the issue of space. Put differently, we suggest that the difficulties in conceptualizing spatial relations are related to more fundamental problems in understanding the historical and social under globalization, and that the counter-hegemonic project of critical IPE risks being hamstrung by its difficulties in theorizing space. This chapter has argued that both mainstream accounts and Coxian-inspired neo-Gramscian readings therefore fail to comprehend the internal relations of these processes.

In contrast, we emphasize the dynamic, mutually constitutive processes of historical, social and spatial change as internally related phenomena, since 'tendencies towards differentiation and universalization or equalization, emanate side by side in the belly of capitalism' (Smith, 1984, p. 90). Spaces are not simply a platform for the unfolding of history; space is simultaneously precondition, mediator and outcome of this highly conflictual process. From here we suggest a scalar-relational understanding of the transnational such that, for example, the state is perceived as both site for and outcome of socio-political struggles perpetually unfolding on overlapping and potentially contradictory forms of territorial organization. The focal points and conceptual categories employed by critical IPE risk precluding an analysis of the codependence of these components to the actual historical process. Finally, in exploring current usage of the transnational we emphasize the importance of our conclusions for de-reifying agents of globalization, and make an initial step in contributing to counter-hegemonic endeavours. This suggests, however, the need to overcome the persistent and deep divisions within critical IPE that preclude a more holistic critique of relations of domination, inequality and injustice.

Notes

1. It is worthwhile noting the proposition that prior to this epochal moment the world was not composed of territorially discrete units that characterize the Westphalian state system (Lacher, 2003).
2. In more recent work Gill has turned to Polanyi to account for these changes (see Bruff, this volume).
3. In our view, whilst this is also the intended argument of a historical, materialist critical IPE more generally, it remains highly problematic given the implicit assumptions about space which emerge under scrutiny.

3
Poststructuralism in/and IPE

Penny Griffin

This chapter seeks to demonstrate how poststructural analysis of the production of knowledge in and about the global political economy (GPE) is both socially useful and intellectually significant. Focusing specifically on the recent global financial crisis (GFC), this chapter asks how this crisis represented a powerful combination of material, ideational and embodied cultures of privilege and how these had (and will continue to have) a profound effect on everyday life.

As is clear from this volume, International Political Economy (IPE), as a discipline,[1] embodies an enormous array of understandings of, approaches to and uses of the term 'critical'. This chapter suggests that we might reasonably narrow such a broad, meaning-laden term to describe 'a willingness to challenge the taken-for-granted', unsettling common sense notions about the nature of the real in favour of espousing 'research that resists closure, instead proliferating possibilities' (Shepherd, 2010, p. 2). As a form of interpretive intervention, not the 'objective pursuit of cumulative knowledge' as practised by IPE's (rationalist) mainstream (de Goede, 2006, p. 21), poststructuralism is here located as part of a broader critical project of interrogating the taken-for-grantedness of the GPE. As a direct challenge to conventional rationalist accounts of/in IPE, poststructuralism offers us powerful tools to understand the relations of power that drive our socio-economic systems.

Poststructural questions are crucial in and to IPE because they query practices and processes of 'cultural representation', 'discourse' and 'the ambiguity of political dissent' (de Goede, 2006, pp. 1–2). It is not only that poststructuralism has something important to say about the GPE, but it is through a poststructural analysis that we are better able to ask questions that interrogate the basis of power, knowledge, representation and identity in the GPE; questions that ask how we are able or not to act in and know the GPE, how we measure and interact with otherwise abstract categories such as 'capital', 'finance' and 'risk', or how we might better take account of the day-to-day realities of ordinary people in our accounts of the GPE. The inclusion of types of questions, categories of identity, methods and understandings, even groups of people that do not easily fit with conventional accounts, offers IPE vital analytical tools, while also revealing the selective and power-laden nature of dominant practices of knowledge production in and about the GPE. We might, for instance, choose to ask how to better understand and investigate the circulation and common sense reproduction of certain realities, what the political implications of this might be and how the practices that give meaning to and make sense of our everyday lives encourage or preclude certain possibilities (by asking how, for example, neoliberal and/or state-led governance strategies define 'opportunities' according to models of economically appropriate/expected behaviour derived from privileging the experiences of white, western and elite men).

Why poststructuralism?

A still relatively underused approach in IPE (de Goede, 2003, p. 79), poststructuralism offers IPE methods of analysis that seek, thoroughly and imaginatively, to question the ways in which knowledge and practice are historically conditioned and informed by patterns of power, values, interests and identities in the GPE. The poststructural critique is particularly significant because it challenges us to explore (differently) various forms of insight into global politics (textual, visual and auditory) and their political implications (see, for example, Bleiker, 2001; Weldes, 2003; Weber, 2008). This chapter argues that understanding how we are represented, and how then our products (and ourselves) are consumed and recirculated, is central to understanding the 'big' issues in world politics (economic crisis, homeland security, terrorism, drug trafficking, and so on).

Rather than corroborating with conventional IPE to sketch a picture of the world as a sequence of isolated events unrelated to everyday practices of social and cultural reproduction, I suggest that we cannot understand the processes and forms of our economic activity without being fully aware of the socio-cultural properties, biases and effects of the structures that govern us. The models of capitalism on which western societies depend are more than a selection of economic choices: these models reach into our everyday, intimate and personal lives, our relationships and experiences, to represent, in many ways, the essence of what it is to be 'self' and 'other' (to be, for example, 'Australian', or 'not Australian'). As part of a broader, reflective (and self-reflexive) critical IPE project, poststructuralism allows us to arrive at answers to our chosen questions only when we reflect carefully (and at some length) on our values, as scholars, students, activists, policymakers, practitioners, and so on.

In pragmatic terms, to ignore the social dynamics from which economic life proceeds (the everyday practices, meanings and social relations that make sense of our selves, our endeavours, activities and desires) is likely only to reproduce a flawed and detrimental policy environment (see Griffin, 2009a, 2009b, 2010a), of which the recent (apparently passed) GFC was one such product. Behaviours, actions, policies and procedures are invariably the result of particular assumptions and rationalities, however long established or commonsensical they may now appear to us (see also Bruff, this volume). Assumptions and rationalities concerning, for example, rational behaviour, economic growth and national stability have not evolved in, nor are they perpetuated in, a social vacuum, although they may well be presented as universal and neutral. As an example: the regulation of 'problem' assets and credit derivatives may be rendered 'value neutral' on paper, but invariably depends on certain assumptions of human productive worth and potentially impinges heavily on human agency, not least where individuals, families and/or communities are already exposed as vulnerable (Griffin, 2010b).

This chapter employs the GFC as an illustration of the social and intellectual significance of analysing how, and where, knowledge is produced in and about the contemporary GPE. This crisis, in particular, is a useful example of the failures of conventional assumptions concerning the separation of politics and economics and the predictability of self-interested, appropriate and rational human behaviour. Poststructural analyses prove constructive here for their focus on how changing conditions in and of the GPE have enabled certain ideas, assumptions and practices about and in the GPE to gain dominance. The increasing speed, immanence and borderless potential of global financial transactions have, for example, provoked particular insecurities for those more comfortable with assuming an 'unequivocal reality' to capital (as a social totality or unified power of sorts capable of controlling financial flows) (de Goede, 2003, p. 83). Moreover, the rise of the 'new economy', and the ensuing displacement of traditional, and therefore more knowable and 'concrete', industries (brewing, building, etc.), with the high-tech stocks of dot.com, communications and/or internet companies, has entailed 'an (ongoing) redefinition of economic interests around conflicting perceptions of money, value and economic growth' (ibid.).

Rather than focus on the realist/liberal preoccupation with the 'identifiable actions of states and policy-makers' (ibid., p. 85), however, an interpretive approach to the GFC is more interested in the ways in which the global financial industry, as a western/northern 'epistemic community' produced by particular capitalist histories, has interpreted and represented certain ideas, assumptions and justifications about the world (in particular, the significance of assumptions about wealth as not only desirable but morally good should not be underestimated). Although these may appear now, with hindsight, to be flawed representations of economic 'reality', they have been hugely influential in determining the origins and future trajectory of the contemporary GPE (particularly the trajectory of contemporary models of capitalism). Financiers are clearly not soldiers, but there remains something knowably 'concrete' about security understood through the material 'reality' of tanks, bombs and front lines. Uncoincidentally, many of the desired behavioural characteristics cultivated in today's generation of finance workers are suspiciously soldier-like, not least the belief that the 'stomach' necessary to make tough decisions, plus a certain fearlessness, are not only desirable but essential qualities.

Poststructuralism in/and International Political Economy

> The resistance of IPE to poststructural intervention can partly be seen as a disciplinary politics that seeks to regulate IPE's agenda of study and to define its core subject matter. All too often, boundaries set in these debates expel from enquiry [important] themes [such as] identity, cultural representation, discourse, everyday life, the ambiguity of political dissent.
>
> (de Goede, 2006, pp. 1–2)

Regularly dismissed as obscurantist, relativist and morally vacuous (as noted in Newman, 2005; de Goede, 2006; Maisonville, 2006), poststructuralism in IPE is also most frequently defined, classified and criticized by those explicitly *not* engaged in its methods (see, for example, Katzenstein et al., 1998). For mainstream IPE, little (if any) merit exists in theories that do not engage with rationalism, and since poststructuralism does not acknowledge 'the possibility of a social science', is unwilling 'to engage openly in scholarly debate with ratio-nalism' and fails 'to pass scientific or ethical judgements' (ibid., p. 668),[2] it resides only at the very boundary of legitimate enquiry. The point for most critical scholars of/in IPE is, of course, that 'rationalism' is not the hub of the IPE universe and, in choosing to measure ourselves against a constructed centre of the discipline, we are only ever able, then, to position our work peripherally.

Avoiding fetishes

Social constructivism, poststructuralism and historical materialism are united, as Bieler and Morton describe, in their basic challenge to neo-realist and liberal institutionalist understandings of the world and, in particular, 'the way they conceptualize the role of ideas' (as constitu-tive of wider social totalities) since 'they all commonly question the notion that it is possible to establish causal relationships within a given objective reality' (2008, p. 104). The problem with poststructuralism for Bieler and Morton, however, lies in the form of its questioning (that is, poststructuralism's focus on the 'how' and not the 'why' questions). This chapter returns to some of these concerns below, but, for the time being, perhaps the major point of note here is their assertion that, although poststructuralism might outline how 'a particular discourse can gain dominance at a specific point in time', it overlooks 'why a certain discourse and not another is successful' (ibid., p. 105). For Bieler and Morton, poststructuralism ignores the 'underlying power structures promoting individual discourses' and thus fails 'to uncover the agency and structural power behind discourses': this results, they suggest, in 'a rendering of capitalist exploitation and domination into a shapeless and contingent world of fetishized self/other differences' (ibid., pp. 105–14).

This chapter agrees that interrogating the underlying power structures creative of certain discourses is crucial in and to any form of critical IPE. It tries also to avoid the pitfall of defining itself against the historical materialism (rather than in dialogue with it) that is common to some poststructural and discourse-analytic scholarship (Laffey, 2004, p. 460).[3] It suggests, instead, that poststructural understandings of power, iden-tity and representation can avoid 'fetishizing' self and other, allocating, even, shape and historicity to relations of exploitation, domination and force. Poststructuralism does this best, I argue, in its postcolonial and gendered forms. As my co-contributors to this volume show, advancing our understanding of and engagement with forms, processes, structures and ideas in and about the GPE requires a variety of strategies, aims and interrogations. As Palan (2007, p. 48) notes, we should avoid judging a school, an approach or a theory 'purely on the basis of material already published', since theories 'are changing, schools of thoughts are evolving, and traditions often develop in unpredictable ways'.

In the spirit of *not* providing answers that are given in theory but instead prompting 'certain kinds of questions' (Laffey, 2004, p. 461), about, for example, representation, capital, power and 'the social', this chapter asks how we might engage in interesting, dynamic but, above all, useful ways with poststructural critique of the GPE. It does so through an examination of 'financial crisis' in order to ask how questions about power, identity, knowledge and representation matter to our understandings of economic reality. This kind of investigation is important because it shows us how the sense we make of the world, and our ability to act within it, is heavily regulated. Such regulation occurs by and through discourses that represent their key subjective, emotional and contingent elements as fixed, pre-given and stable in order to, as Aitken describes, 'create and cultivate capital, often in places where it does not already exist' (2006, p. 81).

Power/embodiment

To borrow Cynthia Enloe's (1996, cited in Griffin, 2009a, p. 200) argument, there are centres of power and there are also margins, silences and bottom rungs, but none exist without a certain conceptual reliance upon gendered dichotomies. Poststructuralism understands power to operate at every level, structural and/or personal, in the words we use and the practices and habits we (knowingly or otherwise) submit ourselves to. It not only takes power and resources to create a centre away from the margins, it also takes specific discursive strategies to maintain and police it. IPE analysis that focuses specifically on the workings of centred political/economic structures exposes the sorts of 'common sense' identities, practices or processes that we take for granted to be products of relations of power.

The intimate life of the GPE

Poststructuralists are wary of separating material and ideational structures, preferring to link the two through conceptualizations of both as inherent in 'discourse' (Bieler and Morton, 2008, p. 111). For poststructuralists, objects and actions, structures and ideas convey meaning and are themselves meaningful; social practices thus 'articulate and contest the discourses that constitute social reality' (Griffin,

2009a, p. 23). Bieler and Morton suggest, however, that poststructural IPE disallows important questions concerning, for example, whose values and beliefs have constituted or embodied identities, interests and international structures, which agents 'shape the core intersubjective beliefs of underlying social and world orders', or why a particular set of ideas becomes part of the structure rather than another (2008, p. 109). Poststructural IPE's 'sole concentration on discourse' thus fails, for Bieler and Morton, to examine 'the internal relation of dominant discourses as material social processes' (ibid., pp. 112–113).

This chapter disagrees that poststructural IPE need avoid the materiality of social processes and argues that scholarship that is more sensitive to the historical and cultural specificity of powerful discursive regulations (sex, class, race, physical 'ability' or otherwise) is intuitively more attuned to the need for more heightened and systematic awareness of global changes and developments, including how these impact upon the interplay between bodies and the GPE. A particularly useful means of investigating and understanding otherwise neglected internal relations/material social processes is through analysis that examines the intimate life (and effects) of the contemporary GPE. Enquiry that focuses less on what bodies *are* than on what they are made to *do* shows how the creation and perpetuation of knowledge fits in with existing assumptions about what is normal, natural and to be expected about 'people' (see, for example, Elias's (2005, 2008) excellent discussion of the re/construction of gendered identities and inequalities in the supposedly 'progressive' multinational firm).

A more heightened and systematic awareness of bodies and the GPE also allows us to ask intimate, personal and often difficult questions concerning the ways in which the contemporary GPE is dependent, for example, on so-called 'informal' and/or 'illicit' activities (see Peterson, 2008). Informal activities range from 'domestic/socially necessary and voluntary "work," where cash is rarely exchanged and "regulatory authorities" are absent', to 'secondary, "shadow" and "irregular" activities, where some form of enterprise and payment is expected but regulation is either difficult to enforce or intentionally avoided/evaded' (ibid., p. 11). Illicit activities in the GPE, which are frequently neglected in/by IPE scholars, might include the expansion of such activities as trafficking in drugs, sex workers, migrants, 'dirty money' and black market goods (ibid., pp. 13–14).

Understanding how bodies are regulated, pre- and proscribed is crucial to understanding the processes and practices of the GPE, not least because conventional approaches to IPE tend to avoid talking about bodies, instead assigning human features to abstract objects (money, weapons, state, corporation or institution) while studiously avoiding the possibility that these objects are socially produced and context-specific (Griffin, 2009a, pp. 1–2). An *embodied* approach, on the other hand (one that engages actively and carefully with the messier politics of everyday human social reproduction), involves analysis of norms and standards in the GPE (about bodies, what can be expected of them and what they are expected to do) that many hold to be true, essential and universal, but a committed critique of which reveals as power-laden, regulatory and highly restrictive identity categories. We might, for example, examine the 'truth' of reproductive heterosexuality as a social, political and economic construct, not the pre-given basis for human interaction that it is made to seem. Consequently, we might, then, investigate the variety of mechanisms, processes and structures of social reproduction and authority (modern science, medicine and/or technology, for example) through which bodies are constrained and controlled such that a 'naturally' distinct re/productive workforce is maintained.

By challenging categories (of sex, race, culture, physical 'ability', and so on) that otherwise define our ability to act in the GPE, we begin also to question (or to 'queer') the apparent stability of dominant discourses. To queer power is to seek to expose the limitations, unstable foundations and power-laden assumptions of the 'straight' political, psychological, cultural and economic discourses that govern us (ibid., p. 37). While sexuality is often ignored in research on the GPE (Bedford, 2005, p. 295), the study of sexuality(ies) in the GPE affords particularly interesting insights into its workings. Taking sexuality seriously in the GPE also subverts powerfully the apparent naturalness of the authorities, hierarchies and discourses residing in the socio-economic systems that govern us, to reveal the ways in which we, as simultaneously consumers, producers, educators and learners, are subject to and object of a bewildering array of socio-economic productions, representations, norms, conventions, stereotypes and life opportunities. Importantly, the ways in which we negotiate and respond to these convey a great deal about prevailing relations of power, which, for poststructuralists, are prolific while also being both intensely intimate and impersonal.

Using neoliberalism as an example, a poststructuralism interested in sexuality might argue that neoliberal models for human interaction and behaviour (centred on the primacy of capital acquisition, private property rights and the capitalist free market) have become pre-eminent because they are based on the assumption that people everywhere adhere to the rule of the market (Griffin, 2009a, p. xv). Neoliberal structures of governance consider us marketable (and capable of appropriately rational practices and behaviours) when we exhibit types of behaviours associated almost exclusively with a gender identity (*homo economicus*) embodied in dominant forms of heterosexual masculinity (Griffin, 2007b, p. 221). That the interests and needs of men can be taken to reflect the interests and needs of society as a whole is clearly masculinist; it is also, however, racist, heterosexist and elitist, since the masculinity most clearly privileged in neoliberalism derives from the experiences not just of 'men', but of white, middle-class, western men (rendering invisible not only women and other non-men, but also those men who do not behave like typical white, western entrepreneurs). To be successful in a GPE dominated by neoliberal discourse, people everywhere must identify themselves with a cultural model of human worth, internalizing the key principles of neoliberal economic doctrine. In so doing, they reproduce centuries of liberal ideology and rhetoric that have naturalized the essentiality of trade, the accumulation of capital and the centrality of economic growth through the liberal 'free market' (Griffin, 2009a, p. xv).

The reality of neoliberal free market 'truth' is thus reproduced through the binding power of certain acts embodied in 'material institutional forms' and 'structural conditions' (Bieler and Morton, 2008, p. 108), including those found in local, national and/or international legislatures and systems of governance. Power here resides in the processes through which authoritative discourses (and the agents that reproduce them) define as appropriate certain actions, while proscribing the responses that do not fit. As an example: neoliberal multilateral organizations, such as the World Bank, today emphasize the productive importance of women's work and the significance of 'making markets work for women (at the policy level) and empowering women to compete in markets (at the agency level)' (World Bank, 2006, p. 4). Policy content remains, however, wedded to assumptions concerning women's essential *a*rationality, such that women continue to be described and positioned in World Bank policy as 'naturally' located in the reproductive sphere (see, for example, World Bank, 2003, 2006). Little, if any, work is done to establish and/or fund 'informal' economy activities to alleviate women and men's burdens here: a 2002 World Bank report notes that the organization's limited 'gender awareness' stretches no further than 'sectors related to education, population, and social protection', with 'no consideration of women's/gender issues' in private sector development, small or medium-sized enterprises, or public sector management (see World Bank, 2002 cited in Griffin, 2007b, p. 234).

Power in/and the Global Financial Crisis (GFC)

Another example of the binding power of neoliberal institutions and structural conditions lies in consideration of the GFC as a potent combination of material, ideational and embodied cultures of privilege. Extensive and sustained critique of the ways in which the financial industry has reproduced flawed and value-laden behaviour has only relatively recently begun to be heard, so effectively has this industry been removed from its political conditions of possibility (conditions dependent on articulating this industry as based on some kind of enduring 'truth' about risk, confidence and the rationality of neoliberal investment strategies).

Angel Gurría, Secretary-General of the Organisation for Economic Cooperation and Development (OECD), in 2008 listed a variety of causes for the financial crisis, none of which are political in nature or human in process. Rather, he notes as causational 'high levels of market liquidity, low global interest rates, low cost of capital, and very low yields on safe investments' (2008). Faced 'with strong investor demand', banks saw 'an opportunity to expand mortgage lending and then to repackage and sell the underlying credit risk as securities with different levels of risk and return' (ibid.). That is, banks acted rationally given their position, seizing their 'opportunity' (as good neoliberals should). The system would, then, crumble due to faltering investor confidence, not internal and/or systemic flaws (for example, concerning the prolonged chain of (ir)responsibility for repackaged, or 'securitized', loans, or that lenders might reasonably have imagined that sub-prime lending may disappoint in a system where the value of the houses borrowers default on would not exceed the value of the original loan). What was not allowed for, that is, what was discursively excluded and/or delegitimized at the time, was that investors might realize that the financial world in which they operated was, in practice, less sure (and therefore less predictable) than they had anticipated (see, for example, Moss, 2008).

Unsurprisingly (given his key position in neoliberal governance), Gurría does not suggest that the financial world should reorientate its key assumptions. Instead, he locates the 'solution' neatly within the neoliberal requirement of capital liquidity, asking simply that institutions 'raise capital' to counter huge losses (rather than reconfigure their foundational approach to the global economy). Although, Gurría (2008) suggests, 'government actions can address some of the shortcomings revealed by the market crisis', the real solution lies in the performance improvements 'key actors in the markets' must make. This includes work that financial institutions themselves have to do, but also 'improved financial education', such that consumers and investors 'make more informed decisions', not only protecting themselves, but helping to 'improve how markets function' (ibid.). Neoliberalism (and its spokes-people) is here most powerful in authorizing actions that do not, under any circumstances, modify the system itself: rather, they are designed to 'improve' its functioning while reproducing existing logics. The self-fulfilling prophecy of neoliberalism's foundational assumptions is thus perpetuated, enabling improved market function by naming market function as improvable through raised capital (the reiteration of which is a confirmation of neoliberalism's correctness).

Knowledge/representation

Against conventional IPE's (and Gurría's) abstractionism, an embod-ied, poststructural IPE contributes essential work in showing how mainstream and critical IPE's exclusions 'are not accidental or coincidental but *required* for the analytical consistency of reigning paradigms' (Peterson, 2005, p. 502; original emphasis). Knowledge, for poststructuralists, can never be produced as 'value neutral'. This is unset-tling for conventional approaches on a number of levels, not least since this has the potential to expose the sexism and racism of dominant disci-plines, discourses and practices considered by many to be 'value neutral' (Griffin, 2009a, p. 16). Poststructural IPE cautions us to understand that the ways in which we think and the things that we say about IPE are con-stitutive of the world(s) that we analyse. Far from being an evacuation of ethics from political enquiry, this actually means that analysts, scholars, practitioners, etc. can never be neutral bystanders to events, histories or crises. Rather, as inherently implicated in their writing, we are therefore also responsible for their effects. Poststructuralism thus challenges us to ask difficult, self-reflective questions about how we make assumptions concerning action, behaviour and identity in the GPE.

We might, for example, ask questions about how we know and are able to interact with 'capital', which might also require of us that we consider important a postcolonial and/or cultural critique of transnational capital as a totalizing cultural force, dependent on, for example, narratives of the 'masculinized Western Self' and the 'back-ward, irrational Native Other' to legitimate certain claims to authority and common sense (see Ling, 2000). As Stuart Hall (1996b, pp. 223–4) describes (in perhaps the clearest and most cited articulation of post-Fordism), a broad social and cultural shift characterized by 'new infor-mation technologies' has fashioned 'a leading role for consumption' while also signalling 'greater social fragmentation and pluralism, the weakening of older collective solidarities and block identities and the emergence of new identities'. Here, the broad social and cultural significance of post-Fordist models resides in the ways such models make possible certain behaviours and actions while rendering illegitimate other possibilities and/or options (for example, by marketing, packaging and designing products according to gendered, ethnocentric and/or class-based assumptions about what people are, or what they do).

In order not to write partial and exclusive stories about the GPE, then, we must 'employ the full register of human perception and intelligence to understand the phenomena of world politics and to address the dilemmas that emanate from them' (Bleiker, 2001, p. 519). By locating 'culture', in its simplest terms, as 'everything symbolic that we learn' (Bartle, 2009), scholars have shown how culture (as embodied, for example, in popular and visual culture), as a process or a set of practices that reproduce meaning and practice between the members of a group or society, 'helps to create and sustain the conditions for contemporary world politics' (Weldes, 2003, p. 6). Crucially, popular visual language is 'increasingly circulated through wireless networks onto the digital screens of our daily lives (computers, telephones, and televisions)', and is experienced 'as much if not more by amateurs than it is by experts' and 'is increasingly the language that amateurs and experts rely upon in order to claim contemporary literacy' (Weber, 2008, pp. 137–8). Power 'is produced and reproduced culturally' (Weldes, 2003, p. 6), such that the political and the cultural are so intimately connected that to continue to neglect, undervalue and thus under-analyse the politics of the popular is, empirically and theoretically, to miss vital considerations of how knowledge is produced by, for and about world politics.

Representing the Global Financial Crisis (GFC)

This chapter has argued that the GFC embodies a material, ideational and embodied culture of privilege. It has also suggested that to engage with power and representation in the GPE, we must understand how bodies are situated, regulated and made to function therein. As noted above, neoliberal assumptions about the appropriate mechanisms of socio-economic exchange and distribution (based largely on the assumed 'natural fact' and inevitability of economic liberalization, integration and, thus, human emancipation) are based on a model of human activity derived from the privileging and experiences of middle class, white and western men. The 'affluent minorities' of the global economy, argues Gill, 'resemble a late modern masculine identity attributed to men in the West': that is, a 'world that is ahistorical, economistic, materialistic, "me-orientated", short-termist, and ecologically myopic' (1995, quoted in Ling, 2000, p. 244).

It is worth noting that analysis of its gendered effects, however important, does not automatically enlighten us on the gendered foundations of the GPE. Similarly, highlighting women's apparent lack of privilege in the global financial industry is not all that gender analysis might meaningfully tell us about the GFC. Such analytical efforts do, however, offer a window onto how the finance industry has created and sustained a culture of privilege, competitive success and masculine 'prowess' that immediately and effectively excludes all other (embodied) possibilities, female, male and otherwise.[4] Women may suffer in particular ways within a heteronormatively ordered and highly masculinized industry, but the point is less about who is worse off at a given moment (this is important, but not pivotally so) than about how the financial industry has achieved these ends (Griffin, 2010b).

At a certain point in mid-2009 (the apparent peak of the GFC), a ubiquitous representation of the GFC as a 'mancession' emerged, attested to by a flurry of descriptions affirming this 'truth': from 2008 to 2009, it was claimed, men experienced job losses at a significantly higher rate than women, 'leading to disproportionate levels of joblessness among males' (Investopedia, 2009). Since women dominated 'publicly funded industries such as education and healthcare' and these saw 'far fewer cutbacks than other male-dominated industries' (ibid.), the assumption was that the GFC was disproportionately hurting men. A little more time for reflection (and better research) has since suggested that actually women (and women everywhere, not just in the US, which has monopolized GFC reporting) may have been more adversely affected by the recent crisis, since men have actually experienced job losses at a lower rate than in earlier recessions: women change jobs more easily, but command lower salaries, and are unlikely to gain from job losses in cyclical sectors such as manufacturing and construction. More significantly, perhaps, in those countries where women's survival was precarious *before* the crisis, slowed economic growth, increased food prices, the increased likelihood of girls rather than boys being withdrawn from school and higher levels of infant and child mortality are yet more damaging (see, for example, Buvinic et al., 2009).

Debates about 'mancessions' notwithstanding, however, the overwhelming majority of discussions of the GFC have almost entirely absented the ways in which *power* in the GPE (that is, the very causes and not just the effects of the crisis) was/is/might be gendered (Griffin, 2010b). At no other time in recent years, it seemed, had questions surrounding economic growth and development, investment, capital transfer and exchange, the size of the public sector, governmental intervention in the 'free' market, and so on, seemed so pressing. That discussions of gender in the GPE rarely, then (at least in the media and popular press), got beyond a 'men/women must be worse off than women/men' approach to social inequality and injustice is disappointing, if perhaps not surprising. Furthermore, the longer we fail to remedy 'any of the underlying factors' that led to the disastrous period of 2007–09 (Auther, 2010), the 'natural fact' of economic liberalization, integration and human emancipation through the expansion of western-style capitalisms remains, apparently, unarrested. As does the highly masculinized and ethnocentric model of human activity on which it has been built.

Also worth noting, here, is the significance of (socio-institutional, governmental and industry-led) efforts to 'mystify' finance in the twentieth century and beyond. Simultaneous to administrative endeavours to incorporate working-class and 'everyday' populations in spaces of 'popular finance', capital has also often been represented, popularly and academically, as 'an implacable kind of force' and the financial world as 'an unknowable and, importantly, undoable centre of power and domination' (Aitken, 2006, pp. 78–80).[5] Thus has the hazy 'science' of global financial transactions been removed rather effectively from public scrutiny, since it is (a) reproduced within a 'community of speech' largely closed to non-industry external scrutiny, (b) spoken through a language too abstract for the average layperson to understand, and (c) heavily guarded by state-led interventions to preserve capital 'mobility'.

Conclusion(s)...

As part of a broader critical project dedicated to interrogating the taken-for-grantedness of the GPE, poststructural IPE is pivotal in understanding the relations of power that drive our social, economic and political systems. Without suggesting that people everywhere labour under the same signifying codes, cultural articulations and/or life experiences, this chapter has argued that poststructural IPE allows us to appreciate the power of the systems of identification through which we understand the world, how we respond to our environments, our abilities to survive, our goals in life and how we approach our relationships. Understanding the (gendered) foundations of the contemporary

GPE (including the recent GFC) involves looking more closely at how and where privilege is located in the GPE. That we do not forget pressing questions and concerns regarding the processes and forms of our economic activity, nor that those who govern us cease to debate how best we might all proceed, does not preclude that we take care with our understanding of the origins, form and effects of crisis. It is crucial that we continue to investigate both why *and* how it is possible for financial markets to work in the ways that they do. We would do well, here, not to underestimate the practices of power and knowledge creation that have reproduced the potency of Anglo-American neoliberalism, as outlined above.

As Elias notes in her chapter, we need always to be conscious of the areas we close (unconsciously or otherwise) as we elsewhere open new spaces for engagement through critical enquiry. Identities are rarely (if ever) neatly mappable onto individual bodies, and we should think carefully about how power relations and forms of identity 'shape the very categories of analysis and research questions' that we ask (this volume). A commitment to understanding the networks and operations of power, representation, desire and interest that drive political and economic life, invests IPE with significant insight into the everyday operations, and effects, of global politics. For poststructural IPE, as for much critical IPE more broadly, the creation, perpetuation and articulation of certain types of knowledge and identity in the GPE are never neutral, nor are they the expression of any objective 'truth'. Knowledge is always generated historically, according to prevailing discourses of power, science and/or truth. It is also generated relationally, as part of the social understandings we share with others, our forebears and our environments.

As we forge knowledge in and about the GPE that includes categories of identity, methods and understandings, even groups of people, that do not easily fit with conventional accounts, it is crucial that we keep asking questions that interrogate the basis of power, knowledge, representation and identity in the GPE. It is imperative also that we remain sensitive to the historical and cultural specificity of relations (and regulations) in the GPE. Such a sensitivity renders our analysis more intuitively attuned to local, cultural and/or historic context, and allows for approaches to and in IPE (as a discipline) that embody a greater systematic awareness of changes in the GPE (as a geopolitical space) and their effects on human bodies. In short, such scholarship is exactly what IPE, in its conventional and critical forms, really needs but often continues to discount: analysis that is both more sensitive to cultural variations and local differences and also more systematically aware of global trends and processes.

Notes

1. This chapter deploys 'IPE' to denote the academic discipline of International Political Economy as it is currently studied and practised, whereas 'GPE' is used to denote the location, or space, of politico-economic activity in world politics (including the relationships between the complex processes, institutions, structures of understanding, meanings, behaviours and identities that circulate).
2. Foucault's later work rather contradicts Katzenstein et al.'s claim concerning poststructuralism's omissions (see, for example, 'Society Must be Defended' and 'The Birth of Biopolitics', part of Foucault's lectures to the Collège de France, 1975–9).
3. Laffey suggests that Foucault and Laclau and Mouffe's critiques of economism have been perhaps the most significant steps towards the rejection of historical materialism. He is perhaps most critical, however, of de Goede and Campbell's work for failing to see the diversity of historical materialist thought, and suggests that the poststructuralist 'dismantling of the subject' (also embodied in Judith Butler's work) is in danger of becoming 'unintentionally complicit' with a world guided by new forms of capitalist exploitation (2004, pp. 467–8). The point should be, Laffey suggests, 'to think a bit more carefully about the politics and the locations of our representations' (ibid., p. 468).
4. The business and financial worlds continue to evince significant inequalities in the recruitment and retainment of male and female employees, with men ten times more likely than women to be employed in skilled trades and more likely to be managers and senior officials (see the UK's Office for National Statistics, 2008). Securities, commodities, funds, trusts and other financial investments (so pertinent to the recent GFC) have been and continue to be heavily dominated by (white) men (see, for example, Boraas and Rodgers, 2003; Personnel Today, 2006).
5. Aitken's analysis focuses specifically on the US Advertising Council's post-Cold War public service campaigns. It offers a persuasive example of how, at a particular historical moment following the Second World War, 'capital' came to be performed and constituted in US society, such that 'popular finance' became a crucial vessel for 'national security'.

Part II
Debate

4
New Marxism and the Problem of Subjectivity: Towards a Critical *and* Historical International Political Economy

Randall Germain

New Marxism and world order

We all come to International Political Economy (IPE) from a particular perspective.[1] To adapt a well-known adage first coined by Robert W. Cox (1981/1996, p. 87), 'political economy is always for someone, and for some purpose'. My entry point into IPE is through questions associated very broadly with world order: what can an understanding of 'world order' provide to our knowledge about the world; why is it important to 'know' this; what kind of world order do we have; how did it come to pass; what moves it; how does it help to distribute rewards and costs; and, crucially, is it changing and if so in what directions? For me, IPE became a useful way of asking these questions because its attention is both more broad-ranging than international politics – the discipline more usually associated with these kinds of questions – but also because it is more appropriately focused on those elements of order that, to me at least, demand attention. These include dealing conceptually and holistically with the state, the international system of states, the production and distribution of wealth, the many and manifold links between power, wealth and life chances, and ultimately with agency and its parameters, determinants and forms. Some render this last element as the 'agent-structure' problem, but I prefer to think of it slightly differently, as the problem of conceiving of the possibilities of agency within an already organized, patterned and therefore structured world.

Within this context, which determines the possibility of agency, the problem of subjectivity is paramount. This is because agency is purpose-led behaviour; it is the attempt by individual and collective actors to bring a particular state or situation into being: it is activity determined by end goals and ambitions. And these are determined by a host of things, among them the values held by agents, their various capabilities and the constraints they face as they undertake their activities. If we understand by the term subjectivity the self-understandings that agents have of themselves, or what R.G. Collingwood (1946, p. 10) called human self-knowledge, then the manner by which they determine the values and beliefs out of which their purposive behaviour emerges, and through which they apprehend the world that confronts them, is crucial to understanding not only their immediate activities but also the wellsprings of that activity. In other words, subjectivity provides the connection between the world that confronts human agents – whether collective or individual in terms of their organization – and what they do in and to that world.

Can IPE, then, provide a useful understanding of the link between world order and subjectivity? I believe it can, but it must take much more seriously than previously two cardinal aspects of political economy that have been largely absent from scholarly discussion: law or legal frameworks, and culture. To date, where law is considered, it is most often as a reflection of power relations, with very little consideration of how individuals and communities might invest in the law or legal orders a sense of right that informs how they formulate their own goals and values. Law in this understanding is the codified right of the strongest rather than codified social norms; it is derivative of broader relations of power rather than, at least partly, determinative of them (Cutler, 2003). In this sense it can only support, never undermine, world order. A similar logic is at work where culture is considered. Culture is too often a residual category of ideas that are simply apprehended and used in an instrumental manner, as ideological categories that rationalize particular decisions taken in the interests of more organic and somehow prior commitments. Culture, in this sense, confirms the modalities of world order, rather than shapes or undermines them (but see Best and Paterson, 2009; Bruff, 2008).

By downplaying the place and role of subjectivity in the construction and constitution of world order, IPE loses an important avenue through which meaning and purpose are formed for historical agents, and therefore through which our understanding of the social world proceeds. Several theoretical traditions within IPE are poorly placed to either acknowledge the importance of subjectivity or explore it.

These include all except the earliest classical forms of liberalism, all rational choice and public choice theory, neo- and structural realism, most world systems and institutionalist analyses, and, I would argue, most Wendtian forms of constructivism (which accept the identities of agents as being products of the properties of the systems in which they happen to find themselves).[2] These traditions are poorly placed to consider subjectivity because they assume a particular version of subjectivity rather than problematize subjectivity itself. For these traditions, any question organized around subjectivity is a derivative, second-order question, perhaps not even amenable to measurement, or one really about a variable of only minor importance. Nevertheless, there are theoretical traditions within IPE which, to my mind, are at least open to the significance of subjectivity, including historical materialism, postmodernism, feminism, some versions of constructivism and some versions of poststructuralism. My concern in this chapter is the tradition of thought understood as historical materialism, and especially its latest incarnation: 'new Marxism'.

At first blush, 'new Marxism', or what some prefer to identify as 'critical' political economy, should be well positioned to consider the place and role of subjectivity in the construction and constitution of world order. For such scholarship, capitalism and its consequences are a fundamental element of the global political economy, and few explorations of the links between wealth and power, state and economy, or structure and agency, can fail to benefit from a frank engagement with Marxist or historical materialist scholarship. In particular, Marxist explorations of class formation squarely confront issues that cannot be answered without considering why agents think and act as they do. But on the vital question of world order subjectivity, or perhaps more properly intersubjectivity, I would argue that Marxist scholarship has not provided us with a suitable formulation of the problem. For despite all of the sophistication of the Marxist analytical toolkit and its deployment, Marxism has been fundamentally unable to comprehend the motivational wellsprings of human behaviour, and therefore it has been unable to understand and predict how human beings respond to the structural conditions Marxist scholarship so keenly and astutely catalogues. Marxism and Marxist historical materialism (for it is difficult to consider historical materialism apart from Marxism), in other words, fail to apprehend satisfactorily the historical subjectivity that informs how human agents understand and respond to their circumstances.

I recognize that this is a big charge and, as it is posed here, a rather indiscriminate one, in at least two ways. First, it takes a swipe at a literature that is so large, so multifaceted, so consumed by its various intellectual stakes, that some might say it is even pointless and irrelevant to pose such a question in the first place. For what are Marxism and historical materialism today anyway?[3] There are as many variants and currents as there are schools and institutions that Marxists may call home, and they write and reflect on every aspect of social life, not just world order. Best, some might say, to let them get on with their battles and arguments and not to detract them with new ones. Also, it is not as if this is a new charge, even if perhaps it has only rarely been formulated, as in this chapter. The intellectual history of Marxist thought is replete with debates, exchanges and battles within, among and between Marxists and others of every imaginable hue. What, it could be asked, is to be gained by beginning another such debate?

I would highlight two reasons for undertaking the task of exploring further the link between new Marxism and subjectivity. The first is simply to confirm the importance of subjectivity to the discipline of political economy in general and to IPE in particular. If we can demonstrate that new Marxism cannot account for world order on its own terms without engaging satisfactorily with the problem of subjectivity, then a debate can be opened up which hopefully can address this important gap, and new Marxist scholars need to take part in this debate. In this chapter I argue that new Marxism is unable to account adequately for the continued resilience of a neoliberal world order unless it confronts squarely the cultural attractions of this order, but that it has the analytical tools to do so. The second reason, however, is, from my perspective, more important. It is this: once we establish the importance of subjectivity to any first-order explanation of world order, then we need to ask whether new Marxism, on its own terms, can come to grips with exploring the various elements of such subjectivity. My argument here is that, on its own terms, new Marxism deploys an ontology that is unable to apprehend adequately the changing intersubjective dynamics that mark out the contemporary world order. In order to address this problem, we need to reconnect historical materialism to its more historicist roots, since it is within this tradition that historical materialism confronts the problem of subjectivity most directly; a reconnected historical materialism would be better able to engage with the issues posed by critical political economy in an age of global or world-order change.

To do this, I explore the recent work of three exemplars of new Marxism: William Robinson, David Harvey, and Michael Hardt and Antonio Negri. All these authors agree that fundamentally important changes within the constitution of global capitalism are under way, and that we must consider these changes holistically and as involving a significant transformation in our capacity to act. Harvey and Robinson organize their analyses around changes in the regime of accumulation and class and state respectively, while Hardt and Negri draw our attention to fundamental changes in the motive dynamics of social organization, in particular changes to how labour power is being organized. All touch on changing modes of subjectivity, but only Hardt and Negri open up a way of thinking about these changes in a manner that allows changing cultural forms to actually shape the contours of world order. Yet, ultimately, all are found wanting, prompting me to ask whether we need to move beyond a Marxist-inspired form of historical materialism to recover our capacity to negotiate successfully the complex terrain of subjectivity, culture and political economy.

New Marxism, subjectivity and ontology

For new Marxists, in line with the tradition out of which they have emerged, the basic unit of analysis is class as set within the context of imperial state power. What is innovative about the authors under consideration here, however, is the context and meaning they attribute to class. For Harvey, the state has been usurped by the capitalist class and its power projected geopolitically through the imperial adventures of the US. World order, in this reading, is under siege from a unilateral and unrepentant American state, supported here and there by states that have undergone similar US-style neoliberal transformations (principally the UK, Australia and a number of European states). For Robinson, in contrast, the capitalist class has gone transnational, and dragged the state along with it. It is the transnational capitalist class that lies at the heart of global capitalism, supported and abetted by the transnational state structure that is taking shape across the dominant core countries. And finally, for Hardt and Negri it is precisely the reconfiguration of class, arising out of the new forms of labour power that are increasingly immaterial, through which new forms of sovereignty – imperial sovereignty – are being produced. In the work of these authors, class and state are linked organically and complicit in the contemporary transformation of world order.

But what is the ontological basis of class for these authors? They divide into two camps: a radical materialist ontology for Harvey and Robinson that explicitly follows Marx, and an equally radical subjective ontology for Hardt and Negri, which, they argue, maintains a Marxist pedigree. The materialist basis of class for Robinson is clear: for him, classes exist in antagonistic relation to each other as organized by their common connection in relation to the process of social reproduction (Robinson, 2004, p. 37). Shorn of this common connection to production, and devoid of their polar opposite, class cannot exist; it needs to be understood relationally. However, he is also clear that classes are historical products by virtue of the forging of a collective sense of self-representation; in this he follows the classic distinction between a class-in-itself and a class-for-itself. For Robinson, the study of class formation thus requires both attention to the material conditions that make collective agency possible, and attention to intentionality and forms of consciousness that enable classes to act for themselves.

Such a rendering should bring subjectivity front and centre to Robinson's analysis. However, his macro-sociological approach, although laced with a concern for agency and what he identifies as 'subjective' elements (for example, issues associated with legitimacy or hegemony), systematically undermines the agency of agency by subordinating it to instrumental calculations concerning the costs and benefits of capitalism understood through its distributional affects among classes. Here Robinson is assuming that classes define themselves solely through their position within the structure of production. The consumption habits, ethnic and racial make-up, educational attainment, and personal feelings and preferences of members of classes are trumped by their collective relationship vis-à-vis their main historical rival. At best, these other attributes of individual and collective actors complicate and intertwine with class relations; they are the cultural adjunct to more basic modalities of class relations. This is a materialist ontology which views all determinants of identity through the prism of class and its principal material antagonism, that is to say, with the distribution of its costs and rewards. It is a monochromatic reading of history's multiple motive forces, albeit a powerful one.

How then does Robinson negotiate the terrain of subjectivity in which individual identities and self-understandings are produced through collective means? For Robinson, subjectivity is essentially a derivative category associated with the personal consumption needs of individuals. It has an important role in facilitating and guiding the individual's consumption of the products of global capitalism, but it cannot challenge capitalism per se. Most importantly, this subjectivity, which can be closely identified with the generation and production of cultural products, is itself firmly tied to the constraints of the transnational structure of production. Here its main role is to function as a mode of social control, to depoliticize social behaviour and pre-empt collective action (Robinson, 2004, pp. 30–2, 83–4). This is not to say that culture has an insignificant role to play in the market economy, because it is a crucial means by which individuals can negotiate the hand dealt to them by existing class relations: the consumption of, or engagement with, cultural products and artefacts provides an escape from the constraints of the market economy. Nevertheless, it is in the end an instrumental mechanism used to achieve a particular end that is itself a product of material interests. In this important sense, subjectivity and its cultural determinants are for Robinson prisoners of his materialist ontology. As a 'problem', therefore, subjectivity and its cultural production remain unresolved, indeed even unbroached.

For David Harvey, subjectivity, as represented by cultural norms and mores and its affects, must loom large in any explanation of why world order has taken a distinctively hegemonic hue. Most importantly, culture and subjectivity arise, for him, as part of the ways and means that hegemony is achieved through the construction of consent. While hegemony is forged on the back of class power, it is through a dominant class's cultural manipulations that subordinate classes acquiesce to its rule. This is particularly clear for Harvey (2005) in his account of the rise of neoliberalism and its global triumph in the 1980s. Whether in Britain, America or elsewhere, Harvey sees the successful deployment of cultural values as a feature of neoliberalism's consensual dominance, culminating in a form of Americanization that he believes has only now witnessed its apogee.

Two cultural values stand out for Harvey as facilitating the rise of neoliberalism. First, freedom as a common-sense societal value has been particularly invaluable to neoliberalism as a critical popular value, perhaps *the* most important one, precisely because it has enabled its spokespersons to fashion a public consensus around the best and proper role for the state in a neoliberal world. This role, which is both limited and directed to maintaining the privileges of a capitalist elite, has become the settled and natural role for the state, which all arguments concerning the role of the state must, in effect, appropriate to greater or lesser degrees. Whether in its extreme form in the US or a more attenuated form in East Asian nations like South Korea, the idea of freedom and its political consequences is a cultural value that has strengthened neoliberal dominance enormously.

Along with the value of freedom goes a form of hedonistic consumption which, for Harvey, both supports capitalism and is leading the world to environmental ruin. Individual consumption and consumer choice have the effect, *pace* Robinson, of depoliticizing people, of inducing apathy so long as a certain lifestyle can be maintained. Or, to be more accurate, only as long as such a lifestyle is merely offered, since even the possibility of attaining such a lifestyle in the US and elsewhere is, according to Harvey, increasingly problematic. There are two reasons for this. One is the growing inequality within developed countries such as the US, which he indicates is subject to a 30:30:40 ratio of secure, precarious and underemployment. Within this emerging condition, fewer and fewer citizens are thus actually able to attain the lifestyles of the rich and famous, which form the template for consumption patterns. Second, if things are bad in the US, they are even worse everywhere else across the developed and developing world. The world is growing more slowly, incomes are becoming increasingly unequal, and dispossession and exploitation are reaching levels that can no longer be placated with the chimera of consumption. Although a middle class with bourgeois aspirations has emerged across many parts of the developing world, the contradictions and struggles they face can no longer be bought off with the promise of conspicuous consumption, since the social and environmental costs associated with this have reached their maximum levels of tolerance. All of this is to drive home, for Harvey, the way in which culture and its values enable elites to forge hegemony and buy off subordinate classes: 'cultural and traditional values...and fears...can be mobilized to mask other realities' (2005, p. 39).

Harvey sees these other realities as in fact the bedrock of neoliberalism. They include, most importantly, class relations and the regime of accumulation, which are the fount and matrix of social life. Class relations direct social struggle and conflict in so far as they order and condition what is possible across space and time. Although Harvey does not offer quite as clear an initial definition of class as Robinson, his meaning of class in terms of its changing social configuration is remarkably close to Robinson's. Most importantly, class is associated with the power of elites, who increasingly derive their material rewards from financial services and orient an important part of their activities in a transnational direction (although Harvey is not yet willing to consign the nation state to a sort of historical purgatory, as does Robinson). Nevertheless, class as a social configuration can be understood by tracing the interests of elites and the distribution of rewards that flow from capitalist ownership rights. It is through these activities that Harvey can trace the operation of the regime of accumulation through the crisis of the 1970s and its reconstitution under what he provocatively terms 'accumulation by dispossession' (2003, p. 137).

I would argue that this understanding of class and its social consequences is based on an overtly materialist ontology. Class is conceived as a collective form of agency determined by tangible material rewards. It is defined by what it does or does not possess. Class is not defined in terms of self-understanding or identity; indeed, these are manipulated and guided by the 'realities' which class relations so cleverly mask. Moreover, Harvey is sceptical that we should try and understand culture on its own terms; he associates this attempt with a 'postmodern' sensibility:

> neo-liberalization required both politically and economically the construction of consumerism and individual libertarianism. As such it proved more than a little compatible with that cultural impulse called 'postmodernism' which had long been lurking in the wings but could now emerge full-blown as both a cultural and an intellectual dominant.
>
> (2005, p. 42)

Culture is derivative of, rather than determinant to, the economy as understood in materialist terms.

Harvey has, of course, already engaged with the theme of culture and political economy in his earlier work, *The Condition of Postmodernity* (1990). What stands out from this engagement, however, is the manner in which Harvey searches for an underlying structural condition to cultural postmodernism, which he identifies with the capitalist regime of accumulation. Culture and its forms, on this earlier reading, were nothing more than an attempt to make sense of, and especially to respond to, the new and problematic regime of accumulation then just beginning to take form. Culture follows rather than leads capitalist innovation and developments; it provides an important outlet for the stresses and contradictions of the present, but it does not fundamentally influence how capitalism evolves. That we were moving to a postmodern form of capitalism was evident, to Harvey at least, from the transformation in production processes, most importantly towards what he identified as 'flexible accumulation'. Such a regime of accumulation promoted, and indeed exalted, change and flexibility in the production process, thus prompting the glorification of change and transitory, ephemeral representations in art, architecture and most forms of cultural aesthetics. The materialist ontology that dominates Harvey's recent work was already well established in his earlier writings.

When compared with the explicit and foundational materialism of Robinson and Harvey, Hardt and Negri's work is organized around a radical subjectivism that seems to lead to wholly different conclusions about the state of the global political economy and the condition of world order more generally. Whereas Robinson and Harvey provide a fundamentally pessimistic, deterministic and even fatalistic reading of what is possible in the contemporary period, in *Empire* Hardt and Negri ooze optimism and even the absolute necessity of acting in concert with the evaluation they provide. Where Robinson and Harvey stress structure and exploitation, Hardt and Negri illuminate the possibilities of network power and the consciousness-raising elements of alienation. And while Hardt and Negri are not deaf to the repercussions of the death throes of coercive military and economic power organized through old-style class formations and state apparatuses, their eyes and ears are deftly tuned to the emergence of startling new forms of collective agency amid the capillaries that channel biopower within global society. In short, they offer a contrast with Robinson and Harvey that speaks directly to what might be termed their 'immaterialist' ontology.

We can glimpse this ontology through the manner by which Hardt and Negri engage culture and class. And here two very interesting dimensions to their use of culture and class present themselves. First, in neither *Empire* nor *Multitude* do these concepts, in and of themselves, resonate explicitly. There are, for example, no entries for either culture or class in the index of *Empire*, and only a few in *Multitude*. Nevertheless, both concepts are omnipresent. Culture, for Hardt and Negri, is nothing short of the social production of order, and as such inheres in each element of global order that is under discussion in *Empire*. For example, their discussion of both biopower and disciplinary governability is an excursus on the way in which adherence to particular social orders is organized and exercised culturally as well as economically and politically, in particular through the interiorization of disciplinary power. Mere coercive force does not and cannot *explain* why individuals with little or no stake in the status quo continue to accept their position, much less to endow that position with a sufficient degree of legitimacy so as to preserve and even extend it. And whatever one may conclude about the viability of the 'multitude' as Hardt and Negri consider it, this is a collective form of agency which is made as much by its own cultural values as it is by the imposition of dominant political and economic interests and values.

The omnipresence of class as a key causal force is elided somewhat by the determination of Hardt and Negri to explain how class configurations are changing. Class formation is now led by what they describe as 'immaterial' labour, namely the production of information, knowledge and even cultural forms without a firm and explicit basis in tangible goods. 'Immaterial' labour is in a way the key to Hardt and Negri's account of accumulation, and it is the grounds upon which they consider world order now to be postmodern rather than modern. It leads to the new form of imperial sovereignty that lies, for them, at the heart of empire. This is a new form also of subjectivity – an imperial subjectivity – that, for the first time ever, is global in scope and arises from within, as an immanent possibility that is dependent upon cultural ideas to become actualized. Class and culture thus conjoin to bring into being, for Hardt and Negri, the possibility of a real global democracy. Therefore, despite not being explicitly articulated as such, culture and class are central to their argument for the emergence of a new world order; these concepts are in effect framed by the problem of subjectivity.

This link provides the second point of interest, namely the radical way in which Hardt and Negri conceive of subjectivity. As just indicated, part of their radical conception of subjectivity lies in the absolute immanence that they attribute to culture and class, which are considered as emerging from within collective forms of agency active in the world at large. Such absolute immanence provides their historical agents with radical potential, and in this lies the basis of their radically subjective ontology. For Hardt and Negri, historical subjects – what they identify as *res gestae* – both conceive of their world and make it on their own terms. These terms cannot of course escape their conditions, but they are ultimately based on the degree to which these conditions are internalized and then reconfigured to produce the requisite counter-power. The real question, therefore, for Hardt and Negri, concerns not these (essentially capitalist) conditions, whose structural parameters in any case have not, arguably, evolved much over the past several decades, but the internal and subjective possibilities of the multitude, which require proper formulation in order to break free of their (conceptual) chains. As they style it, class is not an *empirical* concept, it is a *political* concept; or better yet, a *project* (Hardt and Negri, 2004, p. 104). The inner possibilities of class are ideational, cultural and philosophical in their main outlines; hence their refusal to consider culture to be derivative of, or dependent upon, the outer structural conditions that so animate the work of Robinson and Harvey. Class is understood here, crucially, as a cultural product, open to many and competing representational claims and dynamics.

At the same time, this radical subjectivity has an immense problem: arguably, it has no historical subject at its core. While for Robinson and Harvey the primary historical subject of their work is class, and specifically the working class broadly understood, for Hardt and Negri the question of the actual historical subject under consideration is ambiguous. At one level of course it is the 'multitude'. However, the 'multitude' is posed as a subject on such a vast scale – a global scale – that its cultural determination becomes almost vacuous. By this I mean that the production of self-understanding and identity, which stands at the heart of subjectivity and which makes an appreciation of the cultural infusion of political economy so necessary for any understanding of world order, becomes ambiguous and even confused within a context of the world's population (which is the subject of Hardt and Negri's term 'multitude'). If a historical subject such as class partly comes into being on the basis of its own self-portrayal, does there not need to be a parallel equivalent that can reach and forge such a large collective mentality for a 'multitude'? Hardt and Negri are thus left with a paradoxical situation in which their world is inhabited by agents that are equally endowed with an immanent capacity for subjectivity, but where only one among many such agents actually succeed in realizing this subjectivity. Since there is no *a priori* reason why this should be the case, our conclusion must be that such a radically subjectivist ontology serves us as poorly as does a radically materialist one.

We have now come full circle in our consideration of the potential for new Marxist scholarship to advance our understanding of world order. Those who deploy a materialist ontology are ultimately unable to provide a compelling account of why the current world order has been so resilient to date. Instead, they offer puzzlement (Harvey) and bewilderment (Robinson) as to why an order that is so fundamentally exploitative and alienating continues also to be relatively robust. Coercion alone cannot account for this quiescence, since in the past coercion has been unable to contain such manifest inequities. And those who deploy a radically subjectivist ontology also appear unable to tell us why a real historical subject with an immanent capacity to recognize itself – on the basis of the production of immaterial labour power – has not yet done so, or at least not in a manner that is easily recognizable. Equally puzzling, it is difficult for such scholars to point to any real concrete achievements arising from the activities of this 'new' historical subject. It is on this basis that I claim that new Marxism has not yet provided us with a valuable account of world order and its changing forms of subjectivity.

Recovering and reconnecting historical materialism: negotiating the terrain of subjectivity

So, should we abandon historical materialism as an avenue through which a suitable understanding of world order and its subjectivity – or intersubjectivity – can be pursued? My argument is not to abandon historical materialism, but rather to reconnect it to that part of its tradition which has been eclipsed since it became indelibly associated with Marx and Marxism. This is not an easy task, but if it is deemed worthwhile it can be facilitated in two ways. First, by recovering that strand of historical materialism which is overtly and explicitly historicist in its reasoning, we can highlight once again the idealist component of historical materialism that has been overlain by the more materialist-oriented scholarship of the new Marxists. This can be accomplished by reconsidering the work of Robert W. Cox, who remains an exemplar of historical materialism but yet who refuses the materialist pitfalls that plague Harvey and Robinson. Second, by reconnecting historical materialism with its historicist leanings, we can provide a method to anchor securely the cultural and ideational elements as part of the investigative practices of political economy, without sacrificing the useful elements highlighted not only by Harvey and Robinson, but Hardt and Negri as well. This will require us to return to the work of scholars such as R.G. Collingwood in order to become reacquainted with methods suitable to uncovering the intersubjective basis of world order. Thus, by a process of recovery and reconnection, we can more usefully reframe the problem of subjectivity within the tradition of historical materialism, and provide the tools that will enable it to traverse adequately the terrain of world order.

If we turn first to the task of recovery, it may seem odd that I am proposing here to 'recover' the work of Robert W. Cox for historical materialism, for he has written some of the most insightful and provocative treatments of world order available within the tradition of political economy. But I think this is a useful task because there is some ambiguity as to how his work has related to the tradition of historical materialism. He is, for example, reluctant to identify himself with any one particular tradition: sometimes he has labelled himself a kind of Jacobite, anti-Whig conservative; at other times a cross between a friendly neighbourhood Marxist-Leninist subversive and a simple historical materialist; and most recently as just plain old 'eclectic' (Cox, 2002, p. 26). One cannot help but think that Susan Strange's (1988a, pp. 269–70) description of Cox continues to ring true: as a 'loner, a fugitive from the intellectual camps of victory, both Marxist and liberal'. Nevertheless, if we want to consider him essentially as a scholar rooted in the tradition of historical materialism, then it is incumbent upon us to recognize the very special strand of historical materialism that he embraces, one marked more by deep attention to historicism and debates over historiography than by a concern with Marx and Marxist thought more generally. In effect, for Cox the tradition of historical materialism provides an important entry into the question of changing historical structures within the context of organized collective social behaviour (for example, Cox, 1981/1996, pp. 93–6).

Most importantly, a close reading of Cox's scholarship reveals that the historical materialism that animates his work is drawn from a range of thinkers primarily concerned with understanding the meaning of history, the structural parameters of social life, and the possibility of radical transformation in human consciousness and institutions. The contrast here with someone like Perry Anderson is stark: where Anderson holds fidelity to the ethos of Marx and Engels as the key criterion for assessing the utility of historical materialist thought (for example, Anderson, 1976), Cox holds the degree to which we are able to think 'historically' about the potential for change as the key criterion of assessment. Historical materialism, for Cox, amounts to deploying a 'historical mode of thought' to apprehend the structural and agential modalities characteristic of any particular period of history. Class struggle, for example, can certainly insert itself into such a mode of thought, but it is not a privileged analytical lens, nor, one much suspects, an overly privileged question.

Such a reading of Cox's work can be sustained by looking to the sources that he cites as influential in the development of his thinking. They are an eclectic lot, united less by their fealty to Marxism and more by their embrace of a form of historicism and even relativism which understands historical structures and human agency to emerge out of the historical process and not behind or on the backs of human beings acting individually and collectively. What are these sources? Interestingly, they are almost all historians, philosophers, or both, who have reflected on the particular modalities of civilizational change. They include, among philosophers, Ibn Khaldun (fourteenth century), Niccolo Machiavelli (fifteenth century), Giambattista Vico (seventeenth century), Edmund Burke (eighteenth century) and R.G. Collingwood (twentieth century). Among historians we would count all of the above, who, in effect, were historians as well as philosophers of history, plus Karl Marx, Friedrich Meinecke, Oswald Spengler and Georges Sorel, all of whom overlapped the nineteenth and twentieth centuries, and E.H. Carr, Antonio Gramsci, E.P. Thompson, Fernand Braudel and Geoffrey Barraclough from the twentieth century. What is interesting about this list is that aside (perhaps!) from Marx himself, they are all either problematic Marxists (Gramsci, Thompson and Sorel) or non-Marxists (all the rest).

Why does Cox rely on this eclectic lot for theoretical inspiration? The answer, in a nutshell, is that according to Cox the question that history has set for us in the late twentieth and early twenty-first centuries has predominantly come to be framed in terms of civilizational change, focused most importantly on the intersubjective understandings that frame, shape and promote or impede such change. In order to explore these changes, our intellectual net needs to be cast as wide as necessary in order to piece together the evolving nature of collective consciousness and the way in which material practices give rise to and shape this *mentalité*. What marks out Cox's historical materialism in this sense is its embrace of a form of philosophical idealism – or what he would identify more simply as *historical idealism* – that takes seriously the interrelationship of forms of subjectivity with the actual human practices that sustain and challenge them. This particular fusion of historical idealism with materialism is the key to his careful distinction between synchronic and diachronic understandings of historical structures: the difference between the material practices that uphold or challenge a historical structure can be found in the subjectivities (and intersubjectivities) which inform historical agents at specific points in time, and which generate contradictions in established institutions and patterns of behaviour.

Thus, for Cox, the value of historical materialism as an approach to understanding political economy is precisely that it allows us to prise open the intersubjective consciousness of historical agents (be they individuals, institutions, movements, classes or indeed civilizations) and thereby to reconstruct their *mentalités* so as to understand both why they are organized as they are and what possibilities exist for their future development. Following R.G. Collingwood, who stands as a key inspiration for Cox in this regard, our task is to construct a web of meaning that allows us to enter into the minds of historical participants and rebuild the world as they saw (or see) it. Recognizing this, helps us to make sense of Cox's own intellectual odyssey, which has taken him from reflecting on the practices and organization of concrete international institutions to considering the changing structure of world order to analysing multilateralism to exploring civilizational encounters. Each step in this intellectual journey has involved adding a layer of intersubjective consciousness to an abiding concern with continually evolving material everyday activities or practices. And, crucially, it involves looking back to previous modes of thinking to elicit potential harbingers of change, rooted in the social relations of how the world in which we live is, and has been, produced on a daily basis.

This is *historical* in the twofold sense of holding that consciousness is integral to, rather than derivative of, social 'being', and recognizing that material practices leave their indelible mark on our evolving subjectivity. Class struggle has been and, to a certain extent, remains a special 'contributor' to this imprint, but it sits alongside many others that interrelate and change the composition and situation of class within the context of social order, including culture and a civilizational ethos. Although historical materialism in this view incorporates a concern for class struggle, it does not allow such a concern to encompass or swallow all historical materialist analysis, which has been the default mode of most historical materialist scholarship within IPE (for example, Morton, 2006).

This leads directly to the second task of reconnection, precisely in order to open our analysis of political economy to the many and competing social dynamics that move agents to act. Here, the important thing to establish is both the subject and the method of historical enquiry, which together constitute what we might identify as a 'historical form of reasoning'. It is this form of reasoning that should underlay the practice of historical materialism, and we can see this in action by considering the work of R.G. Collingwood.[4] Collingwood, an early twentieth-century idealist philosopher and historian, is a useful starting point precisely because for him the chief purpose of historical enquiry is to understand the thought of past actors. For Collingwood (1946, p. 9) history is *res gestae*, 'human actions done in the past'. He is not, however, interested primarily in the acts themselves, but rather in the thought processes that lie behind the acts.

This focus leads Collingwood to consider history as philosophy, and to argue that the historical imagination is indispensable to understanding the way in which historical trajectories unfold. In particular, he insists that thinking about history is in fact a form of reflection about the thought of humans that led them to undertake certain and specific courses of action in the past. We can reformulate this to suggest that understanding what motivates agents is crucial to understanding what humans have actually done or accomplished: it is the actions of human beings – conceived of as the logical end points of definite and concrete thought processes – which form the subject matter of our investigations. Historical enquiry (whether of the past or present) cannot proceed without considering the thought processes that guide these activities, and these thought processes, in turn, cannot be comprehended without examining the motivations that precede them, including the goals and aspirations that underpin them. This ultimately leads Collingwood (ibid., p. 10) to consider the purpose of historical enquiry to be 'human self-knowledge', which we can define as an understanding of human motivations, or why we undertake the actions we do.

It is important to stress here that, for Collingwood, the crucial feature of the historical record is not so much the factual listing of achievements, but rather their significance for the individuals and communities that experience them in the first place (or who live with the consequences of such achievements). One must of course begin any enquiry with factual history, with the *outside* of events (or what Collingwood (ibid., p. 214) identifies as spectacle), but in order to perceive the significance of historical events for the people involved we must focus our attention on the *inside* of such events, on the thought processes of the agents involved which lead them to perceive and react to their surroundings in particular ways. In other words, what is central to our investigation is the subjectivity that individual and collective agents share as together they make history. This form of historical reasoning is always about establishing how the subject(s) of history, the individual and collective agents engaged in the construction of the historical record, understand and act upon their interpretation of the conditions of existence. It is through this appreciation of the way in which the material conditions of existence are apprehended by the subjects of history that a first cut at understanding structural constraints emerges.

Collingwood thus establishes that the starting point of a historicist version of historical materialism is a form of reasoning – historical reasoning – which begins with the interpretive understandings of real historical subjects. In this way historical reasoning privileges agency in order to assign analytical weight or significance to the modifications of the human mind, whose apprehension of the conditions of existence in light of a concrete record of historical achievement provides the entry point to thinking and reflecting about broader patters of constraints and opportunities for action, or, in Cox's phraseology, historical structures. This, in turn, comes directly out of both Collingwood's and Cox's acceptance of Giambattista Vico's brilliant *verum–factum* principle, namely that our knowledge of the 'world of nations' is to be found within 'the modifications of our own human mind' (1744/1970, p. 62). This dual moment – considering the motivations of agents as central to understanding *res gestae* and reflecting upon these motivations so as not merely to know what they are but rather to understand their emergence in the context of their material surroundings – rules out adopting deterministic and ahistorical forms of reasoning. With human subjects at the centre of analysis, overarching transhistorical dynamics – whether associated with class, power, ethnicity, etc. – do not become admissible as explanatory devices. Rather, we must craft explanations based upon what human beings actually understand themselves to be doing as the key to understanding their history, even if these self-understandings are themselves often contradictory, misleading or incomplete.

We can thus use Cox's version of historical materialism, together with Collingwood's account of historical reasoning, to fashion a version of historical materialism that places the problem of subjectivity at the centre of our understanding of world order. But it is a version of historical materialism that is inspired by more than Marx, and ranges wider than Marxist scholarship. Such a version has many affinities with Marxist-inspired scholars in this tradition – Gramsci and E.P. Thompson come immediately to mind, along with Georges Sorel and Stuart Hall – precisely because such an important element of this tradition shares with Cox and Collingwood the concern to develop an imaginative reconstruction of the web of meaning that informs human practice at definite points in history. This version of historical materialism also has the benefit of opening up our analysis to the currents of cultural political economy, currents that point to the many ways in which self-understanding and self-representation engage with structural constraints to produce the aims and values that motivate agents to do something about and to their world. And yet political economy remains at the centre of our analysis, because the intersection of power and wealth, security and welfare, state and market, and economy and society continue to mark out many of the most important fault lines of our world. Moreover, such a version of political economy refuses to marginalize the evolving self-understanding of subjectivity from our analysis. Thus can we reconnect to a tradition that has largely been abandoned since Marx, in the *Preface to a Critique of Political Economy*, offered up his definitive statement of the method of political economy.

In conclusion, I wish to stress that my claim here is not that new Marxists have nothing to contribute to our understanding of world order. Rather it is to argue that until their ontology is reconsidered and moved closer towards the historicism inherent to Cox's ontology, which itself fuses idealism and materialism in a holistic and symmetrical manner, their analyses will not be persuasive precisely because they are unable to account for why people adhere to an order that so manifestly fails to benefit them in a satisfactory manner. Any explanation of this must take the evolving subjectivity of historical agents – the modifications of our human mind – much more seriously in order to comprehend the cultural and ideational attractions of a particular world order. And this will involve being able to identify real historical subjects in a recognizable manner, using the self-representations and self-understandings that agents require to make their way in the world. The structural conditions that Harvey and Robinson identify and trace are clearly a part of this, as is the ideational element which Hardt and Negri point to in their explanation of the evolving power of imperial sovereignty. But until they recover a more adequate ontology, and reconnect this ontology to a more fully grounded historical form of reasoning, this task will remain incomplete.

Notes

1. This chapter benefited from delivery to the workshop 'Critical International Political Economy', convened at the University of Manchester, 25–26 March 2010. Earlier versions were presented at the workshop 'Cultural Political Economy', convened at the University of Ottawa, 15–17 June 2007, and to the workshop 'Reading Marx', Carleton University, 13 March 2009. I wish to thank participants in all of these workshops, the editors of this volume and Liliana Pop for helpful comments. All remaining problems and errors are mine.
2. For example, Benjamin Cohen's very readable intellectual history of IPE contains no discussion of the problem of subjectivity in relationship to IPE (Cohen, 2008a).
3. The relationship between Marxism and historical materialism has been almost unbreakable since Marx famously defined his method of political economy as the 'materialist conception of history'. Although the nuance and sophistication of historical materialism have evolved over the intervening years, Marx's statement in the *Preface to a Critique of Political Economy* still stands as the bedrock definition of this approach to political economy: 'In the social production of their life, men [*sic*] enter into definite relations that are indispensable and independent of their will, relations of production which correspond to a definite stage of development of their material productive forces...No social order ever perishes before all of the productive forces for which there is room in it have developed; and new, higher relations of production never appear before the material conditions of their existence have matured in the womb of the old society itself' (Marx, 1977, pp. 389–90).
4. Collingwood has to date been an absent interlocutor within historical materialist IPE. Cox has identified part of the reason for this, which is that Collingwood has been understood principally as an idealist philosopher whose work does not translate into contemporary debates within the social sciences (Cox, 1981/1996, 2002). For a rare but provocative engagement, see Blaney and Inayatullah (2010).

5
Overcoming the State/Market Dichotomy

Ian Bruff

The critical importance of foundational assumptions

Lucian Ashworth (2009, p. 23), in an interesting overview of the historical development of International Relations (IR) as a discipline, points out that 'up to the 1950s, IR was an essentially transdisciplinary subject, with only very limited attachments to political science' (see also his contribution to this volume). However, its subsequent capture by political science has left it in a difficult position in recent years, which have witnessed attempts to reach out to disciplines such as history, geography and sociology (ibid.). This paradox has, in many senses, led to its fragmentation through the rising diversity of perspectives articulated within the discipline, especially if one thinks back to the 'great debates' of previous decades. However, one positive aspect of this development has been the recent move to ground the study of international politics more firmly in philosophies of social science, which then enables us to be more explicit with regard to our assumptions about the world.

Although this has sometimes meant that debates over, say, critical realism and poststructuralism follow in the tracks of those which took place in the previous decades in sociology, social theory and the humanities, it has nevertheless injected fresh life into the discussions. There are many examples of this. One could think of the *Review of International Studies* debates on the state as a 'person' (Wendt, 2004; Wight, 2004; Schiff, 2008), a recent issue of *International Politics* focusing on historical sociology and IR (Hobson, 2007; Lawson, 2007; Mabee, 2007), and the proliferation of discussions on uneven and combined development and 'the international' (Rosenberg, 2006; Callinicos, 2007;

Allinson and Anievas, 2009). And seemingly (but not) paradoxically, this greater conceptual and philosophical reflection has actually opened up the space for heightened uncertainty about the world in which we live. That is, '[f]oregrounding ontology is... one way to keep us *honest* about such matters' (Jackson, 2008, p. 152; original emphasis), for it forces us to be reflexive and open-minded about what we may (unwittingly) take for granted.

Curiously, International Political Economy (IPE) has moved considerably more slowly, despite its reputation for being more open and interdisciplinary than IR. For instance, the recent debates in *Review of International Political Economy* (RIPE) and *New Political Economy* (NPE) on the (postulated) 'transatlantic divide' between 'American' and 'British' IPE remained largely at the methodological level, with a 'winner' from the discussions being the recently developed 'analytical eclecticism' framework (Katzenstein, 2009). In short, 'analytical eclecticism isolates specific features of theories initially embedded in distinct research traditions, separates them from their foundations, philosophical and otherwise, translates them meaningfully, and recombines them as part of an original amalgam of concepts and methods, analytics and empirics' (ibid., p. 133). Although on the surface Katzenstein's 'problem-driven' approach succeeded in its attempt – literally in the term – to combine the (assumed) scientific, 'analytical' focus of American IPE and the more open-ended, 'eclectic' frameworks deployed in British IPE, it is fraught with problems. In particular, the lack of rigorous reflection on the concepts we use, and the assumptions we base them upon, is striking. In my view, there was little recognition in the discussions across the special issues that a more eclectic, complex approach needs to be *more*, not less, reflexive about its ontological commitments (cf. Jackson, 2010, p. 190). As van Apeldoorn et al. (2010, p. 216) argue:

> The complexity of the world in which we live means that research has to be undertaken in a myriad of overlapping and interconnected social relations. Hence to ascertain constituent determinants and their effects requires abstraction and therefore concept formation at every stage of the research process.

This means that '[e]ven what is in principle a holistic perspective cannot say everything and must necessarily prioritise' (Dunn, 2009, p. 318). That is, *all* research is *necessarily* underpinned by a conceptual asymmetry (ibid., pp. 81–6); the scholar has chosen (implicitly or explicitly) to privilege certain ways of viewing the world over others. As Jackson (2010, p. 41) elaborates:

> Ontological commitments, whether philosophical or scientific, logically precede substantive claims, and serve as the often-unacknowledged basis on which empirical claims are founded. In this sense, ontological commitments are 'foundational' – not in the sense that they provide unshakable grounds that universally guarantee the validity of claims that are founded on them, but 'foundational' in the sense that they provide the conditions of intelligibility for those claims.

The question for this chapter is, therefore, what is being taken for granted through IPE's reluctance to embrace a more philosophically explicit approach which is more open about the assumptions upon which all research necessarily rests? For me, one of the key examples is the state/market dichotomy, which – through separating out different aspects of the world in which we live into discrete and autonomous parts – assumes that states and markets contain impersonal properties intrinsic to themselves, as relatively self-organizing components of society. This is not to say that we cannot identify differences between them; more that the distinction is only methodological and not ontological, or 'real' (cf. Gramsci, 1971, p. 159). However, prior philosophical reflection is necessary for making this point: we cannot proceed immediately to methodology, as the RIPE and NPE debates largely did.

This is important for two reasons. First, attempts to provide holistic analyses that seek to make sense of the social totality are often criticized – unfairly – for imposing a theoretical purity on a complex and messy world (cf. Underhill, 2009; Hveem, 2009). In so doing, such charges perform the neat conjuring trick of calling for intellectual pluralism and *at the same time* dismissing certain pluralities as unwelcome (see also Elias and Cammack in this volume). Second, it leads us to banal statements such as 'things are more random than you think and the world is not programmable to a theory of history' (Blyth, 2009b, p. 333) – who on earth would disagree with this? – which finally regresses into 'open' but ultimately limited work that refuses to acknowledge the assumptions that underlie such adherence to multi-causality, contingency and so on.

All of this is highly problematic for IPE as a discipline, for 'the distinction between "the state" and "the market" is a false one and, as such, an IPE that is based on theorizing the relationship between the two must necessarily be limited' (Watson, 2005, p. 13). Watson undermines points such as these in his own contribution to the 'transatlantic divide' debates (see the concluding chapter of this volume), but here he is nevertheless correct to say:

> while most IPE scholars pay lip-service to the artificial nature of that dichotomy, in practice their studies serve merely to reinforce it. In all likelihood, this is not deliberate; rather, it arises from the fact that IPE has conventionally been seen as a sub-field of International Relations, and the dichotomy between 'politics' and 'economics' to be found in IR has simply been imported into IPE.
>
> (ibid., p. 19)

However, we can go further than this: IPE not only tends to adhere to a false dichotomy, but it also ascribes different normative properties to 'states' and 'markets'. Consider this (representative) quote from Phil Cerny (1990, pp. 102–3; emphasis added) in a well-known monograph: '[t]he state becomes the very condition of "practical consciousness", rivalled only by that *more insidious*, equally ubiquitous but less emotive, less holistically visible and less linguistically salient structural formation, the market'. In other words, because IPE tends in practice to equate to the 'politics of the world economy' – by way of its debts to IR (which in turn, in the modern version, is indebted to political science) – it is considerably more likely that 'markets' rather than 'states' will be problematized. Thus, the more detrimental logic *inherent* to markets rather than the more benign logic *inherent* to states leads to a concentration of 'critical' analysis on the former and not on the latter.

In contrast, there is a long tradition in critical social theory of viewing the state as part and parcel of unequal relations of power, rather than as something that intrinsically embodies a more equitable social purpose (see Marx, 1979; Mills, 1956; MacKinnon, 1989; Jessop, 2007). This is not the place to review the huge and varied contributions to this discussion; instead, I wish to demonstrate in the rest of this chapter that, for IPE to overcome the state/market dichotomy and the different normative properties ascribed to states and markets, we need to step outside the discipline. It is only through an engagement with critical social theory that we are then able to return to IPE, enriched in the process, in order to arrive at a more satisfactory study of the international political economy (to use Cammack's distinction; see his chapter in this volume).

Accordingly, the chapter is structured as follows. First, I add flesh to the bones of the above critical comments on IPE and the state/market dichotomy, arguing in the process that even 'critical' IPE tends implicitly to adhere to it. This then sets the stage to depart from IPE and consider Antonio Gramsci's writings on 'common sense' – often cited in sociology, cultural studies and other disciplines – which have been neglected in IPE in favour of more 'political' concepts such as hegemony (Bruff, 2010). I contend that these, especially when situated in Gramsci's broader writings on the sociology of knowledge, are particularly useful when seeking to overcome the artificial separation between 'states' and 'markets'. This will be executed via a denaturalization of the state, which, as I assert above, is more strongly insulated from critical scrutiny in IPE than 'markets'. The implications for IPE are discussed in the conclusion.

IPE and the state/market dichotomy

Through its focus on states and the states system the state/market distinction is still highly prevalent in IR, despite the theoretical advances of recent years. However, given that IPE's emergence out of IR was predicated on the questioning of precisely this dichotomy (classic examples including Strange, 1970; Keohane and Nye, 1977), it is curious that few serious moves have been made to overcome it. This is not confined to mainstream IPE either: the problematic separation of politics and economics has remained a stubborn intellectual hangover from political science's capture of IR for even 'critical' IPE. For this reason, it is not just the more mainstream contributions that deploy a state/market dichotomy, but also more self-professed critical perspectives. Taking the former first, consider these statements:

> In this book I define 'global political economy' as the interaction of the market and such powerful actors as states, multinational firms, and international organizations.
>
> (Gilpin, 2001, pp. 17–18)

> national governments evidently lack both the power and the will to make good the deficiencies of inequality and instability that have always gone with growth and change in market economies.
>
> (Strange, 1996, p. 190)

Here we have, from two of Cohen's (2008a) 'magnificent seven', clear assumptions of both the state/market dichotomy and that these two categories contain intrinsic, and normatively distinctive, properties. This is prevalent in mainstream IPE – consider book titles such as *Small States in World Markets* (Katzenstein, 1985), *States and Markets* (Strange, 1988b) and *States against Markets* (Schwartz, 1994) – and, as indicated above, it extends well beyond it (albeit in a less visible form). In the examples below, we find more complex, multi-causal approaches – in the name of openness and of avoiding determinism – which nevertheless rest on assumptions that are left unexplained:

> This book focuses upon three main actors: the state, organized labor, and organized business... *the relevant unit of analysis depends upon* the view of the crisis that the agents in question operationalize and act upon.
>
> (Blyth, 2002, p. 13; emphasis added)

> The question of the relationship between structure and agency depends fundamentally on the particular constellation of structural forces which prevail in particular political economies, the specific constraints represented by *various ideological, political and economic structures* for different parts of the world, and the particular capacities of agents (particularly states) to respond to and shape them effectively.
>
> (Phillips, 2005a, pp. 257–8; emphasis added)

What we see here is, through the *explicit* rejection of false dichotomies – in these contributions, ideas and economic interests (Blyth) and structure and agency (Phillips) – *implicit* separations are left in place. Note Blyth's 'it depends' approach, and Phillips' emphasis on the need to consider various *but always and already separate* structures that are then brought together as a set of constraints that agents respond to. This is problematic for the reasons set out already: despite the clear awareness of the need to be more 'worldly' than the approaches offered by mainstream IPE, *within* this world we can nevertheless observe separate, identifiable 'units of analysis' or structures. *Only then*, after already being constituted as apart from each other, do they interact – as a result, the state/market dichotomy remains intact.

Another important issue can be raised when considering these contributions, for the commitment to multi-causal analysis has its consequences (be they in IPE or elsewhere in the social sciences). As I have argued with regard to the institutionalism underpinning the 'varieties of capitalism' and related literatures (Bruff, 2008, pp. 3–7), there is an underlying epistemological opportunism. That is, the scholar is able to call upon different factors as and when necessary – or, more pointedly, when other explanations do not 'work' – in order to 'prove' the superiority of their framework. Therefore, the commitment to holistic analysis which captures the myriad of factors at play is undermined by the crucial underlying assumption: at different times, different aspects of the world can be the independent variable (this is implicit in Blyth's (2002, pp. 34–44) five hypotheses about ideas). Obscured from view, again, is the need to be explicit, *not* about methodological strategies which enable one to be opportunistic about how we construct our knowledge of the world, but about the ontological assumptions that are necessary for any research to be conducted at all (for other examples of multi-causal approaches, see Weiss and Hobson, 1995; Seabrooke, 2006).

A key consequence is that we consistently find our objects of study *responding to* something that has gone before, something that is taken for granted. Perhaps, therefore, we need to broaden the scope of our enquiry. However, even in more avowedly 'critical' works we find problems. For instance, in an important article on historicized political economy, Amoore et al. (2000, p. 54) argue that there is a need 'to embrace a substantive concern with the historicity of knowledge itself before we can genuinely construct a historicized IPE'. Such a historicized ontology is rooted in the fact that 'world history is the product of ordinary human actions' (ibid., p. 66). While this accords with the thrust of this chapter, the second of these quotations is undermined by the previous sentence, where the authors concede that they are not asking IPE scholars to abandon 'important agents' such as markets, states and firms (ibid.). But if the central element of this approach is 'the historical mode of inquiry' (ibid., p. 65), then surely the implicit acceptance that markets, states and firms are characterized by intrinsic, identifiable and thus autonomous properties should be questioned further (see also Macartney and Shields in this volume). In other words, perhaps a category of analysis such as 'the state' is socio-historically produced and thus entirely artificial in its appearance as a 'real' aspect of our lives (cf. Bratsis, 2006).

Furthermore, although Robert Cox (1981), in his classic article, stresses that his two triangles – of material capabilities, ideas and institutions, and social forces, forms of state and world orders – are ideal-typical categories within a larger historical structure (one of whose critical elements is the production process), there is considerable potential for the scholar to take these separations as 'real' rather than methodological.

Indeed, this appears to have happened in Cox's own work, for by 2007 (2007, pp. 515–16) he preferred to situate himself towards the 'ideas' end of the first triangle. As a result, the potential remains for the different aspects of the world to be bracketed off not just methodologically – for analysis of parts of the world that help constitute the whole – but ontologically – different parts of society are comprised of a series of independent variables, all with their own causal powers. This is problematic because it encourages us to take aspects of the world that we study as 'real' rather than socio-historically produced, despite Cox's (ibid., p. 516) protestations that he wants to avoid the notion that categories have a permanent and fixed essence.

This is an aspect of other neo-Gramscian works as well. For example, Stephen Gill's (2008) emphasis on how the structural power of capital is, through the transnationalization of production, giving rise to new forms of power in the global political economy, is undermined by his reliance on Braudel, and especially Polanyi and Foucault, when outlining the concrete manifestations of what he terms 'market civilization'. While this is useful as a means to identifying different forms of political projects (such as neoliberalism), it implies that the state constructs a capitalist society on behalf of, and for the benefit of, certain social forces; that is, '[c]apitalism only works because it is politically and socially supported' (Dunn, 2009, p. 246). This is not to question the descriptive accuracy of such a position, but it forces us to consider that we need to state more explicitly that the political and the economic are *internally* related. That is, these two socio-historical categories are based upon a common foundation. To put it more specifically, perhaps we should consider more seriously the possibility that 'the state' is comprised of the same social, that is, human, relations as the 'market'.

Implicit in the above discussion, and as argued in other chapters (Fischer and Tepe; Cammack), is the assertion that the theoretical resources *already* exist to tackle these problems. And, as noted earlier in the chapter, we need to go outside IPE in order to return to it with an enriched view of the world. In this sense, Gramsci's discussions of 'common sense' are just one example of how this could be done (see Bruff, 2011a, 2011b; van Apeldoorn et al. 2010 for discussions of other authors). Moreover, this does not entail a mere appropriation of ideas and notions from critical social theory; we need to work *with*, rather than uncritically apply, the works we consult.

Below I argue that although Gramsci tended to invoke common sense with regard to, for instance, subalternity, folklore and religion (to name but a few), inherent to Gramsci's notes is the foundation for a more expansive view. Through Gramsci's observations on the sociology of knowledge it is possible to acknowledge that the conceptions we hold about the world – our common sense – are the basis for how we think and act. This is true for humans everywhere in society, regardless of whether our study is 'located' within the state, in everyday life or indeed anywhere else. This enables us to go further in our attempts to denaturalize the decisions and actions taken by humans within the state, for it makes it possible for us to enquire more closely into the basis for such decisions and actions. In turn, this helps us to move away from the notion that the state is a 'structure' or a 'thing'; instead, it is the materialization of human thought/action in regularized practices that appear 'real' and 'state-like' by way of the implementation and enforcing of laws, procedures and conventions.

As such, although the next section may appear distant from IPE's concerns, I contend that such a discussion is essential if the study of the international political economy by IPE is to move forward.

How to know Gramsci and his 'common sense'?

Antonio Gramsci's prison notebooks are famous for their incompleteness and shifting conceptual definitions and terminologies. For this reason, it is perhaps unsurprising that many authors argue that the context in which he lived and struggled – taken in both the national-territorial and the historical senses of context – is too specific for scholars not of the place or era to apply his concepts elsewhere in space and time (Bellamy, 1990; Bellamy and Schecter, 1993). There is also the argument that Gramsci's notes, because of the appalling prison conditions in which he was writing, are so open to radically different interpretations that their application is fraught with difficulty (Germain and Kenny, 1998). In a manner similar to Stuart Hall (1991, 1997) and Adam Morton (2003, 2007b), this chapter occupies a middle ground between discarding the notion that Gramsci's ideas are relevant for contemporary societies and utilizing them uncritically.

This approach has two key aspects. The first is the rejection of the thought that 'Gramsci "has the answers" or "holds the key" to our present [context]' (Hall, 1991, p. 114). This would limit our ability to make sense of our own specific conditions of existence, for instead of interrogating them creatively and with purpose, we seek 'the consoling and appropriate quotation' (ibid.). Therefore, and this is the second aspect, we must think things through in 'a Gramscian way' (ibid.), for his ideas can be situated in and beyond their context through a critical appreciation of what might be limited as well as relevant in his work when considering different historical and social conditions (Sassoon, 2000; Morton, 2003, 2007b). Of course, this is what Gramsci did with regard to the Marxist canon in the aftermath of the counter-revolutions in the late 1910s and early 1920s across Europe.

Therefore, there is much to be said for acknowledging the potential of Gramsci's writings rather than indulging in an 'austere historicism' which denies us the possibility of consulting them as a means of orienting ourselves to the world in which we live (Morton, 2003, p. 129). Indeed, one can argue that Gramsci's notes are full of fertile theoretical and conceptual possibilities: it is precisely the incompleteness of the *Prison Notebooks* that provides us with the multiple horizons that are still being explored. The benefits of an unfinished theoretical framework in and of itself *have* been noted by other scholars, albeit reluctantly (presumably for fear of being derided for not being rigorous enough). For example, Stuart Hall (1996a, p. 146) 'confessed' to 'an alarming tendency in myself to prefer people's less complete works to their later, mature and complete ones... where they have gotten over their adolescent idealism but their thought has not yet hardened into a system'. In other words, the suggestive rather than definitive nature of the *Prison Notebooks* is precisely what makes them relevant for our time as well as for Gramsci's.

As such, although the rest of the chapter is littered with Gramsci quotations, this is emphatically *not* because I am seeking the consoling sentence. Instead, it is to show that through creatively working with his writings across a range of topics (for simplicity's sake, I focus on the 1971 *Selections from the Prison Notebooks*) we can think anew about both his ideas and their contemporary relevance. Derek Boothman (2006–7) shows that Gramsci did this himself with regard to other concepts and philosophies, taking a more flexible approach to ideas and paradigms than someone such as Thomas Kuhn, for he saw them as socio-historical products and not systems of thought that are frequently incommensurate with each other. As such, 'discourses may be rendered "open", renewed, and updated by means of a critique and modification of the concepts used in other discourses, [but] not always, or often, by their simple unmodified incorporation into one's own discourse' (ibid., p. 135). While the latter, simple incorporation, is advocated by proponents of analytical eclecticism, this chapter will now demonstrate the advantages of the former approach via an examination of Gramsci's writings on 'common sense', as situated in his broader writings on the sociology of knowledge.

Common sense is a complex set of ideas from a variety of sources, from the Stone Age to advanced science, 'which, even in the brain of one individual, is fragmentary, incoherent and inconsequential' (Gramsci, 1971, p. 419). As a result, it should be viewed as a collective noun, for if it is multifaceted for one person then for a society we must allow for the fact that common sense 'is not a single unique conception, identical in time and space' (ibid.). Nevertheless, it is a crucial means of understanding human social practice, for our conceptions of the world, no matter how implicit and contradictory, provide 'a point of reference for thought and action' (Green and Ives, 2009, p. 14). Indeed, the historical relevance and importance of the sediments left behind by different conceptions of the world is rooted in the extent to which the sediments build up to form a set of often contradictory and uncritical yet solid beliefs, which can potentially assume granite-like imperviousness to new ideas (Gramsci, 1971, p. 404).

For Green and Ives (2009, p. 10), 'the Gramscian notion of "common sense" can [thus] be understood as popular social thought or as the common beliefs and opinions held by ordinary people'. As such, it is the spontaneous philosophy of everyday life, a 'folklore' (also a collective noun) whose 'principal elements . . . are provided by religion' (Gramsci, 1971, p. 420). Hence, if common sense is 'uncritically absorbed by the various social and cultural environments in which the moral individuality of the average man [*sic*, as throughout] is developed' (ibid., p. 419), then 'the relationship between common sense and religion is much more intimate than that between common sense and the philosophical systems of the intellectuals' (ibid., p. 420). Therefore, philosophy should be viewed as the process of 'criticism and the superseding of religion and "common sense" . . . it coincides with "good" as opposed to "common" sense' (ibid., p. 326).

It is for these reasons that Andrew Robinson (2006, pp. 75, 76) criticizes the relative absence of reflection in the secondary literature on Gramsci on:

> his critique of common sense. This is crucial, because this critique was a central part of his conception of revolutionary change. It is clear from the *Prison Notebooks* that Gramsci was opposed both to everyday 'common sense', the philosophy of the masses, and to the manipulative and passivity-inducing effects of elite-dominated politics. He was therefore an advocate of a revolution in everyday life . . . he has in mind a thoroughgoing transformation and development of people's ways of thinking and acting in everyday life.

Robinson cites many examples, several of which revolve around Gramsci's desire for the masses to raise their intellectual level in order to become an active historical force. A collective will can then be articulated, enabling the dominated sections of society to break free of the conceptions of the world that imprison them in their subordination. However, he paints too dichotomous a picture of the rhythm of Gramsci's writings on this issue,[1] with emancipation only arriving once good sense is excavated and set apart from its common-sense cage. For instance, Gramsci (1971, p. 328) argues that 'it is not possible to separate what is known as "scientific" philosophy from the common and popular philosophy... [good sense] deserves to be made more unitary and coherent'. Therefore, the process of developing consciousness and more coherent thoughts about the world *does* involve criticism, but this 'means the diffusion in a critical form of truths already discovered' (ibid., p. 325). This requires an ability to understand the reasons for common-sense opinions being held, 'up to and including the most reprehensible' (Sassoon, 2006, p. 8), in order to raise such outlooks to a level where common sense has become critical (Green and Ives, 2009, p. 9).

As such, Gramsci is interested in common sense in order to understand the basis upon which it can be transformed in the name of human liberation (Green, 2002). And, given his belief that '[i]n acquiring one's conception of the world one always belongs to a particular grouping' which nevertheless is comprised simultaneously of 'a multiplicity of mass human groups' (Gramsci, 1971, p. 324), it is unsurprising that common sense is often connected to his concept of the subaltern (see Green, 2002; Crehan, 2002; Green and Ives, 2009). Subaltern – like common sense – is a collective noun which captures the various forms of subordination suffered by a diversity of social groups (Green, 2002, p. 2). This, in turn, is rooted in the basic antagonisms embodied in capitalist social relations, which pit the owners of the means of production against those whose work actually produces the wealth, through which a range of discriminations are experienced (Morton, 2007a, p. 62). Thus an understanding of class relations and struggles is necessary but not sufficient for comprehending subaltern existences and the potentials for their transformation through the attainment of societal hegemony.

This section, as discussed earlier, was necessary in order to clear the ground for a return to IPE with an enriched view of the world in which we live. Accordingly, the next section starts making that journey, beginning with the articulation of a more expansive conceptualization of common sense before proceeding to consider what this means for 'the state' and thus for IPE.

Expanding common sense in order to problematize the state

As stated earlier, via a consideration of Gramsci's wider writings on the sociology of knowledge it is possible to arrive at a more expansive view of the significance of his notes on common sense. This is necessary, because he (perhaps unsurprisingly) was not the only person to argue for the need for societal transformation through the overcoming of the limits inherent in 'normal' rather than critical common sense. This may seem an obvious point, but if we consider the following quote then we can see that, depending on the writer's perspective, an emphasis on intellectual enlightenment of the masses could lead to very different conclusions than Gramsci's, or indeed those of any other historical materialist:

> The despotism of custom is everywhere the standing hindrance to human advancement, being in unceasing antagonism to that disposition to aim at something better than customary, which is called, according to the circumstances, the spirit of liberty, or that of progress or improvement...The progressive principle...in either shape...is antagonistic to the sway of Custom, involving at least emancipation from that yoke; and the contest between the two constitutes the chief interest of the history of mankind.
>
> (Mill, 1991, p. 78)

John Stuart Mill's polemic in *On Liberty* against the dangers of the 'tyranny of the majority' is hardly complementary to Gramsci's agenda, yet their differing positions stem from the same source, at least with regard to intellectual emancipation from custom, or common sense. Therefore, depending on the author, the masses could be enlightened, and thus free themselves from intellectual enslavement, in a range of ways. In consequence, we need to acknowledge that various social groups (subaltern or otherwise) struggling for societal leadership may well, *in their own terms*, be pushing for intellectual enlightenment of the masses. This may be an uncomfortable proposition for Marxist (and other) critics of Mill, but the point is this: Mill, like Gramsci, believed in human progress, and so may different social groups seeking to achieve societal hegemony.

The emphasis here is on the contingent – different social groups *may* believe in human progress – for those seeking societal hegemony do not necessarily desire human emancipation. However, if we consider Gramsci's argument that common sense is a collective noun, then so too could those conceptions of the world which have become more critical. Indeed as this volume illustrates, it is because certain conceptions of the world are critical in the minds of those articulating such ideas. For instance, in a recent article Mark Rupert (2005, pp. 465–9, 475) openly and honestly discusses the lessons that can be learned by historical materialists from a more extensive engagement with feminist and postcolonial perspectives (even if one remains committed to a historical materialist approach). Therefore, the articulation of spontaneous philosophy, resting on assumptions about the world which are taken for granted, need not be restricted to subaltern groups. As E.P. Thompson (1995, p. 48; original emphasis) has argued, 'some kind of assumptions (as to what we are thinking *about*) must be made before we can even begin to think'.

Hence common sense is present in all conceptions of the world, no matter how well developed. This is because 'the only "philosophy" is history in action, that is, life itself' (Gramsci, 1971, p. 357), and '[t]here is no human activity from which every form of intellectual participation can be excluded' (Gramsci, 1971, p. 9). This rejection of the thought/action dichotomy enables us to see that our thoughts about the world are embodied in *all* aspects of human activity. Hence the declaration that everyone is a philosopher (ibid., p. 323), by which Gramsci means not that every human has the capacity to formulate a philosophical treatize, but, rather, that everyone has some conception of the world and, as incoherent and uncritical as it may be, it should be treated as their philosophy (Simon, 1991, p. 26). Therefore, if all humans hold thoughts about the world – which for each individual is their version of common sense – then this is the case in all aspects of social life, regardless of whether our study is 'located' within the state, in everyday life or indeed anywhere else. In other words, while Gramsci certainly is interested in common sense in order to understand the basis upon which it can be transformed in the name of human liberation, the process of basing our opinions on implicit and often uncontested assumptions about the world is emphatically not restricted to subordinate social groups.

This enables us, first, to denaturalize the decisions and actions taken by humans within the state, for it makes it possible for us to enquire more closely into the basis for such decisions and actions. This is in stark contrast to accounts which accept the validity of a state/market dichotomy rooted in their intrinsic, impersonal, autonomous properties. As Bratsis (2006, p. 11) argues:

> the state as an autonomous social agent exists when those individuals share a bureaucratic [as opposed to a market] rationality and act accordingly... If you or I occupied one of these positions, it would

be expected that we too would then 'think' and 'act' in accordance with this bureaucratic rationality...However, this relation between the position of an individual within the institutions of the state and their 'bureaucratic' consciousness remains unexplained.

Once we begin to problematize the state/market dichotomy via a discussion of 'common sense', though, a much more significant object of enquiry comes into view. If the state is inextricably 'social' in the sense that we cannot presuppose the decisions taken by humans within the state, then surely this means that *the state itself* should also be viewed in this way. Perhaps the state as a category of analysis is merely 'common sense', making it nothing more than a socio-historical product of human practice (Bratsis, 2006). This is the inevitable result of the realization that the state is not a 'structure' or a 'thing', with its own self-reproducing social purpose.

This does not mean that I propose an endlessly elastic conceptualization of the state, whereby 'the state' is in the eye of the beholder. As E.P. Thompson (1995, p. 62) argued, '[h]istorical materialism employs concepts...as expectations rather than as rules...[which appear] in historical practice, not as ideal types fulfilled in historical evolution'. This is because they are:

> derived from the observation of historical eventuation *over time*. This observation is not of discrete facts *seriatim* but of *sets* of facts with their own regularities: of the repetition of certain kinds of event: of the congruence of certain kinds of behaviour within differing contexts.
>
> (ibid., p. 64; original emphases)

This takes us directly to my earlier assertion that the state is nothing more than the materialization of human thought/action in regularized practices which appear 'real' and 'state-like' by way of the implementation and enforcing of laws, procedures and conventions. It *appears* that there is a 'real' state because of the constant and widespread repetition of practices providing for regularized sets of 'facts' which validate the notion that there is a 'state'. Therefore, 'the state' has acquired a granite-like aura of objective, impersonal existence via long-standing notions such as juridical sovereignty: that is, it is *through* our thoughts about the world that, over time, the state came to seem universal and thus 'objective' in essence (cf. Gramsci, 1971, p. 445). Unlike those who adhere, even if implicitly, to a state/market dichotomy and thus the intrinsic properties one can ascribe to them, we can firmly assert that 'the state' exists *only* because we implicitly accept such 'existence' on an everyday basis. As such, it has a self-reproducing social purpose *only* because of the way in which human activity – and thoughts about the world embodied in it – validates this 'capability'. In consequence, the state is a 'natural' fact or a 'structure' only in phenomenological terms; it is humans and their common sense which comprise, validate and reproduce the state. In this sense, the state does not exist.

Comprehending this is central to understanding how, through the implementation and enforcing of laws, procedures and conventions in the name of 'the state', it has concrete, most certainly real, effects on our lives. Through the process of objectivization, whereby it appears to have a natural, real, essence, the state is pivotal to the socio-historical evolution of different societies because it has become 'a *site* and a *centre* of the exercise of power' (Poulantzas, 1978, p. 148; original emphases). It is:

> absolutely central in articulating the different areas of contestation, the different points of antagonism, into a regime of rule. The moment when you can get sufficient power in the state to organise a central political project is then decisive, for then you can use the state to plan, urge, incite, solicit and punish, to *conform* the different sites of power and consent into a single regime.
>
> (Hall, 1991, p. 124; original emphasis)

Therefore, 'the state' appears real, and has clear effects on our lives, because it is grounded in concrete – and unequal – human relations. Some of the most vivid illustrations of this can be found in processes of primitive accumulation bound up with the transition to capitalism. As Michael Perelman (2007) describes, the British state, in the eighteenth century especially, passed law after law against the small-scale, often individual, poaching of game. Poaching was seen as such a serious crime 'that it was, on occasion, even equated with treason ... several poachers were actually executed' (ibid., p. 52; see also Thompson, 1977). He argues that this 'challenged the traditional rights of the poor in the countryside ... [and] became part of a larger movement to cut off large masses of rural people from their traditional means' (ibid., p. 50). In the process, 'the taking of game [became] tantamount to challenging [private] property rights' (ibid., p. 52; see also Perelman, 2000, pp. 38–58) and thus embodied the emerging social relations promoting capital accumulation. This does not mean that the state engineered a transition to capitalism, but that – founded upon the same human relations as 'the market' – it played a key role in accelerating the enclosure of the land and thus the emergence of a large pool of people who could subsist only through selling themselves on the labour market.

To put it more bluntly, a gradual societal transformation took place through denying large numbers of people access to food and thus the means to live. Marx (1976, p. 899) described this particularly memorably:

> Thus were the agricultural folk first forcibly expropriated from the soil, driven from their homes, turned into vagabonds, and then whipped, branded and tortured by grotesquely terroristic laws into accepting the discipline necessary for the system of wage-labour... [In addition] [t]he advance of capitalist production develops a working class which by education, tradition and habit looks upon the requirements of that mode of production as self-evident natural laws.

We have now travelled quite far from the original assertion that Gramsci's writings on 'common sense' were of some significance. This is because they provide the basis for serious and considered reflection on the way in which *all* humans take things for granted, IPE scholars included. In the process, the state/market dichotomy has been exposed as based upon assumptions that do not hold water, which in this chapter has been demonstrated through an interrogation of the notion of 'the state'. Moreover, this enabled me to point out more briefly how the state is part and parcel of unequal relations of power that are embodied in everyday human relations. It does not contain intrinsic, impersonal properties that are benign compared with that other socio-historical product, the 'market'.

I will now discuss the implications of the above discussion for IPE and the study of the international political economy.

Conclusion

This chapter has argued that, through engaging with Gramsci's discussions of common sense as situated in his wider writings on the sociology of knowledge, we can think creatively about both the concept itself plus what this means for how we view the state. This is important for IPE, especially the more explicitly critical variants, for the (often implicitly) accepted state/market dichotomy makes it difficult to adhere *in practice* to the holistic analysis that is adhered to *in principle*. In addition, it frequently leads to 'the state' being conceptualized as something that possesses inherently more benign properties than 'the market', which means that it tends to be insulated from critical scrutiny. As a result, I have attempted to demonstrate how serious reflection on our foundational assumptions about the world is an integral part of any study that we undertake; research does not exist in a philosophical vacuum, no matter how 'empirical' it may be. Therefore, the effective study of the international political economy by International Political Economy remains an open question. While I am less pessimistic than Cammack in his chapter, he is correct to point out that IPE scholars all too rarely make the international political economy the object of enquiry, with the latter instead being the taken-for-granted context within which research takes place.

This has significant consequences for the discipline, for although – as Germain's chapter details – it asks many interesting and important questions, it tends not to tackle them in satisfactory ways. What is more, the theoretical resources that could help IPE move forward *already* exist, yet in the recent debates on the 'transatlantic divide' they were either ignored or dismissed. A striking example of the latter was the lauding of 'analytical eclecticism' and the consequential claims that more conceptually inclined scholars are afflicted by an allergy to 'the real world'. Moreover, and as a result, it was argued that scholars such as Pierre Bourdieu – an excellent example of holistic research which connects closely theory and practice and has had an enormous impact across a range of disciplines – should 'take a back seat' for being too theoretical in their approach (Weaver, 2009, p. 344).

So how could IPE make some progress? (1) acknowledge the necessity of concept formation at every step of the research process owing to the irreducibly complex nature of the world; (2) consider how, although still wedded to a state-centric view which is unsatisfactory for the reasons given throughout this chapter, recent discussions in IR have been more instructive than the 'transatlantic divide' debates because of the willingness to engage with philosophies of social science; (3) reflect on how claims to contingency and openness, premised on a multicausal approach, often mask unproblematized assumptions about the world; (4) take seriously the notion that IPE's indebtedness to IR and thus to political science tends in practice to equate to a 'politics of the world economy' framework; (5) problematize the state to a considerably greater extent in order to question more closely the state/market dichotomy; and (6) be less instinctively hostile to critical social theory in all of its richness and diversity.

This last point is crucial here: although I have focused on Gramsci in this chapter, there are a whole range of scholars whose work would be of significance for the enriching of IPE as a discipline. Therefore, 'critical IPE' 'should be viewed not as a singular but a collective and thus plural term, for although broadly committed to certain modes of [enquiring] into the world in which we live, [it] is defined by open and reflexive research' (van Apeldoorn et al., 2010, p. 215). Hopefully this chapter, and this volume, will make these points harder to refute in the future.

Notes

Earlier versions of this argument were presented at the 'Rethinking Marxism' conference, University of Massachusetts Amherst, 5–8 November 2009, and the 'Critical International Political Economy' workshop, University of Manchester, 25–26 March 2010. My thanks to all of those who commented on the papers at these events. In addition, thanks to my fellow editors for comments, and for ongoing conversations on these issues with (in alphabetical order) Peter Bratsis, Alexander Gallas, Marcus Green, Peter Ives, Patrick Thaddeus Jackson, Naoimh McMahon, Adam David Morton, Reecia Orzeck, Celine-Marie Pascale, Daniela Tepe and Matthias vom Hau. Notably for IPE as a discipline, of these 11 scholars, only 2 could be classed as being in IPE and at most 4 in IR/IPE. Non-IPE authors have been a permanent aspect of my own intellectual development: this is most apparent in Bruff (2011a), where I also discuss the importance of non-IPE authors for the future evolution of critical, especially historical materialist, IPE. It also explains the focus on culture in my recent monograph (Bruff, 2008).

1. Morton (2007a, pp. 19–21 especially) convincingly argues that we should abandon a search for the 'real' Gramsci and instead focus on the rhythm of thinking that permeates, and evolves in, his writings. This is in keeping with Gramsci's (1996, p. 137) own views on the history of ideas (see also Boothman, 2006–7).

6
Critical Feminist Scholarship and IPE

Juanita Elias

Introduction

There is a now quite a significant body of feminist scholarship in the broad area of International Politics that points to the ongoing marginalization of feminist scholarship from the so-called mainstream (or 'malestream') of the discipline (Weber, 1994; Tickner, 1997; Steans, 2003; Youngs, 2004; Zalewski, 2007). Georgina Waylen's 2006 *Review of International Studies* article 'You Still Don't Understand' certainly falls within this tradition of writing, but differs from it in the sense that Waylen's target is critical IPE scholarship (namely that of the neo-Gramscian variety). Her argument is that the lack of dialogue between critical IPE scholarship and feminist IPE is all the more alarming given (a) the numerous attempts by feminist IPE scholars to establish dialogue with critical IPE scholars and (b) the real possibilities that exist for dialogue and engagement between critical IPE and feminist IPE. Thus, whilst it is hardly surprising that feminist scholarship, with its emphasis on the constructed and contestable nature of (gendered) social relations and the need for emancipatory social change, has largely been ignored by, say, positivist IPE scholars, these issues do dovetail with the concerns of much critical scholarship. Why then, Waylen asks, is critical IPE scholarship so loath to bring in insights from feminist IPE? And, why is it that when critical IPE scholars do mention 'gender' in their work, this is characterized by the belief that 'it is enough to make some mention of women as a group in a few contexts, often as activists in women's movements or in terms of the impact of a process on women'? (Waylen, 2006, p. 148).

The broad failure identified in this approach is that it represents little more than an 'adding-on' of women to existing theoretical and empirical research programmes without recognizing the ways in which gender is itself constitutive of the global political economy. Furthermore, it rests upon the deeply unsophisticated notion that gender is merely a synonym for women – in other words, failing to recognize how other groups within the global political economy (e.g. 'labour', 'big business') are also gendered categories in which gender relations and gendered processes of identity formation (including notions of *both* masculinity and femininity) are produced and reproduced. In addition, there is a failure to recognize how the category of 'women' is by no means homogenous, in which all women experience the impact of global economic restructuring in exactly the same manner (that is, how gendered social relations are always cross-cut with divisions of race, nationality and class).

The purpose of this chapter is not to reiterate the arguments presented in Waylen's article. Rather, the aim is to consider her points in light of the recent wave of navel-gazing (sorry, intellectual histories) sparked by the publication of Benjamin J. Cohen's 2007 *Review of International Political Economy* article and his 2008 book *International Political Economy: An Intellectual History*, and the subsequent appearance of a number of 'transatlantic divide' debates in key IPE journals. These discussions between (and over) a so-called divide between a 'British' and an 'American' IPE make scant mention of the contributions of feminist IPE scholarship. This is particularly concerning given that 'British' IPE is frequently (though not exclusively) associated with a critical turn and that feminist scholars have played an important role in developing an IPE that draws upon more reflexive post-positivist methodologies, opens up greater space for non-traditional IPE agendas and is much less focused on the political economy of relations between industrialized states. It is argued here that such an oversight strengthens the idea that an emphasis on gender relations and/or identities has no legitimate place within studies of IPE. Furthermore, the neglect of gender is all the more alarming given (a) the increasing quality and quantity of feminist IPE research, and (b) the real overlaps in the agendas of (especially) critical IPE and feminist IPE that many feminist scholars have identified.

This chapter proceeds as follows. Initially, I seek to demonstrate and account for the lack of feminist voices in the recent 'transatlantic divide' debates. The chapter then turns to consider how and why a feminist perspective offers unique, and perhaps essential, contributions to IPE scholarship (especially that which claims to be 'critical'). Although there already exist writings that point to the contribution that feminist scholarship makes to IPE (Waylen, 2006; Griffin, 2007a), it is important that the feminist contribution to IPE is *yet again* restated, given the ongoing marginalization of feminism within IPE. Finally, the chapter concludes with some thoughts on the way forward – looking to potentially fruitful sources of engagement between feminist and non-feminist scholarship in IPE, and pointing to some of the challenges that such engagement will entail.

Where are feminism and/or gender in the 'transatlantic divide' debates?

For Cohen (2008a, p. 62), a 'British' school of IPE adopts a 'critical theory' approach focused on 'challenging orthodoxies of all kinds'. Significantly, it is in defining 'critical theory' that the only mention of feminist IPE appears in Cohen's text: '[e]ncompassed by this term are varieties of Marxian analysis, some forms of feminism, and other radical schools of thought' (ibid.). Despite this sole mention, feminist IPE is not up for discussion in Cohen's characterization of the discipline. It is a silence on feminism that is reproduced straightforwardly in the subsequent debates that followed the publication of Cohen's book and his earlier article in *Review of International Political Economy*.

Accompanying this is the publication of Mark Blyth's *Handbook of International Political Economy*. While many of the eminent contributors to this volume reflect on the IPE debates, the impetus behind the handbook is to demonstrate the multiplicity of traditions that exist within IPE scholarship. However, while I would welcome Blyth's call for a recognition of IPE as set within 'multiple traditions' (Blyth, 2009a, p. 3) (a concern that reflects a frustration with the idea that IPE is falling into two opposing camps), it appears odd that his handbook yet again reproduces the idea that feminist IPE is a marginal concern to the discipline as a whole. Feminist IPE is only mentioned in the chapter on Australian IPE (Sharman, 2009), and no feminist, let alone female, authors contributed to the volume. The handbook is motivated by what one might perceive as something of a post-positivist position that where you sit (geographically) in the world influences your understanding of what IPE is. But surely, if we are upfront about how our geographical positioning influences our understanding of IPE, then would not other facets of our identity as scholars – including our gender – also influence how we 'see' IPE and the IPE questions that we most value? The handbook is just one example of the potentially devastating role that disciplinary gatekeepers can play in shutting down debate and dialogue with feminist scholars, and acts to reinforce the view that IPE is an overwhelmingly 'gender-blind' pursuit in which questions of gender can be placed on the sidelines.

Perhaps one of the issues faced by feminist IPE scholars is that they cannot be fitted neatly into an intellectual history of the discipline. As Fiona Robinson pointed out, it is difficult to pinpoint easily a feminist IPE since the feminist scholars who have contributed most to the debates refuse to be 'disciplined by boundaries' (Robinson, 1997, p. 773). First, it should be highlighted that some of the major works of feminist IPE have been written by authors who do not identify a clear distinction between IPE and IR. Key feminist scholars who have contributed to the development of feminist IPE approaches, such as Jan Jindy Pettman (1996), Sandra Whitworth (1994) or Cynthia Enloe (1989), continually cross disciplinary boundaries in their work. It is a concern with the gendered nature of international politics that motivates these authors, enabling them to cross those artificial boundaries that exist between IPE, 'security' studies and domestic politics. Therefore, because Cohen's intellectual history is structured around the work of seven 'key' IPE scholars, it is difficult to easily identify a feminist IPE scholar who would fit the bill. Nonetheless, there are questions to be asked, as Craig Murphy does (Murphy, 2009), about why certain scholars (particularly those who are leftist and interdisciplinary in their approach, and who frequently focus their analysis on questions of development and inequality) have been left out of Cohen's 'IPE hit parade' – his 'magnificent seven'.

Since feminist political economy embodies a strong commitment to engaging the voices of the disadvantaged – increasingly, those voices are from less developed parts of the globe – it would appear that there is little scope for including feminist perspective(s) or voices within Cohen's work, since they simply do not fit neatly within his conceptualization of the field. Furthermore, feminist approaches to political economy draw upon a wide variety of traditions, including development studies (particularly Gender and Development (GAD) writings), feminist economics and feminist International Relations theory (Waylen, 1997). Of course, it is certainly the case that almost all traditions of IPE scholarship draw upon a variety of scholarly traditions, but the multidisciplinarity of feminist perspectives on the global political economy often makes it difficult to identify exactly who the key feminist IPE scholars 'are' – indeed, one might raise questions about whether such an exercise is necessary at all. After all, some of the key contributors to feminist IPE scholarship are writers who would not necessarily locate themselves within the field.[1] Furthermore, as will become increasingly clear in the second part of this chapter, feminist scholarly traditions are marked by a broad theoretical diversity and it is therefore difficult to identify a straightforward feminist 'position' in IPE.

Inevitably, then, one might also ask whether students interested in pursuing feminist research at a postgraduate level would see IPE as the natural 'home' for their research compared with, say, geography, development studies or sociology. Questions need to be raised, therefore, about the extent to which there is an implicit conservatism to IPE scholarship (be it 'critical' or otherwise) in which gender issues and feminist-oriented research are always constructed as somewhere 'out there' on the edges of the field. As Laura Sjoberg (2008) argues, the demarcation of feminist scholarship as marginal to more traditional international studies agendas reflects the particular sociology of our discipline, which is dominated by the perspectives of male scholars, with women expected to socialize themselves 'into the discipline as defined by the men who came before them' (p. 176). Although Sjoberg's criticism is levelled at the positivist American IR mainstream, it seems to me that such criticism might also be levelled at the way in which IPE (*including* a great deal of critical IPE scholarship) has come to be defined and discussed in recent years. For example, Hawkesworth (2009) points to the 'erasure' of feminist knowledge in debates on global economic restructuring, whereby discussions of the feminization of poverty and migration have largely been ignored.

Second, we can question the extent to which feminist approaches focus on the same questions and issues prevalent within the so-called 'British' school. Has a 'British' or 'critical' approach in IPE, as Blyth (2009b) claims, come to be dominated by Marxian concepts, rather than a plurality of theoretical perspectives and approaches that are equally 'critical' in their approach? Furthermore, does this capturing of the motto 'critical' create little space for the discussion of gender or other forms of identity unless they are discussed using the appropriate Marxian language (that is, gender is not viewed as constitutive of global social relations, but is subsumed within a broader analysis of class relations)? This is not to suggest that I think that critical Marxian approaches to political economy and feminist IPE are mutually incompatible. Indeed, the literatures on social relations of reproduction and resistance politics discussed below certainly indicate that there is some dialogue occurring (however limited). However, my main concern is that there is something of an intellectual narrowness within critical IPE that leaves little space for accommodating feminist concerns.

A way forward is suggested by Eschle and Maiguashca (2007), who argue that the prefix 'critical' needs to be applied more 'expansively' – encompassing more than just Frankfurt School or neo-Gramscian approaches (see also Fischer and Tepe in this volume). Echoing arguments made by other feminist authors (for example, Ackerley and True, 2006; Steans, 1999; Whitworth, 1989), feminist scholarship is presented as sitting within a critical canon which is defined as one that seeks to (a) 'expose taken-for-granted truths as historically contingent and socially constructed', (b) 'reflect critically on the origins of our own theoretical enterprise', (c) 'illuminate relations of domination and oppression and the concrete social struggles that seek to overturn them', and (d) 'refuses to take a distance from its subject matter, acquiring its bite by speaking from and to a particular marginalised constituency that is, or could be, engaged in the politics of resistance' (Eschle and Maiguashca, 2007, p. 285). Thus the authors draw attention to the commonalities between critical international theory and feminist research, and suggest that feminist scholarship actually strengthens and enhances critical perspective by placing at its centre an emphasis on 'gender relations as a salient form of oppression in a way that other forms of critical theory have yet to do' (ibid., p. 286).[2]

Some alarm has been expressed by writers such as Adam Morton (2006) about the way in which the broadening of the category of 'critical' in IPE has served to neutralize an emphasis on the (important) category of class in IPE. However, my concern is that an overriding emphasis on class is of little use to scholars engaged in feminist research agendas, for it is not understood in terms of how it intersects with other forms of social inequality that cannot be so easily subsumed within a class-based frame. Indeed, it is by broadening our understanding of 'critical' in the way suggested by Eschle and Maiguashca (i.e. 'critical' is not applied as a catch-all term for all non-orthodox IPE approaches as Cohen (see above) or Brown (1994) suggest, but critical approaches are those that 'share the overriding goal of the realisation of self-liberating practice' (Eschle and Maiguashca, 2007, p. 285)), that feminist scholars are able to engage most fruitfully with other critical literatures.[3]

In what follows, I provide a brief account of some of the major contributions of feminist perspectives in IPE. I highlight some of the areas of overlap with non-feminist IPE approaches, but my main aim is to present feminist IPE in its own terms – as a broad school of political economy scholarship which has something unique to contribute to debates in IPE.

The contributions of feminist IPE

For the purposes of simplicity I have divided the contributions of feminist IPE scholarship into two (very) broad areas: production and reproduction, and changing modes of (global) governance. These categories do, of course, overlap, and I also provide a more limited overview of feminist IPE contributions in the area of globalization studies and resistance politics (for more detailed discussions of these areas see Waylen (2006) and Eschle and Maiguashca (2007)). All of the works discussed here fit within the definition of critical scholarship provided by Eschle and Maiguashca, but they also exhibit a theoretical plurality drawing upon materialist, poststructuralist and postcolonial perspectives. It is useful to engage in an exercise of this nature for two reasons. First, to demonstrate that there is no singular critical feminist position in IPE, but a plurality of perspectives. Second, to show (yet again) that feminist scholars *are* conducting research that is relevant to the study of the global political economy, and that they *do* in fact focus on similar topics of enquiry to non-feminist scholars – especially those working within 'critical' traditions.

Conventional political-economic analyses are focused firmly on the productive economy – the study of the how, where and why goods and services are produced, marketed, distributed and consumed. For critical IPE scholars, one of the most important stories in relation to the productive economy pertains to how and why notions of the productive economy as functioning on the basis of so-called 'free' markets emerged. Feminist IPE can play a role in demonstrating how the rise of the market economy cannot be viewed as a process whereby the market came to be progressively disembedded (in a Polanyian sense) from society. Rather, the productive economy is shown to function so that forms of social inequality are reproduced within the capitalist productive economy, and may indeed be integral to its functioning. This argument rests upon two important assumptions, (1) that markets benefit from the existence of (unequal) gendered social relations that associate women's labour with the socially reproductive realm of the household, and (2) that the functioning of the productive economy also depends on the existence of other forms of division and inequality (for example, race, class, nationality) that intersect with gendered social relations in what Peterson (2003, p. 33; original emphasis) has termed 'the *interconnection* of structural hierarchies'. Importantly, one of the most important insights that this feminist scholarship has generated is an emphasis on how these forms of social inequality and hierarchy, that are so central to the functioning of the global market economy, rest upon sets of (ongoing) socially constructed ideas and discourses (see also Griffin in this volume).

To provide an example from my own work on the gendered nature of foreign direct investment in the Malaysian garment manufacturing sector, this research pointed to how multinational corporations benefit from localized social divisions and inequalities (Elias, 2004). First, the operation of 'gendered discourses of work' (Caraway, 2007) ensures that prevalent ideas concerning women's 'natural' suitability for monotonous work and their secondary (non-breadwinner) labour market status act to concentrate women's labour in low-wage, low-status assembly line production. Wright (2006), too, has pointed to the persistence of these discourses, emphasizing in particular how persistent myths around female workers' 'disposability' – the idea that they are only 'good' for employment prior to marriage – enable managers to place women in monotonous and intensive forms of assembly line work and maintain feminized systems of low pay.

Second, my research found that these discourses intersect with ideas around ethnicity and class, so that while certain groups of (in this case, urban, ethnically Chinese) women do have access to higher status forms of work, other groups (in this case the firm's majority female, rural, ethnically Malay workforce) are confined to the assembly lines. And yet, because gender must always be understood as intersecting with other forms of hierarchy, the production of gender relations within firms (which needs to be understood as a central component of the labour process) can take quite different forms. For example, Muñoz's (2008) study of gendered workplace relations in a Tortilla manufacturing firm operating on both sides of the US–Mexican border looks to the intersections between state power, the labour market, race, class and gender in constructing workplace regimes. The high prevalence of male undocumented migrant employment in the US provided the US arm of the firm with an endless source of low-wage employees, while the Mexican firm drew upon a largely feminized pool of workers – often single mothers – to provide 'flexible' low-wage work.

An important new wave of materialist feminist literature has pointed to the centrality of the socially reproductive economy in understanding the broader dynamics of the global political economy, pointing to the significance of those everyday ('unconscious' (Bakker, 2007, p. 543)) caring activities that are so central to the functioning of capitalist economies. And yet, traditional gender orders based upon ideas of a gendered division between the public and private spheres are being transformed under conditions of intensified globalization – a process that is perhaps best understood in terms of the increased reach of the market economy into all spheres of social life. For Bakker and Gill (2003), these local gender regimes or 'orders' (Connell, 1987), centred on nationally bounded social spaces, are undergoing significant transformation under conditions of disciplinary neoliberalism. Part of this transformation is labelled the 'reprivatization of social reproduction', as states increasingly place greater responsibility for welfare provision onto the household and unpaid women's labour.

Thus we can point to the way in which structural adjustment policies have depended, in large part, on assumptions about women's ability to take over in terms of the provision of social and welfare services once state provision is rolled back (Sparr, 1994; Elson, 1995). And emphasis has also been placed on the ways in which increases in women's labour force participation (in both the formal and informal economy) impact upon patterns and practices of social reproduction under conditions of neoliberal restructuring (Ferguson, 2010). The second part is a deeply gendered process labelled the 'intensification of exploitation' whereby the realm of social reproduction is increasingly viewed as a key site of capitalist accumulation (Bakker and Gill, 2003, p. 34). For example, an increased commitment to anti-poverty agendas within neoliberal development discourse has played out in terms of an emphasis on the ability of migrant domestic workers to remit their wages to fund national development in their home countries (Gibson et al., 2001), or the role that entrepreneurial female 'homeworkers' can play in family survival strategies (Batliwala and Dhanraj, 2007).

However, these transformations are not to be understood merely in terms of how a disciplinary neoliberalism drives the reconfiguration of socially reproductive relations. Rather, transformations need to be contextualized within the particularities of the localized historical evolution of a sexual division of labour as well as class- and race-based hierarchies and norms within specific local contexts (Young, 2003, p. 109). For example, in Malaysia the desire to foster internationally 'competitive' growth through developing a knowledge economy, less centred on labour-intensive manufacturing and migrant labour, has led the state to pursue policies designed to boost levels of middle-class female employment (a group who traditionally would have limited labour market participation). These policies, however, create tensions and contradictions – for example, they depend upon the generation of a racialized underclass of workers as the continued expansion of the market for migrant domestic labour draws in female care workers from poorer Asian economies (Elias, 2009).

As the above discussion indicates, scholarship that is concerned with understanding the dynamics of gendered social relations of production and reproduction under globalization situates these transformations within a wider reading of the transformation and neoliberalization of modes of global governance. Understanding the dynamics of the productive and socially reproductive economies cannot, indeed, be divorced from a wider understanding of the gendered politics of global governance. As Rai and Waylen (2008, p. 2) argue, feminist scholarship draws attention to 'the way in which both the practices and institutions of governance are gendered and result in an institutional, discursive and structural bias in favour of men that leads global governance to take particular forms, which affect different sectors of society unequally'. Global governance is, of course, a broadly contested concept (see also Macartney and Shields in this volume), and is utilized to refer to both the changing nature of political power and authority under conditions of (neoliberal) globalization. This has led to a reformulation of traditional (state-centric) forms of governance as well as the rising importance of key global economic institutions in the face of these broader changes. While it is somewhat difficult to separate neatly the literature on production and social reproduction from a discussion of global governance, it is notable that an important body of literature has focused attention on gendered norms and identities as a feature of the discursive production of globalized forms of governance.

Griffin's 2009 book *Gendering the World Bank* presents the argument that the economistic development discourses emanating from institutions of global governance such as the World Bank are predicated upon sets of assumptions in relation to sex, gender and sexual practice which act to reproduce gender-'appropriate' identities and behaviours. These assumptions are characterized by the tendency to view women as both vulnerable and reproductive beings – in other words, women are always heterosexual and in need of (some form of) male protection. Such ideas are not only evident in how institutions discuss women and gender (for example, within the context of 'gender mainstreaming' projects), but also are reflective of 'a type of gender ... which resides in the very fundamentals of its economic logic' (Griffin, 2009, p. 113). Thus supposedly gender-neutral policy agendas, framed in mainstream economic language, obscure the extent to which contemporary understandings of the 'market economy' reflect a pervasive masculinist bias (see also Bergeron, 2001). Griffin adds to this argument by pointing to how mainstream economic discourse is fundamentally predicated upon a heteronormative gender order, whereby World Bank discourse is shown to centre on the reproduction of heterosexual economic actors, identities and behaviours.

A number of other scholars have also pointed out that a focus on gender in political economy cannot be divorced from an assessment of how heteronormative assumptions shape prevalent understandings of gender identity and gender relations. As Bedford (2007) argues, World Bank gender and development policies are frequently characterized by an emphasis on the need to support loving 'complementary' hetero-sexual family units as a development priority. Moreover, Lind (2009) points out that similar assumptions also underpin national develop-ment strategies in states that have sought to distance themselves from the neoliberal policy prescriptions of the international financial institu-tions. For example, in Venezuela development policies aimed at lifting the very poor out of poverty have rested upon the hypervisibilization of poor, heterosexual, mothers – a development priority that clearly inter-sects with standard nationalist tropes concerning women as mothers of the nation.

The findings of Bedford's study are important, because they show that the emphasis on the heteronormative family unit in World Bank policymaking stemmed from the desire to present gender and devel-opment policies as not only about women, but as policies that also concern men. The desire to avoid the tendency to conflate gender and women resulted, therefore, in a privileging of (western) heteronormative assumptions about the family. Bedford's work does, however, point to the growing recognition within development studies of the need to consider men's role in development and, moreover, that men as well as women are gendered beings. These important insights need to be brought into our understanding of the global political econ-omy. For example, much of the feminist IPE literature stresses the feminization of global manufacturing employment that has accompa-nied the restructuring of capitalist production from North to South. But the reality of these global shifts is much more complicated, with male migrant labour forces frequently taking up employment in 'femi-nized' industries and male-dominated organized labour seeking to resist and challenge the flexibilization (and accompanying feminization) of their workplaces (see, for example, Theresa Healy's (2008) study of labour organizing amongst Mexico's male-dominated organized labour elite).

Furthermore, feminist scholars have increasingly come to engage with Connell's (1987) work on 'hegemonic masculinity' in order to understand how neoliberal economic practice centres around deeply masculinized ideas of rationality and competitiveness (Hooper, 2001; Elias, 2008). And, as Coleman (2007) argues, hegemonic neoliberal discourses that focus on the construction of a hegemonically masculine norm depend on the construction of 'other' groups as hypermasculinized 'savages' or backward 'feminized' pre-modern actors. Coleman's point is that such discourses play a role in justifying the everyday violence of neoliberal development. But her research, like that of many other feminist scholars, also highlights how gender cannot be understood straightforwardly as something that maps easily onto either male or female bodies – this is an important point that non-feminist scholars, attempting to 'add on' a concern with gender, need to reflect upon.

The changing practices and politics of global governance also raise questions about the role that feminist activists and scholars can play in challenging and resisting disciplinary neoliberalism. The literature on gender mainstreaming within institutions of global governance highlights the role that women's activist groups and feminist scholars have played in pushing for the recognition of gender issues within international organizations and national policy machineries. Much of this literature points to the fact that practices of gender mainstreaming, or other policy agendas aimed at improving the status of women (and other marginalized groups), are only taken up when they are seen as compatible with dominant neoliberal frames (True, 2008). For example, employing a Foucauldian governmentality approach, Woehl's (2008) analysis of gender mainstreaming within the EU suggests that such policies have rested upon neoliberal technologies of governance in ways that lead to the subsuming of critical activist demands to the broader politics of neoliberal capitalist globalization. By placing an emphasis on differences between women (something that has become a key feature of contemporary feminist theorizing in IPE), scholars have pointed to how certain groups of women are able to benefit from policies of gender mainstreaming – hence True (2008) looks at the emphasis in APEC's (Asia Pacific Economic Cooperation) gender mainstreaming strategies on women leaders, entrepreneurs and exporters, which simultaneously fails to address the needs of those women who make up the working poor in the region, frequently employed in those precarious yet 'flexible' economic sectors that have underpinned the economic dynamism of the Asia-Pacific region.

Nonetheless, many feminist scholars remain committed to the view that practices of gender mainstreaming within international organizations act to open up spaces for feminist engagement and do not *necessarily* rob feminist demands of their emancipatory potential. Such a perspective rests on the assumption that feminism needs to maintain a *critical* lens in analysing the uses and abuses of gender mainstreaming within international organizations, a lens that may well stem from feminist scholarship's traditionally close ties with grass-roots feminist activism (True, 2003). But, at the same time, we need to be attendant to the politics of the so-called 'global' women's movement – not least in terms of the ways in which the dominance of Northern/Western feminist voices have often acted to downplay the significance of economic justice agendas (Chowdhry, 2002; Grewal, 2005).

Concluding comments: spaces of/for engagement between feminist and non-feminist scholars?

I wish to end this chapter with some brief comments on how the emergence of new research agendas are opening up more spaces for potential engagements between feminist and non-feminist IPE. My aim here is not to suggest that a new wave of pro-feminist male scholars is finally thoroughly (and properly) integrating feminist ideas and concepts into their work – since (with perhaps the notable exception of Stephen Gill's work with Isabella Bakker) this is simply not the case. Rather, my aim is to signal that, in spite of the shutting out of feminism in the recent 'transatlantic divide' debates, there remains clear scope for engagement.

A small, yet significant, move within IPE is to recognize the contribution of feminist approaches as the discipline of IPE (including critical IPE) starts to move away from its tendency to privilege top-down analysis in favour of a more thoroughly engaged look at 'everyday' politics and practices as an important site of global politics. There are parallels between the clear tendency in feminist political economy to link 'the macro-structural to the micro-personal' (Ling, 2000, p. 242) and the recent calls within IPE for a focus on a more 'everyday' political economy (Hobson and Seabrooke, 2007). This (broad) approach is one that recognizes the interconnections between everyday political practice and global political-economic transformations. To a certain extent, a more 'everyday' approach to IPE sits more comfortably alongside feminist IPE since it serves to highlight the human faces and identities behind processes of economic transformation. Importantly, what is potentially revealed by such analysis is that these 'human faces' exist as gendered, classed and racialized.

Such developments in the broad area of IPE also complement developments in global labour studies. Marcus Taylor (2009) argues, in a recent special issue of *Third World Quarterly*, that a new wave of studies of global labour is finally seeking to place issues of gender and race at their centre, by specifically recognizing the importance of gendered and racialized processes of social construction to the formation and utilization of national and transnational labour forces. What such studies indicate, therefore, is the possibility of ongoing and fruitful engagements between feminist scholars and political economists, working within both critical and constructivist traditions, in analysing how the practices of globalization both generate and are supported by gendered, classed and racialized divisions and inequalities (see also Davies and Ryner, 2006). Such an approach, with its strong focus on the need for empirical research within local contexts, certainly shares commonalities with much feminist scholarship – although it might be suggested that even 'everyday IPE' scholars have a lot to learn from the extensive feminist literature on research methods and research ethics.[4]

However, despite these potential new spaces for engagement, it should be recognized that a focus on the everyday politics of the global economy can be somewhat limiting when it comes to forging links between feminist and non-feminist scholarship. My concern is that the resulting research will engage with very embodied understandings of gender (for example, viewing gender as mapping neatly onto individual male and female bodies) without engaging with an understanding of how gendered relations and identities are forged at the intersection between competing localized and globalized gender ideologies. When feminist political economists make the claim that gender is constitutive of global politics, they are arguing that IPE scholars need to think carefully about how gendered power relations and forms of identity shape the very categories of analysis and research questions that they are asking. For example, we may not 'see' gender within institutions of global governance or global financial markets, but to what extent are the behaviours of these institutions driven by gendered assumptions and rationalities? This, then, is the radical *and* critical significance of feminist IPE.

Notes

1. These include feminist economists such as Diane Elson and Lourdes Benería, feminist geographers such as J.K. Gibson-Graham, development studies

writers such as Naila Kabeer and Andrea Cornwall, and sociologists and anthropologists focusing on the central role played by gender in the constitution of production and consumption (such as Carla Freeman, Leslie Salzinger and Pun Ngai).

2. It should be noted that Eschle and Maiguashca's formulation of 'critical theory' is not remarkably different from that put forward by Robert Cox in his 1981 article 'Social Forces, States and World Orders', in which he stresses the ideological foundations of supposedly value-neutral theorizing and the need to move beyond and transform existing understandings of world orders. Given that most feminist IPE shares this emphasis on challenging value neutrality and emancipatory social struggle, it is alarming that feminist perspectives have been so overlooked by neo-Gramscian scholars. This chapter thus adopts the understanding of critical theory presented by Eschle and Maiguashca because of its overt recognition of the role of feminist theories within a *broad* canon of critical theorizing in International Studies.

3. Reference should be made at this point to the long history of feminist engagement with radical traditions of political economy, particularly Marxism, as seen for example in the debates in the 1970s on domestic labour plus the role of feminism within class-based organizing (Rowbotham et al., 1979). For an excellent overview of the ways in which feminism has engaged with, and also challenged, Marxist scholarship, seen through the lens of Iris Marion Young's work, see Hawkesworth (2008).

4. This is a very wide literature focused on the ethical dilemmas and challenges in developing a feminist methodology and research method. For example, see Harding (1986), Ackerley and True (2006) and Hawkesworth (2009).

Part III
Dissensus

7
Reclaiming Critical IPE from the 'British' School

Owen Worth

Introduction

Recent accounts of the intellectual history of International Political Economy (IPE) have cemented what had been expressed previously concerning the difference between the 'empiricist' or 'positivist' and the 'critical' or 'post-positivist' approach to the discipline (Murphy and Nelson, 2002; Cohen, 2008a). In this, the 'critical' or 'British' approach is portrayed as a method that is geared towards questioning the conventions of political and scientific enquiry that had dominated the American-based study of the subject (Cohen, 2008a, pp. 50–5). Debates within *Review of International Political Economy* and *New Political Economy* have continued the trend of presenting the discipline as a transatlantic division between 'American' and 'British' schools. Included in the newly minted British school are areas that view IPE in a manner that accounts for more than just the relationship between the state and economic actors. As a result, it includes a whole variety of different theoretical positions and avenues of enquiry which, seemingly, are loosely joined by their rejection of the state-centric positivism of behaviourist IPE (ibid.).

Rather than pursue the debate about the nature and substance of 'transatlantic' polarization within IPE, the main focus of this chapter argues that the British school's representation of 'critical' has been undermined. In my opinion, the fresh debates on the geographical divides within the discipline have constructed an almost mythic history of the discipline (see also Ashworth in this volume), which, indeed, many of the debates have illustrated. What it seems to omit or downplay is the importance of 'critique' that was central to the main focus of the initial departure point of what is now seen as the British school. As a result, the avenue of 'critique' within the British school has become increasingly undermined within these discussions (see also Cammack in this volume). Benjamin Cohen's influential book goes firmly beyond that of earlier ontological divisions that separated 'problem-solving' from 'critical' IPE, by arguing for a more generalized methodological and analytical division that marked (and marks) the growth of the disciplines in the US and Britain (2008a). The debates that have followed might have queried the geographical lineage of Cohen's arguments, but have accepted the notion of a divide, on the form and content of study on the one hand and the scope of method on the other, which has evolved from two separate traditions (Cox, 2009; Maliniak and Tierney, 2009; Palan, 2009; Phillips, 2009).

In contrast, this chapter argues that the original aim of what is now regarded as the British school was to provide a distinct form of critique that contained certain normative commitments. Largely derived from the work of Robert Cox, the emphasis on critical theory was geared towards understanding social orders as historically fashioned constructs that transform over time (1981; see also Germain in this volume). In this way, Cox was calling for a form of analysis geared towards (to borrow from Marx) both interpreting and changing the world. What has now broadly been defined as the British school did not emerge from a more inclusive engagement with political economy, but from Robert Cox's classic distinction between 'problem-solving theory' and 'critical theory', which he first illustrated in his *Millennium* article (1981).

Whilst critical theory has appeared in many forms and in many guises, what unifies it is the progressive commitment towards emancipation and the belief that the present social system can be transformed in order to address its injustices. It was with this departure point that critical IPE was conceived, and I believe that it is through this normative commitment that critical IPE is methodologically founded. Yet, it seems that this commitment to 'critique and transform' is in danger of being undermined by an increasing sense of orthodoxy that has emerged within the recent debates concerning the British and American schools. For whilst critical IPE has hitherto been conceived as an approach that attacked orthodoxy on the grounds of its ahistorical and narrow focus, in favour of one rooted in radical transformation, the British school has tended to be presented in a different light. That is, its content is presented as methodologically opposed to positivism and consequently is more inclusive, the distinctions between critical and problem-solving research being more explicit in their ultimate objectives only (Dickins, 2006; Weaver, 2009).

Rather than follow current arguments that a transatlantic divide is preventing progress and somehow dividing the IPE discipline, my belief is that the foundations of the British school were based upon a form of radicalism that was committed not towards pluralizing itself within a wider academic purpose, but towards a distinct form of social critique. In order for this to be maintained – or to put it more clearly, in order to be critical – one must fundamentally believe that social orders are constructed unevenly and unequally and, as such, require transformation. The radicalism rests upon rejecting the status quo and seeking to envisage a world beyond it. Such radicalism has fluctuated in its distinct objectives, but still ultimately takes its cue from the writings of Kant and Marx. Cox recognizes this in his critical theory, by insisting that such thought should progressively and fundamentally change that which it is critiquing. Critical IPE ought to maintain this mantle, or it will slide further back towards forms of orthodoxy (Farrands and Worth, 2005) – a condition, one could argue, that has been accelerated by the recent attempt to locate any form of critique within a wider, more sanitized, British school. By reasserting this commitment, through reminding us of the principles of critical theory and of the initial insights that Cox made, critical IPE must reassert itself as a distinct form of enquiry within the discipline, rather than one submerged within a wider territorial debate on methodology.

The content of 'critical' IPE

The development of critical IPE has often been presented as stemming from Cox's seminal ground-breaking piece in 1981, and as having followed a path aimed at providing us with an ontological understanding of historical structures (Cox, 1981, 1996; Abbott and Worth, 2002). However, it has been presented by textbooks as spanning dependency, world-systems analysis, Gramscianism, constructivism, feminism and environmentalism (Cohn, 2010), and, indeed, as incorporating a number of positions that are generally critical of the material conditions that shape contemporary reproductions of capitalism. It should also be noted that although critical IPE might not have been formally conceived as a discipline until (as Cohen suggests) its reaction to the post-Bretton Woods literature that was largely emerging from American political science at the time, its history can be traced back earlier. However, as Ashworth's chapter in this volume indicates, and as others have argued previously, the anti-imperialist movement in the early decades of the twentieth century in Britain provided an early form of radicalism that fulfilled much of the normative commitment towards critiquing the nature and form of the international political economy at the time (see also Murphy, 2001; Schwartz, 2002).

It was partly through this early tradition that Cox's understanding of critical theory was developed. In imagining a critical alternative to the dominance of positivism within American-based IPE, Cox presented us with a wide variety of social and political theorists, including Carr and Collingwood (the potential of the latter is developed by Germain's chapter in this volume), who emerged from the anti-imperialist tradition. Others included Sorel and Vico, who both, from their rejections of realism and naturalism in their respective eras, added to Cox's own belief the idea that human nature cannot be understood as a fixed entity but as an 'ensemble of social relations changing through the course of history' (Cox, 1996, p. 29). For Cox, all of these contributions provided a strong base from which a rich form of historicism could be applied that could contest the static form of positivism that orthodox scholars and policymakers were using to understand developments in international economic relations from the 1970s onwards.

Cox's engagement with Gramsci has been the most significant impact on critical IPE. This was tentatively explored in his earlier 1981 *Millennium* paper, but developed more extensively in an article in the same journal two years later (Cox, 1983). This was largely undertaken in order to provide a more comprehensive understanding of hegemony than that used by positivist IR scholars at the time, and has since provided the basis of the 'neo-Gramscian school' that has become highly significant within critical IPE.

For Cox, the importance of Gramsci was that he gave some idea as to how we can understand the configuration of the character of historical structures, a construction he refers to as a 'world order'. Gramsci's concept of hegemony is employed to show how one leading state can transport its ideological and political influence to an international level. Cox's usage was twofold: first, to critique the 'American' equation of hegemony = state leadership, which was used in Hegemonic Stability Theory and was popular with US economic declinists in the aftermath of Bretton-Woods; second, it was used as a vehicle to provide one area of critique in IPE. This was particularly important in the decades that followed, as globalization could be located as a form of US-inspired hegemony. It was Cox's introduction of Gramsci to IR/IPE that led to a number of similar 'neo-Gramscian' accounts that sought to demonstrate how globalization was spread through the transnationalization of class formations that strengthened and institutionalized the neoliberal world order (for instance, see Gill, 1993).

My concern here is that whilst neo-Gramscian accounts have possibly fulfilled their commitment to critique and to develop emancipatory thought, they nevertheless have appeared increasingly as forms of orthodoxy, and in some cases could no longer be considered as particularly radical. Indeed, many new empirical accounts that borrow from the 'neo-Gramscian' mantle seem to make scant commitment towards foregrounding the notion of critique. Certainly for new students, the main purpose of the neo-Gramscian theory has been presented as to explain the workings of power relations in the global economy and to expand existing shortcomings in previous 'mainstream' literature. Despite this, neo-Gramscian research has, at least in principle, remained fairly consistent in its outlook. By favouring a broadly Marxian approach to IPE, neo-Gramscians have maintained their commitment towards critique and – at least tentatively – are rooted in emancipatory thought. At the same time, many neo-Gramscians can equally be accused of situating their enquiries within a narrow and often top-down manner which can open up charges of reductionism and as such negates critical forms of reflexivity (Strange, 2006). Nevertheless, they all at least locate these empirical studies within the purpose of contributing towards wider critique. For example, the focus on hegemony has allowed them to pursue emancipatory strategies and research agendas that are geared towards a 'post-hegemonic' world order (Cox, 1996). More significant still has been the work explaining how 'counter-hegemonic' forces might be constructed in order to contest and potentially transform existing hegemonic relationships or (to borrow from Gramsci) 'common sense' (Gill, 2000; Rupert, 2000; Worth, 2002).

Other theoretical traditions that have emerged within critical IPE are less convincing in their commitments to 'critique and transformation'. For example, whilst Polanyi has been used either alongside or in preference to Gramsci, his own credentials as a departure point for the construction of critical theory are more questionable. Polanyi's understanding of the commodity fetishism of market liberalism provides a useful reminder of the artificial and misplaced reliance on ideology within the practices of political economies at any level. Popular with Cox and other neo-Gramscians such as Stephen Gill as a means of providing another layer for criticizing the ideological nature of contemporary neoliberal globalization, Polanyi demonstrates how

market societies become untenable when the inability to prevent instabilities leads to a 'counter' or 'double' movement whereby the state
and/or civil society acts to re-regulate in order to shield and protect
society from its excesses (1944). Many have sought to apply this concept of the 'double-movement' as a way of demonstrating the fragility
of the neoliberal ideology, placing it alongside the neo-Gramscian concept of hegemony and counter-hegemony (Birchfield, 1999; Chin and
Mittelman, 2000).

Yet, whilst market fetishism and the counter-movement provide us
with a way of understanding the unsustainability of neoliberal economics, and reveal the folly of the many economists who deemed it
indestructible, Polanyi himself could not really be regarded as a critical theorist. As someone who favoured the reformism of British guild
socialism over the more radical socialism of the early twentieth century (Dale, 2009), Polanyi's own credentials can at best be seen as
social democratic and at worst neo-protectionist.[1] Yet, despite this,
Polanyi has perhaps been more widely used than Gramsci as a starting point of analysis in IPE. Although to some extent Polanyi has
attracted those who have favoured a non-Marxist form of IPE critique,
he has also been used by those who have pursued more traditional
avenues of Marxism than many neo-Gramscians. As a result, Polanyi
seems to attract those who have attacked critical IPE for not being suf-
ficiently deeply rooted within Marxist historical materialism (Lacher,
1999), world-systems theorists who were derided by Cox for not being
open enough to the dialectical understanding of transformation (Cox,
1996, pp. 510–13), and those who have criticized the British school as
a whole for being too infatuated with critical theory itself (Blyth, 2002,
2009b).

The ambivalence in articulating the distinct role that critical IPE
should be playing within the wider discipline has left it open to criticisms regarding what its main focus actually is. Those who have taken
these criticisms seriously and have followed Cox's calls for such a
distinction have argued that critical theory needs to maintain its neo-
Gramscian strand or/and (preferably) engage with the Frankfurt School,
so as to firmly distinguish it from other post-positivist accounts that
have emerged within the realms of global politics (Wyn Jones, 2001;
see also Fischer and Tepe in this volume on the Frankfurt School).
Other accounts have laid claim to being 'critical', too, or as being
works that belong to 'critical IPE'. However, whilst these may contain
radical elements that include poststructuralism, neo-Polanyian, post-
Keynesian, Schumpeterian and feminist theories, these approaches have

not necessarily been situated within either the Coxian definition or the Frankfurt School's prescription of 'critique' (Farrands and Worth, 2005).

Alongside these elements, has been the move towards social constructivist accounts that show the importance of agency in shaping and facilitating the functioning characters of the global political economy (Palan, 2000; Seabrooke; 2006; Hobson and Seabrooke, 2007; Langley, 2008; Abdelal et al., 2010). Here, a great deal of attention has been placed on showing how empirical and historical practices are often 'excluded' when assessing the salient features of the global political economy. Whilst interesting, and whilst some studies undoubtedly strive towards radical conclusions that question common perceptions that IPE is the sum of elite-led forces (Langley, 2008), they do not offer any substantive critique. Nor do they appear to offer much to suggest a significant departure from the forms of problem-solving that Cox had insisted one must avoid when setting out critical research agendas.

At this point, one finds it difficult to disagree with Paul Cammack's (2007) recent account of critical IPE, where he argues that it has 'ceased to be critical' and has ultimately failed in what Cox set out to achieve. Similarly, if we are to follow the form and content of the 'British' school that recent debates have posited, we might also take on board Cammack's assertion that it has moved to a broad church that includes neo-Gramscianism at one end and traditional IR at the other, and, as a result, has watered down any Marxist or radical component that was previously seen as critical (ibid., p. 15).[2] In order to provide an answer to this, we need to distinguish further what is, and should be seen as, critical IPE and what merely resides in this newly categorized methodological sphere that is associated with 'British' or 'American' research.

The 'British' school and critical IPE

One of the more intriguing consequences of the Cohen-inspired debates on the nature and development of IPE has been the marginalization of the term 'critical' from much of the discussion. As a result, the term 'critical IPE', which seems to have dominated literature within IPE in recent years, and equally seems to refer to anything that was not involved in positivist empirical case studies, has at least more accurately been replaced. In this sense the observation that IPE has experienced a methodological divide since its inception is largely correct, despite the many problems it has faced in its precise definition of this division (Cohen, 2009).

The current unproblematic reproduction of a notion of a 'British' school has seemed to vindicate this observation. This new move has favoured dropping the phrase 'critical' altogether, instead replacing it with a wider and more inclusive term relating to its dominant geographical positioning. This British school represents something that is far broader than that which Cox was asking for, and does seem to present itself more as a more competitive form of orthodoxy than that of the 'American' school. Indeed, in identifying the parameters of the British school, Cohen originally argued that it could be seen to have its original philosophical roots in Grotius, rather than in the critical epistemology of Marx or Kant (2007, p. 212).

In this way, IPE is merely revisiting what mainstream International Relations (IR) theory was arguing in the 1960s. This largely consisted of a set of methodological debates between Hedley Bull and Morton Kaplan, with the former urging for a historically defined approach to the subject and the latter favouring a behaviourist framework (Bull, 1966; Kaplan, 1966). Whilst linking Bull to Cox (as well as Carr) is not a novel move in the pursuit of critical enquiry (Falk, 1997), it remains a rather peculiar development and surely one which Hedley Bull himself would not wish to be associated with. Bull was writing alongside Martin Wight in fashioning a generally conservative reading of International Relations that was reflected in the British version of realism (known as the English school). This historical/behaviourist split between the UK and the US goes far deeper within the social sciences and, for IR, is indicative of how the respective Foreign Offices of the two states understand the practices of international affairs. By pursuing a transatlantic divide on this level we risk leading ourselves back into not just the orthodoxy, but, indirectly, into the realms of elite policymaking (Smith, 2002).

Unlike critical IPE, the British school's founding figure is not seen as being Robert Cox, but Susan Strange. For while the 1981 piece by Cox in *Millennium* is viewed as the starting point of critical IPE, Susan Strange is more often considered the architect of the wider British school. Strange, as Cohen correctly argues, was neither a radical nor a theorist, but pointed to the problems with state-centric empiricism and the positivism that was entering IPE from IR (Cohen, 2008a). Strange's contribution to critical IPE was to open up avenues that had not been pursued by her Ivy League counterparts. Similarly, Strange questioned their methods and models by suggesting that they were both ontologically narrow and ill-equipped for dealing with the realities of the contemporary world. The most obvious examples include her dismissals of notions of US hegemonic decline and regime theory for their inability to account for structural power (1987). Yet it was perhaps in her prologue to *States and Markets* that this was illustrated most effectively, where she depicted, through a desert island tale, the evolution of IPE. Her point was that there were a number of economic, political and societal approaches to the subject, but IPE as it was then was firmly rooted in a state-centric, security-first political approach (Strange, 1988b). Her argument was thus simply to allow for a wider engagement for study.

Thus, Strange opened certain doors to allow critical IPE to develop, but she was not a critical theorist and not someone to whom one could look for reclaiming and re-establishing any further direction. She remains significant in demonstrating the importance of inclusivity over exclusivity and rigidity, and in questioning certain forms of knowledge that hitherto were unchallenged. She also provided an important influence for those who were initially constructing a critical alternative to positivist IPE (Murphy and Tooze, 1991; Cox, 1996), but that is largely where her influence regarding wider critique ends. More importantly, if we were to look at what the British school stands for as a departure point – ideational, historical and philosophical, qualitative, normative, multidisciplinary and inclusive – then Strange's work certainly did much to create this community. Yet, like Bull before her, this was largely in line with the British tradition of political research and often reflective of her particular time and place. For example, whilst American academics became preoccupied with economic relations in international affairs after the collapse of the dollar system, British IPE stemmed from a study by Strange that had as much in common with economics and traditional political economy as it did with IR. The British school – or what should more appropriately be termed the British 'approach' – seems to incorporate all areas of IPE research that reject the positivism inherent within initial US-centred work on regimes and hegemonic stability, and likewise the econometric quantitative research that is endemic within American social science more broadly.

The British school should thus be distinguished from critical IPE. The former represents a general method of how to approach the discipline and follows the more general 'British' trend that roots political and international studies within a humanities tradition which relies upon the primacy of philosophy and history as opposed to notions of an empirically testable science. The latter might appear from within this overall bracket, but it represents a distinct research project of its own and it emerges not exclusively from Britain, but from the radical social science traditions within North America (particularly Canada),

Britain, Europe and beyond.[3] It would therefore be wrong to equate the British school with what we might call critical IPE. If we did, we would be in danger of interpreting what was originally rooted within Robert Cox's understanding of anti-problem-solving critical historicism as an 'option' within a wider methodological framework that effectively alters or dramatically waters down the effectiveness of critical IPE. Yet one of the purposes of the much-heralded special issues on the declared 'schools' in IPE that followed Cohen's book is to do precisely that, as they attempt to bridge the differences between American and British IPE so that common concerns and respective differences and weakness could be addressed from both sides. For those involved in the debates on the nature of the British school, this has inevitably led to a call for greater inclusion.

At the same time, there has been a dissatisfaction that too much British IPE is concerned with questions of class, inequality, injustices, etc., leading to persistent charges of 'monolithic Marxism' (Blyth, 2009b, p. 331). This suggests that the British school needs to cast off its obsession with critique and radicalism and the language that accompanies it, and engage far more with broader approaches and methods (ibid.; Underhill, 2009). In response to this, I suggest precisely the opposite. For critical IPE to maintain its initial objectives and commitments, I believe it is necessary for it to distinguish itself from the separate aims of mainstreaming that the work on the transatlantic divide seems to be doing. As Craig Murphy (2009) rightly reminds us in response to the fresh categorizing of IPE schools, contemporary IPE should be seen not as a geographical division, but as a split between those 'satisfied' with the status quo and those who are not. Or, put plainly, this can be seen as a split between those who embody a radicalism on the one hand and those who favour conservatism on the other – locating it as an 'older distinction between left and right' (ibid., p. 362).

What we next need to ask is where critical IPE should go from here to in order to reclaim and reformulate its central purpose? One route would be to reassert the importance of a historical materialist approach as a means of distinguishing itself from the creeping orthodoxy of the British school. This could allow for a wider Marxist-based critique of capitalism – one that can respond to current claims that dismiss Marxism (as opposed to the 'neo-Gramscians') as determinist and economistic (Phillips, 2005b; Cammack, 2007). Yet, this would have to be done in a manner that does not attract such criticisms by expanding upon existing class-based accounts that have been ontologically narrow in their focus (Germain, 2007). More importantly, in order for us to build upon a critical discourse, we also need to entrench such a discourse in the wider commitments that critical theory sought to deliver. Using Murphy's apt comments as a departure point, refocusing our understanding of what critical theory is founded upon might be a useful start.

Critical epistemology

Rooted in the spirit of spirit of Kant's *Critique of Pure Reason* and reinforced throughout the work of Marx, critical theory developed into a body of thought that was to resurface with the Frankfurt School in the 1930s (see also Fischer and Tepe in this volume). Here, the three-pronged composition of social critique, critical knowledge and emancipation was developed by Horkheimer (1937/1972) and later in Habermas's early work on Critical Knowledge (1987). The commitment towards emancipation was founded in the dialectical reflexivity that Marx teased out in the 'Theses on Feuerbach', with his much-quoted line that 'philosophers have only interpreted the world in various ways, the point is to change it' (Marx, 1969). The point, therefore, for critical theorists is to demonstrate that when action fails or is insufficient in its purpose, then its working principles have to be reviewed and corrected (Adorno and Horkheimer, 2002).

Despite the legacy of the traditions of the critical theorists of the Frankfurt School, IPE has largely chosen to avoid any real engagement with them (Wyn Jones, 2001). This might be because of the huge influence that Cox has had on its evolution and that his own understanding of critical thought seemed to adopt an Italian – as opposed to a Frankfurt – influence. Gramsci might have been the central inspiration when it came to Cox's understanding of world order, but Vico's *New Science* seems to have formed the basis of his critical theory (Cox, 2002). There are certain advantages for critical IPE in not following the more established route taken by critical theory within the wider social sciences. In particular, the move towards poststructuralism that has accompanied critical theory, coupled with the increasingly liberal turn taken by Habermas in his later works on cosmopolitan communitarianism, has freed critical IPE from following increasingly detached objects of critique. However, in order to firmly distinguish it from orthodoxy, the commitment towards ensuring the retention of critique, critical knowledge and emancipation would at least bring the 'critical' back to a study that has for too long been lazy in its application of the term (Farrands, 2002; see Griffin in this volume for a different perspective on poststructuralism).

The in-depth understanding of how the three-pronged method of critique, critical thought and emancipation might be utilized within IPE has been mentioned before (Farrands and Worth, 2005), but it might be useful to stress some of the approaches here. On critique, Cox has provided us with a sound benchmark in his critical model, which, although brief and not without problems, does nevertheless offer a coherent challenge to mainstream, or in this case 'problem-solving', theory. Whilst seemingly drawn from Vico's and Sorel's criticisms of science, Cox's critique of problem-solving theory shares many similarities with the Frankfurt School's attacks on pragmatism and positivism. Added to this is the close proximity between Cox's usage of historical structures and Adorno's development of dialectics. What is more surprising, however, is that, Gramsci aside, the other sources of philosophical critique that Cox uses have not been tapped into and developed. He is largely alone in his usage of Vico and Sorel, whilst other prominent Marxists who were also highly dialectical in their respective work (such as Benjamin and Luxemburg) have seldom been explored. In addition, Gramsci has often been applied in a manner that is distinctly driven by Cox himself, and one which often ignores the debates and exchanges that Gramscians (as opposed to neo-Gramscians) had with the structural Marxists of the 1960s and 1970s over where to situate Gramsci.[4] Despite this, it must be stressed that Cox has provided a platform for critique that allows for a viable interrogation of pragmatism and contemporary norms and conditions.

The subject of critical knowledge is one that follows on from critique and one that again Cox applies in part. It was a key ingredient in the more recognized forms of critical theory (from Kant and Marx onwards) and something that Habermas did much to build on. He illustrated the distinction between critical and practical knowledge. Practical knowledge serves the interests of the established order and seeks to reproduce existing boundaries of influence. Critical knowledge aims to understand the dynamics that exist within this relationship, so as to exploit their weaknesses (Habermas, 1987; Farrands and Worth, 2005). It is here that the importance of dialectical method comes in, so as to understand and comprehend existing ontologies of practical knowledge.

Again, if we locate this within IPE, then many of the neo-Gramscians and, to a lesser extent, the neo-Polanyians are on the right track. Both demonstrate how market economies construct and, as a result, embed forms of practical knowledge. As we know, Cox himself acknowledges the importance of the difference between the two sets of what he terms problem-solving and critical forms of enquiry, yet he does not make – and does not appear to make anywhere in his work – any engagement with, or show great interest in, the works contained within the Frankfurt tradition (Cox, 1996; Wyn Jones, 2001). Nevertheless, an engagement with how different generations of the Frankfurt School have considered the production of knowledge would certainly be beneficial. For where critical IPE has been weak is in the lack of dialectical understanding of how practical knowledge in this form is produced and reproduced. This trait has confused what we consider to be critical of something or some process, with that which is rooted within wider critical theory.

Perhaps the most neglected area of critical theory in IPE, however, remains in the premise of emancipatory thought and in the negotiation of emancipatory strategies. Emancipation is explicit in Cox, the Frankfurt School and western Marxism, yet it is often overlooked and disregarded by the many accounts that lay some claim towards taking a critical point of enquiry within IPE. Whilst there are obviously concerns with the form that this type of emancipation might take, and whether indeed it might itself fall into the trap of merely reinforcing existing mainstreams (as Habermas himself seems increasingly prone to doing), critical theory nevertheless commits itself – as a necessity – to agenda that is geared towards progressive transformation. At present there is a danger that many studies within the academy have become too preoccupied with scrutinizing a specific subject matter rather than foregrounding the importance of transformative emancipation. As a result, a key component within Cox's normative vision for critical theory is ignored, leading further to proclamations of its demise (Cammack, 2007). The pursuit of emancipation is not something that should be glossed over, or added as a footnote at the end of a 'critical' piece of research, but rather needs to be centred, so that it highlights the problems with a specific aspect of the global political economy and demonstrates how, why and in what form the problem needs to be transcended. Without this, the claim towards providing a radical critique becomes less and less convincing.

Conclusion

In light of recent debates surrounding the 'transatlantic divide' in IPE, this chapter has argued that 'critical' IPE is in danger of losing its distinct radicalism which had been built by Robert Cox in his *Millennium* articles and followed up through neo-Gramscian contributions. However, this move also brought with it a flourish of new work that declared itself 'critical', but without necessarily giving us much indication as to why this was so, leaving some to suggest that IPE has indeed ceased to be critical in any sense (Cammack, 2007). Such observations appear justified in light of the debates that have suggested that such accounts can be seen better if placed within a larger 'British' school or approach. These debates, brought on by Benjamin Cohen's intellectual history of the discipline, have, in my opinion, made two observations that are important for any renewed form of critical IPE to reassert itself. First, he suggests (rightly in my opinion) that the methodological split within the discipline has been as much the result of the differences between American and British approaches to social science in general, as any ideological and theoretical split. Second, he argues that a coming together of these two strands is necessary for the discipline to develop further – a process which is seemingly being constructed within key journals and volumes at the moment.

Yet the real purpose of this bridge seems to be to construct new forms of orthodoxy (see also Cammack in this volume). If this is indeed the result, then perhaps the real significance of Cohen's account of the British school is in its use of semiotics. Prior to his account, critical IPE was slowly becoming a term that seemed to mean anything and everything that did not adhere to a strict form of scientific positivism. This would suggest that the critical component that was prominent in the Cox-inspired British school has been undermined by a larger, more inclusive, more open (and more sanitized) British school.

In response, critical IPE needs to do a number of things. First, it should use this opportunity to distinguish itself from the British school. Rather than follow the trend towards greater engagement with methods and theories that would enable it to be less marginal, critical IPE should restate itself as an influential body of thought through the reclamation of its radicalism. Far from being parochial, critical IPE has a number of different radical departure points that it might tap into, but which are often overlooked or dismissed within contemporary IPE. Such a point has been highlighted by Murphy, when he questions why many of those in radical political economy and sociology who had been involved in debates within IPE have been left out of recent discussions (Murphy, 2009). Thus for critical IPE to move forward, it should spell out far more explicitly what separates it from other accounts. In order to do this it needs to take seriously its commitments to the process of critique. Or, to put it rather more eloquently in the words of Chris Farrands, it needs to be 'critical about those who proclaim to be critical' (2002, p. 15). It is only by refocusing upon the requirements of critical research, and particularly upon the principles of critique, emancipation and the dissection of critical and practical knowledge, that critical IPE can rediscover itself with a renewed purpose.

Notes

1. The main thrust of Polanyi's understanding of political economy can be found in his anthropological writings that are often associated with his later, post-*Great Transformation*, work. Here he favours a rediscovery of archaic and primitive economies in order to reconnect with a social foundation that had been neglected by market economics (Polanyi, 1968). Such a position, indeed, serves as the antithesis of Marx's central understanding of dialectical materialism.
2. A number of textbooks actually present the neo-Gramscian school as a radical form of social constructivism (Palan, 2000; Woods, 2008). On this level, they seem to view critical IPE as a broad family of social constructivism, joined together primarily by the stress upon agency as an explanatory focus.
3. Indeed, the various neo-Gramscian accounts that appeared as a direct result of Robert Cox's calls for critique are still identified as either the 'Amsterdam' or 'Italian' schools, occasionally being referred to as the 'Toronto' school.
4. Cox (1981) merely dismisses the Althusser/Poulantzas approach as being determinist in nature. This observation has largely formed the basis of subsequent dismissals of other forms of Marxism within the British school (Phillips, 2005b). A more adequate summary and scrutiny of structural Marxism from a Gramscian perspective can be seen in Stuart Hall's theoretical work (Hall, 1988, pp. 93–175).

8

'What's Critical about Critical Theory': Feminist Materialism, Intersectionality and the Social Totality of the Frankfurt School

Anita Fischer and Daniela Tepe

Introduction

This is certainly not the first contribution to address the nature of Critical Theory, nor the first to address the necessarily feminist character of Critical Theory. Given that most of the writing concerned with the latter has gone largely unheard in much of IR and IPE scholarship, it seems appropriate to address this subject again. In 1985, Nancy Fraser, in her seminal piece 'What's Critical about Critical Theory? The Case of Habermas and Gender', engaged with Habermas's conceptualization of distinct logics of symbolic and natural reproduction relating to the spheres of life-world and system-world as crucial to his Critical Theory. Fraser exposed these distinctions as conceptually inadequate and potentially ideological, highlighting the 'dual aspect' of both spheres and logics. She showed how Habermas's logic potentially:

> directs attention away from the fact that the household, like the paid workplace, is a site of labor, albeit of unremunerated and often unrecognized labor. Likewise, it does not make visible the fact that in the paid workplace, as in the household, women are assigned to, indeed ghettoized in, distinctively feminine, service-oriented and often sexualized occupations. Finally, it fails to focalize the fact that in both spheres women are subordinated to men.
>
> (Fraser, 1985, p. 107)

Twenty years on, Critical Theory scholarship in IPE (and IR), whether it derives its 'critical' from idealist Habermasian notions or a neo-Gramscian background located in the tradition of a more materialist definition of Critical Theory, has mostly paid lip-service to these insights. As Georgina Waylen has put it, 'despite some similarities in their ontologies and epistemologies, and a commitment to pluralism, most critical IPE does not mention gender except in passing or engage with any of the gendered political economy debates and research' (2006, p. 145; see also Tickner, 1997; Peterson, 2005; Steans and Tepe, 2008; Elias, this volume). Given this, one might ask why one should, as a feminist scholar, actually stick with a notion of Critical Theory, if it seems so difficult to fight the ground here? Seemingly, it has been easier for liberal feminists to engage in fruitful dialogue with mainstream IPE resulting in collaborative scholarship and political practice,[1] including the institutionalization of gender studies as an academic discipline and of gender mainstreaming practices in European politics (Knapp, 2008, p. 292). Similarly, postmodern and/or poststructuralist feminists and non-feminists (if such a distinction is at all possible) have shared research agendas and themes.

Klinger and Alexi-Knapp (2007) have answered this question emphatically: Critical Theory offers a utopian moment incorporating a radical rejection of existing relations of domination. This utopian moment is the realization of the promise that modern society gave when it made ideas of freedom, equality and solidarity the guiding principles of its very constitution. Yet, we would also argue that this promise is insufficient if we did not believe that Critical Theory, in its materialist version, is necessarily a feminist theory, and has at its very core the hope and aim for the 'overcoming of societal injustice' (Horkheimer, 1968, p. 56), including relations of domination beyond the capital relation. As Brown asserts, Critical Theory, in contrast to other forms of modern Marxist thinking, has questioned orthodox economic causality, traced capital's cultural and social effects, given respect to subjectivity and paid attention 'to forms of power that exceeded the capital-relation' (2006, p. 4). We contend that Critical Theory, combining a strong anti-capitalist argument with an openness towards feminist critique, provides the foundation for theorizing inequalities in society aiming at their abolition.

In reflecting on these concerns, this chapter will first engage with Horkheimer's notion of Critical Theory as developed in the course of his 1937 essay *Traditionelle und kritische Theorie* republished in 1968. We also explore the writings of Adorno in the so-called *Positivismusstreit der deutschen Soziologie*, highlighting how, at the very core of both authors' arguments, there stands the realization that any theory that aims to be critical has to look at the social totality (*Betrachtung des Gesellschaftlichen Ganzen*) and not at its parts (*Teilbereiche*).[2] We then explain the ultimate reduction of social totality to the capital relation as a result of Critical Theory's conceptualization of femininity and women as natural and located outside the rational sphere of capitalist logic. Second, we point to the crucial feminist insight that social totality should not ultimately be reducible to the capital relation. We highlight the development of feminist thinking in capturing the social totality from early feminist thought, acknowledging the analysis of a social reproductive sphere as crucial to critical theorizing of the notion of intersectionality, acknowledging the 'three axes of inequality' as constitutive for the social totality. Third, we engage with some feminist writings that produce Critical Theory against the background of insights from intersectionality, before concluding by pointing towards possible avenues for future collaboration between IPE and critical 'feminist' theory.

Social totality in Critical Theory

Horkheimer wrote his seminal essay 'Critical and Traditional Theory' against the subject-specific (*fachspezifische*) isolation and related particularization of societal research.[3] Critical Theory, for Horkheimer, aims to overcome disciplinary boundaries and to understand societal facts in their real context as the only legitimate way to aim for freedom from societal repression. He develops his understanding of Critical Theory against the counter-term Traditional Theory, which stands for the 'entire, positivist science method, geared towards the ideal of natural science methodology, rests upon the rigid dissociation of the scientific object and the observant subject' (Dubiel, 1988, p. 21). Similarly for Adorno, Critical Theory is distinct from positivist theorizing in that it critically relativizes the appearance of society, rather than radically separating science from real life (Adorno, 1972). This epistemological stance is also what, it has been argued, Robert Cox took on in 1981 to define the neo-Gramscian Critical Theory, and which continues to serve to this day as one of the central conceptual blueprints for IPE (Cox, 1981; for a feminist critique of neo-Gramscian IPE see Steans and Tepe, 2008).[4] Yet, as is outlined below, Critical Theory is more than solely the opposite of problem-solving theory as proclaimed by many neo-Gramscians. Similarly, problem-solving theory is more than solely problem-solving, being crucially an instrument of reaffirming and reassuring structures of domination. Cox's simplification needs to be rejected as it reduces Critical Theory – by simplifying societal structural conditions – to a

Realkritik (real critique) of visible relations of exploitation. Adorno and Horkheimer, in contrast to Cox, are able to show how positivist theory becomes a necessary illusion in capitalist society:

> It is illusion since the diversity of methods does not encompass the unity of the object and conceals it behind so-called factors into which the object is broken up for the sake of convenience; it is necessary since the object, society, fears nothing more than to be called by name, and therefore it automatically encourages and tolerates only such knowledge of itself that slides off its back without any impact.
>
> (Adorno, 1976, p. 76)

Similarly, Horkheimer's critique begins and ends with the realization that traditional theory is incapable of understanding the social totality, and that it is exactly this shortcoming which results in its positive societal function (Horkheimer, 1968, p. 26). Critical Theory, in contrast, takes the 'two-sided character of the social totality in its present form' (Horkheimer, 1972, p. 207) as a starting point in order to consciously realize its contradictions.

Societal totality, for Adorno and Horkheimer,[5] is not a trivial notion – it does not simply refer to the triviality that everything is connected with everything in one way or another (Adorno, 1972, p. 20). Social totality is the realization that, in its concrete form, everybody – given that they do not want to be subjected to decay (*zugrundegehen*) – is subject to laws of exchange (*Tauschgesetz*), independent of whether they are subjectively driven by an interest in profit or not:

> The crucial difference between the dialectical and the positivistic view of totality is that the dialectical concept of totality is intended 'objectively', namely, for the understanding of every social individual observation, whilst positivistic systems theories wish, in an uncontradictory manner, to incorporate observations in a logical continuum, simply through the selection of categories as general as possible. In so doing, they do not recognize the highest structural concepts as the precondition for the states of affairs subsumed under them. ... The core of the critique of positivism is that it shuts itself off from both the experience of the blindly dominating totality and the driving desire that it should ultimately become something else. It contends itself with the senseless ruins which remain after the liquidation of idealism, without interpreting, and rendering them true.
>
> (Adorno, 1976, p. 14; see also Adorno, 1967)

This social totality is therefore constitutive of domination, the domination of people over people. It is not an affirmative but a critical category which cannot be separated from dialectics, and the decisive processes of this form of domination can only be uncovered through theory (Adorno, 1972, p. 19).

As such, within this social totality, the function of the critical intellectual is to develop such theory, to highlight societal contradictions, yet, at the same time, to not only provide an impression of the societal situation but also to serve as a stimulating and changing factor from within. The aim that Critical Theory strives towards is:

> the rational state of society, [that] is forced upon him by present distress. The theory which projects such a solution to the distress does not labor in the service of an existing reality but only gives voice to the mystery of such reality.
>
> (Horkheimer, 1972, p. 217)

For Horkheimer the essence of critical theorizing and its stability and cohesiveness is owed to the fact that despite all societal change, 'the basic economic structure, the class relationship in its simplest form, and therefore the idea of supersession of these two remains identical' (Horkheimer, 1972, p. 234). In this sense, Horkheimer ultimately reduces the social totality to the capital relation. Similarly, for Adorno the class relation is the highest structuring principle (*oberster Strukturprinzip*) of the social totality. This is linked to the way in which Horkheimer and Adorno have engaged with femininity and women, and what, until today, malestream research has tended to do (Steans and Tepe, 2008). As Marasco notes, 'these works are full of problematic claims about women and unsettling nostalgia for the pre-rationalized form of life identified as feminine' (2006, p. 89).

For Critical Theory, the feminine has been connected to the natural world of beauty, passion, impulse and irrationality.[6] As critics of the Enlightenment project, Horkheimer and Adorno realized how the concept of the Enlightenment itself locks femininity as natural into the private sphere, to be directed by masculine reason. They stress how women and nature have become objects of instrumental domination. 'Rational man's domination of nature is secured through what is also its precondition: the rational separation between subject and object and, more precisely, the elevation of the subject over the object of knowledge' (Marasco, 2006, p. 91). Owning power and being the subject of knowledge, the male assumes power over its object. Enlightenment is for Critical Theory linked to a historical progression by dominating nature through civilization. Horkheimer and Adorno argue that the presumed barbarism of the past remains an integral component of Enlightenment reason, 'which has its origin in myth (the Odyssey) and propagates a secularised myth of itself through science, culture and morality' (ibid., p. 92).

Yet, Adorno and Horkheimer's Critical Theory is more complex than simply to suggest that male domination over women would derive and be secured through a particular representation of women as natural (as has been suggested by Hewitt, 1992). Rather, 'women and nature', for them, 'are associated to the extent that both become objects of masculine instrumental domination. Therefore, women and nature are associated with one another through historical conditions of domination, not through some intrinsic connection between the feminine and the natural' (Marasco, 2006, p. 93). The consequences, however, are similar: the equation of femininity and women with nature, although historically produced and specific to capitalist relations, results in a construction of a sphere of private life which is, partly at least, freed from the logics of capital and as such not part of the social totality – the very thing which Critical Theory sees as its sole assignment in theorizing and overcoming. Confusingly, and partly contradictory however (the legitimizing argument is probably that this is part of dialectical thinking, *sic*!), Adorno does not fully detach the privateness of, for example, the family (which he considers a capitalist enclave) from the social totality he describes. He acknowledges that,

> system and individual entity are reciprocal and can only be apprehended in their reciprocity. Even those enclaves, survivals from previous societies, the favourites of a sociology which desires to unburden itself of the concept of society – as it might of an all too spectacular philosopheme – become what they are only in relation to the dominant totality from which they deviate.
>
> (Adorno, 1976, p. 107)

For us, Adorno's thinking becomes inconsequential when what he considers non-capitalist forms have to be understood in relation to the social totality he tries to capture. The reason for this is his setting of what is constitutive for the everyday lives of people. He writes,

> the category 'a society based on the division of labour in general' is higher and more general than 'capitalistic society' – but it is not more

substantial. Rather, it is less substantial and tells us less about the life of the people and what threatens them. This does not mean, however, that a logically lower category such as 'urbanism' would say more.

(Adorno, 1976, p. 70)

In that sense, it is the category 'capitalist society' and its underlying laws that decide constitutively on the structure of everyday life. However, as feminist research has shown, the lives of women in particular are determined as much by the respective class position of subjects as by their gender position (or race/ethnicity position – as we highlight below). In historically specific situations the gender of a subject tells us more about their life situation, the inequalities and suppressions a specific subject is exposed to and, crucially, what needs to be theorized in order to overcome this suppression. Interestingly, Adorno implicitly affirms this insight in the very same article on sociology and empirical research when he writes:

> The generality of social-scientific laws is not at all that of a conceptual sphere into which the individual parts can be wholly incorporated, but rather always and essentially relates to the relationship of the general to the particular in its historical concretization.
>
> (1976, p. 77)

Below, we highlight how Adorno's and Horkheimer's conception of the social totality remains behind the reality of societal suppression and exploitation, and as such is incapable of understanding and even seeing them in their totality. At the same time, we are convinced by Adorno's and Horkheimer's claim that an understanding of the social totality must be the starting point of a Critical Theory that has as its only remaining duty to contribute to the abolition of societal suppression and exploitation. Therefore, Critical Theory will need to change, to being inclusive of the reality of societal suppression and exploitation and, as such, even becoming relatively incohesive in order to remain one with itself. As Horkheimer contends,

> For all its insight into the individual steps in social change and for all the agreement of its elements with the most advanced traditional theories, the critical theory has no specific influence on its side, except for the concern for the abolition of social injustice. This negative formulation, if we wish to express it abstractly, is the materialist content of the idealist concept of reason.
>
> (Horkheimer, 1972, p. 242)

The encompassing social totality

Feminists from a materialist background have, on the basis of in-depth empirical research and rigid theorizing, shown how the social totality cannot be understood through, nor be reduced to, the capital relation.[7] In the mid-1970s the new social movements, especially the women's movement, started to criticize the materialist definition of the social totality as a relation of dominance and power which is based on the antagonism of capital and labour (Haug, 1996, p. 218). So-called materialist feminists like Becker-Schmidt provided an elaborate critique of social theories (*Gesellschaftstheorien*), which captured societal phenomena as gender-neutral, resulting in the neglect and fading-out of 'female' realities in scientific and societal consciousness. Within malestream theories, societal cohesion is, in most cases, explained without considering the question of social reproduction, its location and its protagonists (Becker-Schmidt, 1987, p. 12). In their critique, however, feminist research is not limited to a differentiation of femininity or a broaching of the issue of 'women' in the conditions of family, education, work, sexuality and/or culture. The focus of analysis is rather on the question of the societal organization of gender relations (ibid., pp. 10f.). As such, when feminists engage with malestream approaches in IPE and critique the neglect of conditions of societal reproduction in economic contexts, they do not solely highlight the need to make visible 'female' circles of life and/or circumstances under which 'females' live their lives, by looking closely at 'female' practices in the complementary spheres of income work (*Erwerbsarbeit*) and social reproduction (ibid., p. 12). In contrast, this feminist engagement encompasses a broader notion of social reproduction and cedes ground to a more all-encompassing understanding of how society is organized.

Social reproduction here refers to the re-creation/reproduction of the population from one day to the next and from one generation to the next:

> The concept entails more than the physical reproduction of a population; it encompasses the intergenerational transmitting of historically derived values, norms, skills and knowledge as well as the construction of identities and subjectivities, individual and collective, across generations and across cultures. It thus refers to the care work necessary for biological reproduction, the reproduction of human labor (and – in large part – the social and cultural values of specific societies).
>
> (Steans and Tepe, 2010, pp. 807–15)

As such, a materialist feminist critique of malestream IPE aims to address the historical meaning and function of the historically specific (and constituted) separation between the 'public' sphere of income generation (*Erbwerbssphäre*) and the 'private' sphere of reproduction for the organization of gender relations. The construction of privateness and the related privatization of social reproduction themselves are understood as decisive modi of modernity, generating the elimination of gender in the public sphere (Sauer, 1997, p. 35). Therefore, this separation needs to be problematized as a dichotomizing modus of gender construction (*Vergeschlechtlichung*). In the political sciences[8] 'public' and 'private' denominate two complementary terms, yet, the very notion and reality of a public sphere only comes into historical being through the separation of a (fictitious) privateness. Within the very process of labelling private and public male power is historically constituted, and it becomes a resource for the enforcement of 'male' requirements after intimacy and open spaces for 'male' fantasies of domination and violence (ibid., p. 36):

> The dichotomy of the public and the private is a pattern to organise and perceive reality, politics and society. The public and the private are assortative concepts that allow us to regulate social relationships and also to ban or grant something. The dichotomy not only regulates the access to specific spaces and resources, it also generates groups of agents (e.g. through gendering), streamlines interests and has a normative dimension: to regulate what one is allowed to do, what one should do and what one shouldn't.
>
> (cf. Gaus and Benn, 1983, pp. 7ff.; Sauer, 1997, p. 37)[9]

These remarks highlight how a materialist feminist intervention in malestream debates in IPE makes visible the contribution of malestream IPE to the production and reproduction of gender relations – by making invisible gendered (*vergeschlechtlichte*) subjects in the unquestioned reproduction of a concept of privateness.

Through making visible the historical construction of a private and public sphere, materialist feminists have successfully challenged the thesis of a principal contradiction (class) and a side contradiction (gender), and argued that capitalism and patriarchy are two interdependent social relations, each of which cannot be reduced to the other. The main concern of feminist scholars was to highlight that Critical Theory focusing solely on class relations and the sphere of production is gender-blind and thus incapable of capturing the social totality, based on an ignorance regarding the necessary societal reproduction of the workforce, the gender-specific division of labour and the question of paid and unpaid work: the 'societal division of labour between the sexes is not only determining the social division of tasks, it also implies – on the side of individuation – distinct possibilities to acquire (*Aneignungsmoeglichkeiten*)' (Becker-Schmidt, 1987, p. 18).

Realizing then, that the social totality incorporates production *and* social reproduction, feminist theoretical work at the time assumed that patriarchy, as a relation of domination in charge of social reproduction, has a relatively independent structure analogous to the structure of the capital relation. The core question in feminist debates has been how to conceptualize interaction at the interstices of both these structures (Winker, 2007, p. 18). Becker-Schmidt and others have captured the interdependent nature of capitalism and patriarchy with concepts including dual socialization (*Doppelte Vergesellschaftung*), gender relations as relations of production and the gender-specific division of labour (see Beer, 1990; Fischer, 2008). One of the main aims of these theoretical conceptualizations has been to widen the notion of the social totality in order to capture the concomitance of various social relations of exploitation.

Similarly to the analysis of public and private in IPE, approaches in Critical Theory elsewhere remain malestream. From a gender-theoretical perspective their analysis of society suffers from sincere and consequential short circuits. Horkheimer and Adorno in the first place circumvent the necessity of social reproduction in the development of their notion of social totality – femininity becomes localized in the private sphere of the family and as such contributes to a tradition of downsizing gender which occurs most frequently in the following ways: 'a limited and personalised understanding of gender and the tendency to locate gender relationships in the private sphere and within intimate relationships' (Klinger and Knapp, 2007, p. 32).

The insights of materialist feminists have, however, been subject to a wide range of criticism from within feminist scholarship, not least by scholars from an anti-racist background. The confinement to look at class and gender relations as sources of social inequality has been critiqued widely from this perspective. Women of colour have rightfully exposed the materialist feminist confinement to gender or class and gender as white middle-class feminism (Kerner, 2009, p. 263). An example of this line of critique is work on 'triple-oppression' or on 'multiple jeopardy' (see King, 1988) which addresses the experiences of racist discrimination for non-white women. These debates constitute the point of origin of more recent debates on intersectionality, which we turn to below.

The critique addresses a mechanism to accomplish and reproduce social inequality. We have addressed a similar mechanism above, resulting from the public/private divide – making invisible the elements, meanings and functions of social inequality and thereby the subjugated subjects themselves. For a long time the category race/ethnicity has been neglected in economic analysis as a crucial factor constituting economic relations and thereby fundamentally social relations. The groups and subjects in society categorized thereby have become invisible, with feminist research and practice even being accomplices to this form of domination and subjugation (see Knapp, 2010).

The intervention of women of colour had several interlinked consequences for the development of feminist theoretical research and feminist practice. On the one hand, the feminist standpoint has developed theoretical concepts and politics that look closely at the experiences of black women – as interpreted by black women (Collins, 1991, p. 22). Connected to this endeavour is an internal differentiation, or, perhaps better, the pluralization of the category of gender. The idea of conceptualizing an integrative feminist theory capturing all women equally has become questionable (see Kerner, 2009, pp. 262ff.).

On the other hand, while the second development is connected to exactly this point of questioning the homogeneity of the category gender, it heads in a different direction in developing more formal research programmes (*Forschungsprogramatik*). This scholarly work focuses not just on developing standpoint analytical perspectives; instead, the focus lies much more on highlighting the interconnectedness, entanglement and overlapping of various relatively independent systems of domination and subjugation. We argue that these approaches can be read and understood as connecting with, and critically developing, further materialist-feminist debates. In this line of engagement with the realities of women from varying racial backgrounds, the triple-oppression as well as the multiple-jeopardy approaches have receded in importance relatively quickly, due to the additive character they assign to the structuring principles of class, race and gender. Rather, approaches of intersectionality have become the main point of reference (Kerner, 2009, p. 346).

A possible way out of this dilemma – intersectionality?

The key element of the 'intersectionality' debates formulates the questions about the connecting point between social disparity/inequality and differences, the interactions between mechanisms of exclusion and discrimination (Riegraf, 2010, p. 40). The starting point of the projected 'intersectionality analysis' is the assumption that in modern differentiated societies the central axes of inequality are intrinsically intertwined and therefore concrete conditions of social inequality cannot be adequately grasped in isolation from one another. In contrast, their entanglement has to become the very object of analysis to allow for a meaningful analysis of inequality (Becker-Schmidt, 2007, p. 56).

The term and concept of intersectionality was introduced as early as the 1980s by law professor Kimberlé Crenshaw. Her research linked up with the critique of 'women of colour' levelled towards a white middle-class feminism, which had reduced its scientific research to, and developed its political concepts around, a narrow focus on a reduction of gender discrimination (Crenshaw, 1989). On the basis of an analysis of American anti-discrimination regulations and data sets relating to police intervention in cases of domestic violence, Crenshaw was able to show how the privileging of one axis of inequality results not only in neglect of the other axes, but consolidates and even reinforces them, in social research agendas and political programmes:

> Among the most troubling political consequences of the failure of antiracist and feminist discourses to address the intersections of racism and patriarchy is the fact that, to the extent they forward the interests of people of color and 'women', respectively, one analysis often implicitly denies the validity of the other. The failure of feminism to interrogate race means that the resistance strategies of feminism will often replicate and reinforce the subordination of people of color, and the failure of antiracism to interrogate patriarchy means that antiracism will frequently reproduce the subordination of women.
>
> (Crenshaw, 1994, p. 1256)

One can capture Crenshaw's understanding of intersectionality with the metaphor of a street crossing, in which the various axes of societal inequalities and differences cross each other, swap and overlap, where discrimination,

> like traffic through an intersection, may flow in one direction, and it may flow in another. If an accident happens in an intersection, it can be caused by cars travelling from a number of directions and, sometimes, from all of them. Similarly, if a Black woman is harmed

because she is in her intersection, her injury could result from sex discrimination or race discrimination.

(1989, p. 149)

Her research clearly shows how a distinction between structural and political intersection widens an understanding of societal inequalities and differences. It becomes possible to distinguish between scientific analysis of intersectionalities (structural intersectionality) and political aspirations and processes (Riegraf, 2010, pp. 45–6). Despite the fruitfulness of the concept of intersectionality in capturing the interrelated character of the categories of inequality for a Critical Theory, what is problematic is the immanent reduction of the categories class, race and gender to categories of identity on the level of subjectivity. Such a micro- or meso-theoretical conceptualization obscures from view the necessity of a societal or macro-theoretical perspective in order to capture the social totality in line with the aims of Critical Theory. As such, it reduces the possibility of explaining how, and through what means, class, race and gender are reciprocally constituted as social categories (Klinger and Knapp, 2007, pp. 36–7).

Along with the categories of class, race and gender, the debate on intersectionality has succeeded in naming the central categories of inequality which are entangled in modern society. Yet, social theory has so far not been able to develop an integrated approach, capable of seeing these entangled inequalities in order to capture the social totality (Becker-Schmidt, 2007, p. 56). The development of such a systematically integrated perspective on the intersectionality of class, race and gender, which holds on to the concept of a social theory, remains absent (Klinger and Knapp, 2007, p. 30).

Despite this absence, there are some works located within the debate on intersectionality which point toward the necessity of developing approaches that adhere to the project of social theory that addresses society in its totality (see Becker-Schmidt, 2007; Klinger and Knapp, 2007; Knapp, 2008, 2010). Yet, to this point these approaches remain marginalized even within feminist debates, partly due to a preoccupation (*pace* Griffin in this volume) with the poststructuralist-inspired neglect of 'totalizing' social theory (Steans and Tepe, 2010). Nevertheless, our contribution to this volume illustrates how these approaches, especially the work of Klinger and Knapp, are of special interest to critical IPE as these authors explicitly affiliate their writings with Critical Theory in the early Frankfurt School sense. We believe that turning to these works can help to load the term social totality with its gendered meaning and, as such, help to address the gender theoretical shortcomings of Critical Theory. Therefore, in the following, we briefly highlight some of the central arguments brought forward by Klinger and Knapp and others.

From a social theory perspective these approaches stress the necessity of analysing categories of social inequality in their historical integration within the history of modern society – social inequality becomes the linchpin of modern society. As such, it was only in the context of industrialization that class and gender relations converged. The social inequality of race/ethnicity in its modern form appears within the context of nation state building. Of central importance for the analysis of intersectionality is the localization of configurations of social inequality and differences in its socio-historical context. Such focus enables the investigation of concrete social relations and their concrete appearances and entanglements (Becker-Schmidt, 2007, pp. 58f.).

The debates outlined are, in part, a critical response to the US debate on intersectionality. This debate is forcefully driven by poststructuralist notions of social difference. Rather than understanding race, class and gender as identity categories marking social difference, these approaches have as their starting point axial principles of social inequality and difference making (*Differenzsetzung*). In reference to critical social theory, especially Critical Theory, and as a continuation of the materialist feminist theorization of the relationship between class and gender in modern society (as outlined above), these approaches assume that gender, class and race/ethnicity mark the central axes of social inequality, creating a constant form of domination. The argument thereby departs from two central premises:

> Firstly of the assumption that inequality is neither a passing phenomenon nor a marginal anomaly or pathology in modern societies but a formative and expanding feature. [...] The second advance decision in approaching the topic concerns the categorical focus on three axes of inequality. Our socio-theoretical presumption is that the triad of class, 'race'/ethnicity and gender labels relations that mark the structure of inequality of almost every society in various ways but with lasting effects.
>
> (Klinger and Knapp, 2007, pp. 19–20)

Domination thereby is structured through, and simultaneously structures, the way in which class, gender and race are interlinked in historically specific ways (Knapp, 2008).

Conclusion

With our account of the social totality as captured in a selection of Critical Theory writings by Horkheimer and Adorno the adjacent confrontation of this concept with feminist theories, the 'early' materialist feminist debates concerning the relationship of class and gender, and an expansion of this perspective through insights on the debate on intersectionality and the triad of race, class and gender, we have tried to highlight the possibilities but also problems of a Critical Theory. In IPE Critical Theory seems to be stuck with an abbreviated understanding of the overall context (*Gesamtzusammenhang*) of the social totality. In our understanding, three avenues need to be pursued in order to address this shortcoming.

First, we believe that there is an urgent need to address the dichotomous and gender-blind conceptualization of production and social reproduction prevalent in IPE (see the chapter by Elias in this volume, also Steans and Tepe, 2010). This border marks a central resource of 'male' power by deporting gender relations into the area for intimate relations (see Sauer, 2001). On the one hand, gender relations as constituting the overall social context of relations of power and dominance are out of sight and consideration of the social totality becomes 'unigendered' (*vereingeschlechtlicht*) (Becker-Schmidt, 1987, p. 13). A focus on the reproduction of economic relations transmitted through the market, on the other hand, clouds the necessity of social reproduction (see Bruff's contribution, this volume, for another angle on notions of necessity). The foremost female occupied realities of life are then out of sight, and sexist forms of division of labour, and related consequences for social possibilities for appropriation, become concealed. Without paying consideration toward gendered realities and gendered relationships, what calls itself critical IPE remains stuck in malestream theorizing.

Second, we believe a new engagement with Critical Theory and its theoretical premises, as we have tried to show with our engagement with Horkheimer's conceptualization of Critical Theory, is promising for a Critical IPE in (at least) two ways. On the one hand, Horkheimer offers, with his concept of the social totality, an instrument for scientific research in order to analyse and understand societal relations of power and dominance. As such, it clearly overcomes the analysis only of societal parts, and takes as its central premise the existence of overall societal contexts. We believe this, when holding on to the idea of an encompassing social theory, to be of special importance at times like the present when disciplinary boundaries are being redefined in light of their perceived economic impact and applicability. The other strength of a Critical Theory is the concept of the social totality. Horkheimer provides, in our reading, a political concept, which to date has not forfeited its emancipatory potential. Critical Theory, and with it an understanding of the social totality, points towards overcoming, through their negation, of societal relations of suppression and exploitation.

Therefore we suggest, *finally*, to employ the approaches we introduced here as a theoretical and political puzzle, which, placed on top of one another, mark blank spaces, highlight shortcomings and are able to provide an impulse to critically engage with the social totality. This is, in our understanding, connected to the hope that the knowledge-gain (*Erkenntnisgewinn*) of such an approach contributes to political battles against, and the overcoming of, social inequalities along the axes of class, race and gender. As Adorno claimed, 'Only the person who can conceptualise a different society from the existing one can experience it as a problem. Only through that which it is not, will it reveal itself as that which it is' (Adorno, 1976, p. 120).

Notes

1. This is not to suggest that the fight for liberal feminist rights has been easy or straightforward by any means, nor that it is finished.
2. We employ the term 'social totality' on the basis of the absence of a better translation of the German, '*das gesellschaftliche Ganze*'. We are aware that through using this term we are entering the terrain of French Althusserian philosophy, which refers to 'social totality' to capture a structural relation. In contrast, Horkheimer's notion of the social totality, going back to Hegel, describes a societal relation.
3. His argument against distinct disciplinary boundaries is, today, again of very specific importance given the ongoing trend in higher education to introduce highly specialized degrees in distinct academic disciplines.
4. Cox himself never explicitly mentions the Frankfurt School, yet he takes on an epistemological stance, which is, at the outset, surprisingly similar. His distinction between problem solving and Critical Theory reminds observers of the distinction between critical and traditional theory. The critique presented here could potentially have been pre-empted if Cox had engaged with Adorno's and Horkheimer's work.
5. We are conscious that differences exist between Adorno's and Horkheimer's work and their respective application of a notion of social totality. Similarly, as Marasco (2006) has pointed out, the conceptualization of femininity and privateness differs in the writings of Adorno and Horkheimer. Yet, in the context of this chapter, we assert that, for the purpose of clarity of our critique, certain simplifications are adequate.

6. Fraser (1985), for example, reveals how Habermas attaches meaning to the reproductive sphere of the life-world, which, according to him, is characterized by 'feminine' non-rationalized logics of action.
7. To paraphrase Buckel (2007), materialism here does not refer to a pre-Marxist employment of the term in the sense of a mechanical or physically abstract notion of materiality. Rather, it is a social category, referring to the materiality of social 'praxis', which is 'the object and source of materialist theory' (Schmidt, 1993, p. 33). The institutional set-up of relations of domination and subjugation function as a mode of cohesion for various subjectivities, favouring certain interests over others. Following Buckel, we subsume those approaches that stand in the tradition of the Critical Theory of Marx and those which analyse societies by looking at the structuring principles of capitalist socialization.
8. We consciously talk about more than one political science given the ontological, epistemological and methodological variety of approaches – a critical focus of this volume.
9. Translations, where otherwise unavailable, by the authors.

9
Knowledge Versus Power in the Field of IPE

Paul Cammack

The recent publication of Cohen's 'intellectual history' of 'the academic field of study known as International Political Economy – for short, IPE' (Cohen, 2008a, p. 1), and the debate over 'American' and 'British' schools to which it has given rise, confront scholars seeking to develop a critical perspective on the contemporary international political economy with a clear choice: to engage with mainstream IPE, or to situate themselves outside it. Having previously advocated the abandonment of IPE, critical or otherwise (Cammack, 2007), I argue here for the latter course. A critical reading of Cohen's account of the field and the response it has prompted reveals it to be theoretically and empirically barren, and marked by a constitutive disparity between institutional advance and success on the one hand, and intellectual incoherence and failure on the other.

First, once Cohen's account is seen for what it is – a *construction* of IPE as a field rather than a history of how it *was* constructed – it becomes apparent that its central focus is on maintaining a hold on institutional power rather than on the disinterested (let alone 'scientific') pursuit of knowledge. Second, the case made for 'building bridges' between the positivism and empiricism favoured by 'American' IPE and the holistic, normative approach of the 'British' school is thoroughly subverted by the text itself, in a manner that identifies but cannot explain the deficiencies of 'scientific method'.

The institutional stakes matter here, and the institutional power of the *liberal* IPE that Cohen espouses (centred upon a core belief in the inherent goodness of properly regulated markets) is advanced by all contributions to the developing debate, however critical of Cohen's specific claims, that accept *un*critically the liberal assumptions on which it is built. This is particularly the case, of course, because the debate is so structured as to exclude the greater part of the critical literature on the international political economy, including all of it that stems from Marxist or 'neo-Marxist' perspectives. This feature of Cohen's 'intellectual history' is of a piece with the character of IPE (in capital letters) as a liberal project in which leading US academics positioned themselves consciously as organic intellectuals of the US state and US capital and their projection abroad, and succeeded in building enduring institutional strongholds in the leading institutions of the US academy. And it is fully reflected in otherwise critical contributions to the debate that offer constructivist and ideational alternatives, and lobby for a return to pluralism, but are silent on Marxist alternatives (McNamara, 2009; Weaver, 2009).

Important though it is to recognize the institutional logic of Cohen's argument then, the intellectual stakes are broader. In this respect, the character of his history as an ideological project presented as an objective contribution to knowledge is only part of the story – and not one that should occasion surprise. The more interesting and revealing aspect of the text is that it comprehensively subverts the overt message that a bridge needs to be built between a positivist/empiricist 'American' school and a normative/holistic 'British' school. For a persistent counter-theme in Cohen's account is that the more it has embraced a formal positivist methodology, the less successful American IPE has been in illuminating the 'really big questions' in international political economy. But if Cohen brings out this contradiction clearly, he does not in the end either explain it or allow it to inform his proposal for a new research agenda. I argue that the root cause is very simple – the same hostility to Marxism that shapes the ideological project has not only led a generation of US scholars to shy away from an analysis of capitalism as a global system and of the social relations and domestic class conflicts which it generates, as Cohen repeatedly acknowledges; it has also precluded a method of analysis that *starts* with the global economy and grasps the complex logic of a single historical process – the evolution of capitalism on a global scale.

These two points taken together in turn explain why American IPE in particular is unable to ask 'the right questions'. And because it is not, and will not be while the fear of Marxism and the hold of barren methodological rigidity over political science and increasingly over international political economy and international relations in the US academy persist, the path to a genuinely critical analysis of the contemporary international political economy leads directly away from IPE (with capital letters), towards retrieval of and engagement with the perspectives excluded at its founding moment.

This being so, the early signs are discouraging. Responding to the first version of Cohen's 'intellectual history' (Cohen, 2007) even before the monograph was published, Higgott and Watson (2008, p. 16) expressed the fear that the two 'schools', caricatures as they were, would become attractors, 'drawing analytical work towards them and thus cementing the apparent coherence of the positions built upon them'. Within a year, special issues of the *Review of International Political Economy* and *New Political Economy* were devoted to them, with debate largely revolving around their relative merits and the accuracy of Cohen's characterization of them rather than around the broader implications of the project – allowing Cohen to congratulate himself that '[e]ach of the distinguished contributors [to the NPE collection] accepts the reality of something that may be described as the British school' (Cohen, 2009, p. 395). Nor can Higgott and Watson themselves be absolved of blame – their espousal of political philosophy as the appropriate disciplinary interlocutor, their rejection of positivism, their explicitly normative stance and their neglect of critical (Marxist and neo-Marxist) political economy further Cohen's account for all that they set out to challenge it.

The present danger, then, is that new generations of graduate students will grow up to understand and practise international political economy (without capital letters) in terms of the 'field of IPE' and its two contending schools. The dice are loaded from the start against a critical intervention on these terms, so this chapter is aimed against the prospect. It proceeds by deconstructing Cohen's 'intellectual history' (which is rather more artful than it has appeared to many of its critics) in order to reveal precisely what is at stake, then suggesting that scholars committed to a critical approach should not engage with IPE (with capital letters) at all, but rather turn to Marxism instead.

Constructing IPE: Cohen's 'intellectual history'

I do not question Cohen's commitment to an eclectic and pluralist analytical framework, or his dissatisfaction with the narrowly positivist and empiricist character of much US social science. But his claim that his study is a history of 'the *construction* of IPE as a recognized field of scholarly enquiry' (Cohen, 2008a, p. 1; original emphasis) is too modest by half. It is not an objective history of how the field was constructed but rather *itself* a construction of IPE as a field of study, to which the part played by the distinction between American and British schools is crucial. The core of what is in essence a hegemonic project is disclosed in a sequence of claims advanced in the first section of the book that constitute the surface narrative of the 'intellectual history' recounted:

> [1] As a practical matter, political economy has always been part of international relations (IR). But as a distinct academic field, surprisingly enough, IPE was born just a few decades ago. Prior to the 1970s, in the English-speaking world, economics and political science were treated as entirely different disciplines, each with its own view of international affairs.
>
> (Ibid.; see Ashworth in this volume for a critique of this claim)
>
> [2] The field of IPE is united in its effort to bridge the gap between the separate specialities of international economics and IR: that is its common denominator. But IPE is hardly a monolith.
>
> (Ibid., p. 3)
>
> [3] In the 'American School,' priority is given to scientific method – what might be called a pure or hard science model. Analysis is based on the twin principles of positivism and empiricism, which hold that knowledge is best accumulated through an appeal to objective observation and systematic testing.
>
> (Ibid., pp. 3–4)
>
> [4] In the British style, IPE is less wedded to scientific method and more ambitious in its agenda. The contrasts with the mainstream U.S. approach are not small: this is not an instance of what Sigmund Freud called the 'narcissism of small differences.' Indeed, the contrasts are so great that it is not illegitimate to speak of a 'British School' of IPE, in contrast to the U.S. version.
>
> (Ibid., p. 4)
>
> [5] Critical to the construction of IPE were some extraordinary individuals: a generation of pioneering researchers inspired to raise their sights and look beyond the horizon – beyond the traditional disciplines in which they had been trained – to see the politics and economics of international relations in a new, more illuminating light.
>
> (Ibid., p. 5)

[6] The American and British schools are in many ways complementary, and have much to learn from one another... [M]uch can be gained by building new bridges between scholars on the two sides of the Atlantic.

(Ibid., p. 12)

It is an elementary observation that the empirical claims upon which this core narrative is based are either plainly false, or highly disputable, and Cohen's critics have been quick to point this out. However, much of the sting is drawn from such criticisms by the fact that Cohen himself repeatedly acknowledges the variance between his own account and the historical record (and is second to none in his enumeration of the shortcomings of IPE in all its manifestations). In a parallel narrative that runs alongside and subverts the claims cited above, he notes that there actually *was* political economy before and outside IR, and indeed before the emergence of separate disciplines of economics and political science (ibid., p. 17); that economics and political science were *not* actually treated as separate disciplines in the English-speaking world before Keohane and Nye sprang into view (ibid., pp. 38–9); that the intellectual entrepreneurs identified as founding IPE were *not* actually united in the common endeavour of bringing international economics and IR together, nor, for the most part, committed in practice to the 'scientific method' (ibid., pp. 42, 82, 127); that 'as a practical matter, there is no consensus on what precisely IPE is all about' (ibid., p. 3); that 'the notion of a "school" here is used loosely, by no means implying any sort of common goal or unified agenda' (ibid., p. 16; cf. p. 44); that the 'American school' was not actually American any more than the 'British school' was British (ibid., pp. 4–5); that Americans have not engaged significantly with the work of either Cox or Strange (ibid., pp. 10, 44); that the 'pioneers' were not actually pioneers at all, but had significant recent and distant forerunners (ibid., pp. 17–21); and (*passim*) that the two 'schools', far from being complementary, are actually based on diametrically opposed principles.

Important as it is, therefore, to debunk the idea of Cohen's account as an objective or coherent intellectual history, the exercise leaves the broader project unscathed if it does not go further, to interrogate its character as a sophisticated *construct* with a deeper coherence behind its superficial inconsistencies. There are five elements to this: the construction of Cohen himself as an objective historian concerned only to provide a documentary record; the insistence on the novelty represented by the 'field of IPE'; the concomitant writing out of Marxist (and neo-Marxist) approaches; the construction of the debate between American and British schools as diverse and inclusive, and sufficient in itself to constitute the field and address the 'right questions'; and, holding it all together, the consistent interpretation of intellectual advance in terms of institutional control (or, in other words, the subordination of knowledge to power). These five elements together constitute the deeper structure of Cohen's argument, giving it a consistent internal logic to which the remainder of this section is addressed. It is, in turn, subverted by a deeper *illogic,* which is the subject of the following section.

Cohen's first move, then, is to present himself as the objective historian of the construction of the field of IPE. He proposes to write an 'intellectual history of the field – how it came into being, and why it took the shape that it did' (ibid., p. 2); and concludes a long passage detailing his personal involvement in the field ('which I have long regarded as my natural home') with the assertion that 'I have been there from the start; I have been associated, directly or indirectly, with some of the most notable advances in the field; and I have been personally acquainted with almost everyone involved. *Above all, I have no ax* [sic] *to grind, and so hopefully can remain reasonably objective in what I have to say here'* (ibid., p. 6; emphasis added). Whether Cohen succeeds in being even-handed between the American and British schools is a matter of opinion on which I am inclined towards charity. In any case, his attempt to portray himself as such (in the emphasis he places on the role of Susan Strange in his own intellectual development, for example), and the strength with which he defends himself against the assertion of bias (see Higgott and Watson, 2008, pp. 7–12; Cohen, 2008b, pp. 31–3), is indicative of his intent. But the claim to produce an objective history crucially extends beyond the issue of even-handedness *within* IPE (with capital letters) to the broader claim of objectivity with regard to the place of IPE (with capital letters) in the broader field of political economy. Here Cohen self-evidently does have an axe to grind, as the juxtaposing of his claim to impartiality and his thoroughgoing identification with IPE (with capital letters) inadvertently reveals, and it shows.

Thus his next key move involves the twin claims that 'political economy has always been part of international relations (IR)', and that 'as a distinct academic field ... IPE was born just a few decades ago' (ibid., p. 1). The first statement silently conflates international relations as relations between states on the one hand (of which political economy has indeed always been a part), and the academic field of International Relations (with capital letters) on the other (of which it has not). It is *IPE* (at least, as understood by its leading proponents) that has always been a part of IR. Political economy, for all that it has always had an international dimension, conspicuously has its roots, whether in the classical tradition associated with Petty and Smith or in Weber's sociology, in the economy of the *household* and the *state*. And as a consequence, it has focused, long before Marx made an appearance, on classes, the organization of production, and the distribution of income and wealth within states as much as on the wider international economy.

Cohen is aware of this. But it would be a mistake to think that he is merely being careless. The formulation on the opening page is crucial, as without it he cannot present IPE as emerging as a *new* field of study in its own right when it developed within IR in the 1970s. Even so, the claim that it did is prefaced by a statement which entirely contradicts what he has just said: 'Prior to the 1970s, in the English-speaking world, economics and political science were treated as entirely different disciplines, each with its own view of international affairs.' All of a sudden the 'political economy' that a mere two sentences ago was, for practical purposes, subsumed within IR is written out of history altogether (the English-speaking world being the known universe where Cohen is concerned). Absurd though this is, it is essential if IPE is to be seen as an innovation and an intellectual advance, rather than as a backward step in a vigorous and long-standing tradition. The next key move follows immediately (and we are still on the very first page of the book), again contradicting entirely what has just been said, but crucially laying the foundations for Cohen's construction of IPE as an enterprise from which Marxist (and 'neo-Marxist') political economy is excluded: 'Relatively few efforts were made to bridge the gap between the two. *Exceptions could be found, of course,* often quite creative ones, but mostly among Marxists or others outside the "respectable" mainstream of Western scholarship' (ibid., p. 1; emphasis added). There is something very familiar going on here, in the almost casual sidelining of Marxist and related approaches, and it is so much the 'common sense' of the power-holders in the US academy that it is best seen as produced by, as well as producing, the antipathy towards Marxism which is so central to it (Cammack, 1989, 1990). In this particular case, as Murphy (2009) shows, Cohen has simply 'left out' radical voices *within* American IPE in the 1970s and after.

Having expelled all other contenders, Cohen has set up IPE as the sole occupant of the field. In what follows, the persistent counterpoint between claims for the unity and coherence of IPE as a project on the one hand, and for its breadth and diversity on the other, is just as significant as the precise content ascribed to the American and British schools. If there really is 'no consensus on what precisely IPE is all about', the founding of a 'true interdiscipline' is a difficult enterprise. But if it is narrowly based on methodological and theoretical principles that are widely disputed *within* the 'respectable mainstream', it cannot provide a basis for drawing all the wagons up in a defensive circle strong enough to repel a radical assault. The strategic logic is clear: Cohen *has to* insist that the contributors to the 'respectable mainstream' are partners in a common and pluralistic enterprise, and urge them both to see it and strengthen it. So it is not just that this supposedly objective 'intellectual history' has a whiff of ideology about it – it is ideological all the way down, and there is no other way to make sense of it.

It is telling, then, that the best specific claim Cohen can find to make is that the field is united by the effort to bridge the gap between the separate specialties of international economics and IR, but equally telling that he felt the need to find a 'common denominator' (Cohen, 2008a, p. 3) uniting the field in the first place, or to insist against his own evidence that we are in the presence of a 'common research community' (ibid., p. 5). These are simply unsustainable claims. Equally, it is as instructive that such claims are immediately followed by the assertions that 'IPE is hardly a monolith' (ibid., p. 3), and that it divides into two groups between whom 'lie deep ontological and epistemological differences' (ibid., p. 5), as that Cohen has latched on to the contrast between 'American' and 'British' schools as the empirical referent for these differences. All these claims address not an existing but an *imagined* common research community, hopefully to be brought into being by Cohen's construction of the field. The 'bridge-building', towards which the whole enterprise is focused, is yet to be done, and it is essentially about building a hegemonic bloc across the Atlantic academy.

For Cohen's project to succeed, then, IPE must be sufficient in itself to encompass the whole field of international political economy, and capable on its own of illuminating its contemporary subject matter. But here he is on treacherous ground. He asserts early on that a more diverse group than his seven nominees to the IPE Hall of Fame 'could hardly be imagined' (ibid., p. 8). To resort to his own idiom – yeah, right. As Germain (2009) has succinctly pointed out, a small group of individuals have succeeded in dominating the discipline in institutional terms; and the attempt to depict them as diverse is just more of the same. Later, when Cohen addresses the question of 'what we have learned', three successive statements throw him right back to the point at which he started:

> If knowledge is measured by our ability to make definitive statements – to generalize without fear of dispute – the field's success may be rated as negligible at best.
>
> (Cohen, 2008a, p. 142)

> We may not know the answers, but at least we can learn to ask the right questions – to define an appropriate research agenda.
>
> (Ibid.)

> Unfortunately, even by that test IPE's success must be rated as less than stellar. At the broadest level, we all accept that the field is about the nexus of global economics and politics, an amalgam of market studies and political analysis. But try to get any more specific and differences quickly emerge.
>
> (Ibid., p. 143)

I leave for the following section a fuller assessment of the knowledge generated by IPE. For the present, my purpose is to contrast this record of intellectual failure with the celebration of institutional success, or the consistent subordination of knowledge to power. The starting point is a statement early in the introduction, which makes an abrupt transition, after one initial sentence, from an *intellectual* to an *institutional* definition of the field:

> An academic field may be said to exist when a coherent body of knowledge is developed to define a subject of enquiry. Recognized standards come to be employed to train and certify specialists; full-time employment opportunities become available in university teaching and research; learned societies are established to promote study and dialogue; and publishing venues become available to help disseminate new ideas and analysis. In short, an institutionalized network of scholars comes into being – a distinct research community *with its own boundaries, rewards and careers*. In that sense the field of IPE has existed for less than half a century.
>
> (Ibid., p. 2; emphasis added)

We have already seen Cohen concede that IPE is *not* characterized by a coherent body of knowledge that defines it as a subject of enquiry.

But if we review the logic of his construction of IPE, it transpires that this is not the point. Despite the claim immediately following the statement above that the book 'aims to offer an intellectual history', the only history on offer is strictly *institutional*. The point – the logic at the heart of the account – is not knowledge but power, the power to control the academy and to police its boundaries, rewards and careers. It is this that is under threat, from sterile formal theory from within and radical critique from without. Grasp this, and everything falls into place – an institutional perspective informs the whole text (cf. Germain, 2009). Thus Cohen is quick to concede that in *intellectual* terms what he calls the pioneer generation 'was not the first in history to think of connecting the economics and politics of international relations'; but it turns out to be the *institutional* history that matters: 'The pioneers of the 1970s and beyond were the first to succeed in making IPE a recognized and respected academic speciality. That is their accomplishment, their real claim to fame' (ibid., p. 17). The theme persists throughout, with emphasis placed upon Cohen's own 1970s Basic Books Political Economy of International Relations series (after which 'The rest, as they say, is history' – ibid., p. 6), the capture of the journal *International Organization* by Keohane and Nye (ibid., pp. 35–6), and the penetration of political science departments in the US (ibid., pp. 37–8). On the same logic, it is the fear that narrow positivists are taking over and that the ability of IPE to address pressing real-world issues is diminishing that provokes the need for a tactical alliance with the more ambitious, holistic and normative 'British' school.

In this context, the institutional logic for 'building bridges' and promoting an alliance between the two 'schools' is twofold – it will reacquaint the American school with the 'really big questions' with which it has lost touch, while establishing the British school as the preferred interlocutor, and writing more critical approaches out of the picture. Thus the 'British' school, as constructed by Cohen, plays the crucial role of making possible the creation of a pluralistic debate within the confines of the respectable mainstream (much as the 'neo-neo' debate and the 'varieties of capitalism' debate have done). In doing so it sidelines the genuine challenge to the respectable mainstream represented by the resurgence of Marxist and related critical perspectives in the 1960s and early 1970s and their renewed vigour today. In institutional terms at least, this strategy appears to 'have legs'. But as the following section will show, because the contribution it makes to the advance of knowledge is as a consequence negligible, it fails, so there is no loss involved in consigning IPE (with capital letters) to history.

Knowledge versus power in IPE

What can we make, then, of Cohen's claim that the field of IPE 'teaches us to think about the connections between economics and politics beyond the confines of a single state' (ibid., p. 1)? His opening account of the American school gives pride of place to the work of Keohane and Nye, and the concept of 'complex interdependence'. The three chapters that follow his account of the American and British schools then take up in turn three 'really big questions': *systemic transformation* arising as a consequence of 'the growing interdependence of national economies after World War II'; *system governance* in the context of the 'control gap' between state aspirations and state capabilities created by the growth of global economic interdependence (ibid., p. 13); and the *'place of the state* in formal analysis' (ibid., p. 14; emphasis added). Each follows the same pattern, telling a story of failure, retreat and increasing narrowness on the part of the American school, and proposing an infusion from the British school as a means of restoring its vitality. This is followed by an assessment of 'what we have learned', and the outline of a bridge-building research programme. I first review Cohen's account of 'complex interdependence' and the three 'really big questions', then evaluate the research programme proposed.

Complex interdependence

Keohane and Nye's *Transnational Relations and World Politics* (1972) took shape between 1970 and 1972, and the notion of 'complex interdependence' (with its triple focus on multiple channels of communications, an absence of hierarchy among issues, and a diminished role for military force) was launched five years later (Keohane and Nye, 1977). On one assessment, this was a tactical shift, inspired by Vernon's *Sovereignty at Bay* (1971) and Nye's dissatisfaction with 'realism as taught at Harvard then', and intended 'not to discredit realism but rather to supplement it' (Cohen, 2008a, pp. 29–30). On another, lying directly alongside it, it was a 'revolutionary new paradigm' (ibid., p. 29) and a genuine contribution to knowledge:

> Today we take for granted that interdependence in the world economy can be analyzed in political terms, not just as an economic phenomenon. We also take for granted that we can examine patterns of interdependence by separate issue areas. We do so because, implicitly or explicitly, we all now share the ontology bequeathed to us by Keohane and Nye – a sense that the three characteristics of

complex interdependence define the essential nature of the present international system.

(Ibid., p. 31)

The conjunction of these two sharply contrasting perspectives, without recognition of the way in which they contradict each other, is a telling example of 'Charles River syndrome' – the belief that all that counts is what happens at or near Harvard (cf. Germain, 2009, pp. 100–1). But as Cohen accurately reflects, Keohane and Nye were actually catching up with a burst of activity that reflected changing circumstances in the real world: the recovery of the European and Japanese economies after the Second World War, the shifting balance of power among industrial nations, the liberalization of trade and currency markets, the increasing salience of new international organizations, the challenges posed by post-war decolonization, and the calls for a New International Economic Order (ibid., pp. 21–2). The issues arising were already being addressed not only by Richard Cooper and Raymond Vernon (identified by Cohen as major immediate influences) but also by Marxists and dependency theorists such as Harry Magdoff, Andre Gunder Frank and Arghiri Emmanuel, along with radical American scholars associated with the Union for Radical Political Economics and the *Review of Radical Political Economics* (ibid., pp. 38–9). In this context, Keohane and Nye aimed to reorient the US academy towards new threats to the global reach of the US state and US capital, in the face of more radical challenges, by effecting a slight shift *within* the prevailing realist framework – a goal to which both have remained faithful ever since: Keohane recently described his 'institutional framework' as a 'half-sibling of realism' (ibid., p. 109), and Nye is still seeking to renew US power by allying the 'soft power' of persuasion to the 'hard power' of material advantage (Cammack, 2009).

The American school has not progressed beyond the anodyne notion of 'complex interdependence', nor has it shifted its world view from the context of the 1970s to the very different context of today – a situation ruefully noted by Keohane himself, now, like Katzenstein, a fugitive from IPE. Keohane describes 'the new IPE' as remarkably reluctant to focus on major changes taking place in world politics and 'missing…the synthetic interpretation of change', listing five examples: the genuine economic development taking place on a global scale, the role of China, the volatility of financial and energy markets, the role of actors other than states, and the implications of the Internet for the analysis of power (Keohane, 2009, p. 40). In contrasting it with the 'old' analytically loose but creative IPE, he echoes Cohen's own account of an inexorable slide down from creativity to narrow rigour. Neither his account of the field today nor his personal trajectory (any more than Nye's) gives any reason to engage with what has become of IPE. And strong reasons are surely needed if one is to engage critically with a field from which the major protagonists have long departed. Let us see if any can be gleaned (despite Keohane's scepticism) from a review of the 'really big questions' on which IPE has focused.

The 'really big questions'

Cohen identifies 'hegemonic stability theory' as the principal contribution to IPE analysis of system transformation. The salient points of his analysis are that it exaggerated the extent of redistribution of power among states (Cohen, 2008a, pp. 67–8); that in particular the fears of US decline that prompted its development were misplaced (as at the dawn of the millennium, 'America's economic primacy was once again unquestioned', ibid., p. 77); and that as a consequence of this realization, scholars of IPE in the United States have 'lost interest in the grand theme of systemic change – all of which is a bit of a shame' (ibid., p. 79). In order to re-engage with the really big question of globalization, therefore, American scholars should turn to the hitherto ignored Robert Cox: 'With Cox as a guide, the grand theme of systemic change need not be abandoned' (ibid., p. 93). Here, ironically, Cox comes in as a reformist problem-solver, concerned with 'how to manage a radically shifting balance of economic power with an eye to preserving and advancing social equity – an achievement of equity that is being eroded by unregulated markets' (citing Cox, 2006, p. 17). And as Cohen (2008a, p. 93) himself immediately construes the thought, 'The challenge is to promote a broad-based countermovement, premised on the principles of collective creativity and social justice, that might successfully contain the excesses of "hyper-liberal globalizing capitalism" '. This is a classic example of the domestication and neutralization of radical thought, albeit one that has been aided and abetted by Cox's own trajectory (Cammack, 2007).

System governance fares no better. Here the point of reference is the 'control gap' between state aspirations and state capabilities which Keohane and Nye 'pointed out from the start' (Cohen, 2008a, p. 95), and the work of Krasner and Keohane on international regimes governing global economic governance. Having belatedly caught on to the fact that there is a demand for international regimes because they increase the likelihood that states will be able to cooperate on issues of mutual interest (hardly a fresh insight outside the peculiar confines of US realism), regime theory found itself by the end of the 1980s 'in a cul-de-sac of its own making' (ibid., p. 106) – unable to explain how regimes came to be created to meet this demand, and why states would not defect (the puzzles of supply and compliance). The subsequent shift away from international regimes in particular towards 'institutions' in general, still within the confines of formal game theory, did not add up to a coherent theory: it brought the discipline back 'full circle like a boomerang' to the study of organizations, where it remained locked within a state-centric discourse, forgetting that 'in a world economy growing increasingly interdependent, such a plain-vanilla approach seems incomplete, perhaps even misguided' (ibid., pp. 113–14).

As before, Cohen looks for salvation to the British school (and Strange in the first instance), with its central question: 'If governments are no longer in charge, then who is?' (ibid., p. 115). But no single answer was forthcoming, and those who emerged 'may also be criticized for a decided lack of rigor' (ibid., p. 116). In this case Cohen backtracks from his concern with 'really big questions', calling for 'studies that focus clearly on specific groups capable of exercising effective authority in their respective spheres of activity' (ibid., p. 117). By the end of the chapter, the larger issue of *system governance* has faded from view.

The subsequent chapter moves on to the 'mystery of the state', beginning with the fact that scholars in the US tradition 'take for granted that IPE, first and foremost, is about states and their interactions', and profiling the contribution made by Katzenstein's analysis of 'the domestic sources of foreign economic policy' (ibid., pp. 118–19). Only in relation to the restricted optic of US IR, with its rigid separation of the domestic and the international, could the goal of Katzenstein's project seem 'actually quite ambitious, even revolutionary – nothing less than to add a missing level of analysis to the new field of IPE' (ibid., p. 125). Yet again, though, the trajectory of subsequent scholarship is disappointing: 'in individual research programs, the scope of enquiry has tended to contract markedly... [and] horizons have shrunk to accommodate aspirations for professional respect' (ibid., p. 127; cf. pp. 128–9, 130–1). Against this background, Katzenstein has been prominent in a new departure – 'a determined campaign to promote the study of ideational factors as well' (ibid., p. 131), or a turn to constructivism. But as a result, 'his own emphasis has shifted. The more he has taken up the cause of constructivism, the more issues of political economy have come to be marginalized in his work' (ibid., p. 133).

Even so, ideational factors now feature alongside more traditional systemic and domestic variables in opening the 'black box' of the state.

But it is still to the British school that one must turn to look beyond it. Adherents to this school, Cohen reports, combine an analysis of the *transformation* of the state in response to globalization with a disposition to go beyond the state – but here 'they divide sharply over where the spotlight should instead be directed' (ibid., p. 140). Cohen ends his survey of the 'really big questions', then, on a downbeat note:

> If anything, the lack of intellectual coherence has actually grown worse with time. The British school's harmony of opposition to state-centrism breaks down when it comes to providing a compelling counterpoint... If the American school can be criticized for leaving too much out, the British school is vulnerable to the charge that it tries to bring too much in – everything but the kitchen sink, one might say.
>
> (Ibid., p. 141)

Even Pollyanna would be hard-pressed to match Cohen's optimistic conclusion: 'Once again, we are reminded of how complementary the two schools are' (ibid.).

On Cohen's account of IPE's engagement with 'really big questions', 'American' approaches have narrowed down or lost their way, and there has been no advance on the positions formulated a generation ago. From a starting point at which the hegemony of a single state (the US) was seen as necessary to assure global stability, states were seen as the only actors in the international system, and a rigid division was maintained between systemic and domestic levels, a point has been reached where other possibilities than the hegemony of a single state are contemplated, other actors are admitted alongside states, and the domestic level is taken into account. Hard-won as these gains may be against the stultifying background of realism *and* the neglect of political economy in the then-prevailing forms of American IR, they do not take us very far. What is more, on all three of the 'really big questions' addressed, there appears to have been a distinct loss of momentum after initial positions were advanced. Has American IPE lost its way? The following section will suggest that it has, and explain why.

The 'really big questions' today

I noted above that Keohane criticizes 'American' IPE in particular for failing to address five pressing issues in the contemporary international political economy: the genuine economic development taking place on a global scale, the role of China, the volatility of financial and energy markets, the role of actors other than states, and the implications of the Internet for the analysis of power. McNamara offers a complementary list (2009, pp. 81–2; see also Palan, 2009, pp. 387–9 and Phillips, 2009, pp. 91–3), recalls the 'largely unforeseen collapse of the USSR', and asks whether ten years from now we are 'likely to look back at mainstream IPE and blame it for similar lack of scholarly attention in the face of profound change in the global political economy' (McNamara, 2009, p. 82). My response is that it is *already* possible to level this charge. Where in contemporary American IPE do we find formal methods, either of the kind addressed by Cohen or the new and improved version promoted by Lake (2009), addressed with any consequence to such issues as the tendency of the global capitalist economy to recurrent crisis, the current massive onslaught on labour and welfare rights across the developed world (cf. Murphy, 2009, pp. 361–2), or the shift to greater internal inequality in virtually all states across the whole world, or the drive towards competitiveness in global markets in virtually all states in the global economy, or the concerted efforts of the international organizations to promote capitalist development on a global scale? Where are the *connections* between these phenomena addressed?

Cohen has an explanation for this sorry state of affairs, and it undermines the rationale for his effort to promote the marriage of the American 'scientific method' and British holism and normative commitment, summarized at the end of the book in the following terms:

> The American school could learn much from the British side's broad multidisciplinarity, which helps to import useful new insights from other academic specialties. U.S.-style IPE could benefit from a little more ambition, to combat the shrinkage of horizons that has been so noticeable in recent years. The British school, conversely, could learn much from the American side's more rigorous methodologies, which help bring consistency and replicability to theoretical analysis. British-style IPE could benefit from a little less ambition, to temper the temptation to address the totality of human experience.
>
> (Cohen, 2008a, p. 177)

This proposal reflects the drawing of the boundaries of debate to exclude Marxism, as noted at the outset. But, at the same time, it contradicts Cohen's frequent statements throughout the text to the effect that it is precisely the move towards 'more rigorous methodologies' that has tempered the ambition of American IPE and led to the 'shrinkage of horizons' (ibid., pp. 12–13, 41–3, 82–3, 126–31 – the latter section ending with a bald statement: 'Methodological rigor has been preserved, but at the expense of the bigger picture').

This is fine, as far as it goes – except of course that it exposes the wishful thinking involved in Cohen's prescription for building bridges between the two 'schools'. But it does not go far enough. The fundamental reason for the inability of American IPE to address issues in international political economy lies in the devastating legacy of Cold War anti-Marxism. We have already seen how Cohen places Marxist and similar approaches outside the respectable mainstream, and continues to bar them from admission to the academy. Elsewhere he paints a broader picture, first describing the 'chilling effect of postwar anti-communism' on the *economics* profession, where '[p]olitical economy tended to be equated unthinkingly with Marxism or other unacceptable left doctrines' (ibid., p. 38), then broadens the point in a contrast with the UK, where '[a]ttitudes towards Marxism or other leftist doctrines…were far more relaxed than in the United States, where most academics were wary of anything that might seem tainted by socialist sympathies' (ibid., p. 62). A telling anecdote in this regard concerns Gilpin (whose *Political Economy of International Relations* (1987) has close affinities with contemporaneous Marxist scholarship on the contradiction between legitimacy and accumulation in western welfare states). Suspected of Marxist leanings because he ventured the thought that 'there was some connection between the exercise of power in the economic realm and the world of security', Cohen comments in retrospect: 'I knew I was not a Marxist…I read other things on the interplay of economics and politics, and then I discovered a book on mercantilism and said to myself: "Ah! That's what I am!" I began to realize that you could have a realist view of world economics without being a Marxist' (ibid., p. 73, citing *International Relations*, 2005). The point is more than incidental. When Cohen lists the *variety* of approaches in 'British' IPE, he characteristically associates a focus on global capitalism with Marxism. So, on what it is beyond the state that provides the glue that holds the system together: 'Others, reflecting a Marxian influence, speak of the dominant role of "global" or "transnational" capitalism' (ibid., p. 116); and later, 'yet others, in the Marxist tradition, simply equate the international system with global or transnational capitalism' (ibid., p. 140).

American IPE cannot address *global capitalism* as a system at all because to do so would be Marxist; even less can it address domestic issues in terms of class interests and conflict around production and appropriation, and relate *those* to the global political economy – even, apparently, from a perspective thoroughly supportive of capitalism. Its defences, some apparent to its practitioners and others not, have been built too strongly. It is therefore denied access to the tools needed to analyse and understand the 'really big questions' of the day. It is hardly surprising in the circumstances that, for all its thrashing about, it has come up blank on the way to address 'the nexus of global economics and politics'. A bodged-up alliance with the 'respectable' end of the 'British' school will only perpetuate this, as will an embrace of constructivism in the name of pluralism.

Conclusion

The case for holistic analysis of the contemporary global political economy is strong. But as Peter Burnham put it in a phrase that Cohen cites (though in passing, and only as evidence of anti-Americanism), the point is 'to grasp the complex organic set of social relations which is the global political economy' (Burnham, 1994, cited in Cohen, 2008a, p. 62). In other words, the analysis must start with the global political economy, not with the states that are moments within it. Unfortunately for advocates of the 'scientific method', such an approach necessarily rules out the search for law-like generalization: at the level of the global political economy, things only ever happen once.

The conclusion to which one comes, then, if one asks how the 'field of IPE' has advanced our knowledge of the connections between economics and politics beyond the confines of a single state in the context of global economic interdependence, is that it has not advanced it at all; that in many respects it has gone backwards (as indeed has 'British' IPE – see Cammack, 2007); that it cannot identify, let alone address, the questions posed by the issue of global economic interdependence today; that it is primarily ideological in character; and that paradoxically while proposing 'international political economy' as its object of enquiry, it shies away from any analysis of capitalism at a systemic level, class at a domestic level, and the implications for the state. Its privileging of institutional position over the pursuit of knowledge is a part of this stultifying version of 'political economy lite', as is its continued insistence on the virtues of the scientific method and the search for law-like generalizations: clinging to nurse, for fear of something worse. It can safely be cast into oblivion, along with the project of bridge-building with its British Other.

Further reading

Where, then, should one turn instead, for analyses that *do* succeed in addressing the 'really big questions' of system transformation, system governance, the role of the state, and the connections between these aspects of the global political economy? Still to Marx and Engels, in the first instance, to *Capital* (not forgetting the Appendix to Volume I), then to invaluable conjunctural analyses such as *The Class Struggles in France* and *The Eighteenth Brumaire of Louis Bonaparte* (widely available, but K. Marx, *Political Writings*, vols 1–4 (Penguin/New Left Review, London, 1973–5) is a good collection); to Lenin, Trotsky and Gramsci, with a preference for their analyses of the development of capitalism in their own societies (V.I. Lenin, *The Development of Capitalism in Russia* in *Collected Works*, vol. 3 (Moscow, 1964); L. Trotsky, *History of the Russian Revolution* (Pluto Press, London, 1977); A. Gramsci, 'Notes on Italian History', in *Selections from Prison Notebooks*, ed. Q. Hoare and G. Nowell-Smith (Lawrence and Wishart, London, 1971)); and then to the classics of the revival of Marxist political economy from the 1970s to the present. Any listing can be no more than indicative, and leaves out hugely important and impressive work. The following suggestions are intended to provide a bridge to genuinely critical political economy for scholars stranded in IPE.

First come four essential series: *Historical Materialism, Monthly Review* and *New Left Review* among many journals, and the annual *Socialist Register*, the latter providing the best window onto the wealth of relevant scholarship over the last 40 years. Then two edited collections that span the period – John Holloway and Sol Picciotto, eds, *State and Capital: A Marxist Debate* (Edward Arnold, London, 1978), and Mark Rupert and Hazel Smith, eds, *Historical Materialism and Globalization* (Routledge, London, 2002). After this, the list could be endless. I offer a sample restricted to monographs, in alphabetical order by author, with original foreign language texts in English translations: Michel Aglietta, *A Theory of Capitalist Regulation: the US Experience* (Verso, London, 1979); Elmar Altvater, *The Future of the Market* (Verso, London, 1993); Giovanni Arrighi, *The Long Twentieth Century: Money, Power and the Origins of Our Times* (Verso, London, 1994) and *Adam Smith in Beijing: Lineages of the Twenty-first Century* (Verso, London, 2007); Werner Bonefeld, *The Recomposition of the British State during the 1980s* (Ashgate, Farnham, 1993); Robert Brenner, *The Economics of Global Turbulence: The Advanced Capitalist Economies from Long Boom to Long Downturn, 1945–2005* (Verso,

London, 2006); Peter Burnham, *The Political Economy of Postwar Reconstruction* (Macmillan, London, 1990); Simon Clarke, *Marx's Theory of Crisis* (Macmillan, London, 1994); Peter Gowan, *The Global Gamble: Washington's Faustian Bid for World Dominance* (Verso, London, 1999); David Harvey, *Limits to Capital* (Blackwell, Oxford, 1982) and *The New Imperialism* (Oxford University Press, New York, 2003 (revised 2005)); Bob Jessop, *The Future of the Capitalist State* (Polity, Cambridge, 2002); Ernest Mandel, *Late Capitalism* (Verso, London, 1975); Ralph Miliband, *Marxism and Politics* (Oxford University Press, Oxford, 1977); James O'Connor, *The Fiscal Crisis of the State* (New York, St. Martin's Press, 1973); Clause Offe, *Contradictions of the Welfare State*, ed. John Keane (Hutchinson, London, 1984); Henk Overbeek, *Global Capitalism and National Decline: The Thatcher Decade in Perspective* (Unwin Hyman, London, 1990); Kees van der Pijl, *The Making of the Atlantic Ruling Class* (Verso, London, 1984); Nicos Poulantzas, *Political Power and Social Classes* (New Left Books, London, 1973); Neil Smith, *Uneven Development: Nature, Capital and the Production of Space* (Blackwell, Oxford, 1984); Susanne Soederberg, *Global Governance in Question* (Pluto, London, 2006) and *Corporate Power and Ownership in Contemporary Capitalism* (Routledge, London, 2010); Bill Warren, *Imperialism: Pioneer of Capitalism* (Verso, London, 1980); Ellen Meiksins Wood, *Democracy against Capitalism: Renewing Historical Materialism* (Verso, London, 1995) and *The Empire of Capital* (Verso, London, 2003).

Conclusion: IPE *and* the international political economy? IPE *or* the international political economy?

Stuart Shields, Ian Bruff and Huw Macartney

Our intention in bringing together this collection of scholars has been to begin a process of reflection on why volumes such as these are particularly timely in the current period, for both the discipline of IPE and the study of the international political economy. Although the debates on the 'British' and 'American' schools were an important catalyst for such reflections, they also built upon earlier marginalizations and silencings which were, in our view, unwarranted. Recall, for example, Robert Keohane's more explicit invitation in the late 1980s to 'reflectivist' scholars to produce systematic research agendas and falsifiable claims as a means of engaging with the 'rationalism' dominant in IR – in other words, a demand for 'post-positivist' research to abandon its *raison d'être* and engage in narrow specifics which take for granted wider questions about the world in which we live. More recently, the explosion of contributions on 'globalization' tended to produce a neat conjuring trick, whereby a globalized world was (magically and tautologically) both the outcome – what needed to be explained – and the explanation of this outcome. In the process, alternative narratives were pushed to the sidelines (Rosenberg, 2000).

As Richard Ashley (1983) pointed out three decades ago, this is part and parcel of scholarship in the social sciences, whereby disciplines are disciplined via the construction of narratives which maintain the coherence of a field of study *as it is already constituted* (see especially the chapters by Ashworth and Griffin). Through appeals to terms and concepts – though common to vast swathes of a discipline's 'in-crowd' – these efforts systematically exclude 'questions and arguments from political discourse without saying [those] which [are] exclude[d]' (ibid., p. 464). Therefore, the categories of analysis 'are typically undefined and suspended beyond the reach of critical analysis' and must remain so (ibid.). Put differently, serious and productive engagement with those 'outside' the constituted intellectual territories is both impossible and, more importantly, entirely unnecessary. Herein lies the irony, for whilst many of those who have responded to Cohen's invitation would remain open to the contributions of those he excludes (Murphy, 2009), their response targets the misrepresentation of those already constituted as 'insiders'. By way of the 'IPE narrative' that has already been constructed, those outside remain outside (cf. Elias's chapter in this volume).

In this regard, and in contradistinction to the debates on the 'British' and 'American' schools, the contributors to this volume are united predominantly by their questioning of the validity of these debates rather than a shared approach or common language. As such, we – as are all of the authors – are very clear that, *by its very nature,* 'critical' scholarship is a pluralistic enterprise (van Apeldoorn et al., 2010). Although, as detailed in the introduction, there are commitments to certain modes of social enquiry inherent to such work, this volume has been less about presenting a coherent alternative than opening up potentially fruitful fields of enquiry. For this reason (and inevitably), numerous 'critical IPE' perspectives exist, and, indeed, there have been many debates within and across them – including those which view (as Cammack does) 'critical IPE' as oxymoronic. It is our contention that this stands in direct contrast to the manner in which the responses to Cohen frequently, and often unwittingly, reproduced precisely the constructions that he proposed. For instance, in perhaps the best-known contribution aside from Cohen's, Richard Higgott and Matthew Watson's (2008) warning against a US/UK dichotomy is inexplicably grounded in a defence of the role of British traditions in political philosophy. The terms of engagement established by Cohen were thus implicitly accepted.

The contributors to this volume have been at pains to emphasize the deficiencies within critical IPE as well. A key theme of a number of chapters has been the dissatisfaction with the conflation of neo-Gramscian with critical IPE, or with neo-Gramscian scholarship in general – even if one, as Bruff does, seeks to renew it on a more explicitly sociological basis. This is a key advantage of this volume, given the accepted wisdom that 'critical IPE' was brought into being by Robert W. Cox's (1981, 1983) two seminal articles in the early 1980s. Indeed, such reflexivity is part and parcel of engaging critically with our world and the ideas that predominate within it. Certainly, neo-Gramscian scholarship has been particularly significant in its engagement with debates in both mainstream and critical IPE, with a key claim being that the underlying power structures immanent to the contemporary capitalist world order remain, at best, obscured from view (see, for example, Bieler and Morton, 2008). Nonetheless, this volume has – in various ways – argued that even neo-Gramscian scholarship has come up against its own (implicitly) self-imposed limits (cf. Macartney and Shields' chapter). Although the reasons given differ, the dissatisfaction is arguably rooted in its embeddedness within IPE itself. We now turn to this wider issue.

IPE as constraint on, or platform for, critical scholarship?

Perhaps one key conclusion of this volume is that the discipline of International Political Economy – in its current form(s) – is frequently ill-equipped to make the international political economy its object of enquiry. Indeed, all of the contributors have raised fundamental questions which perhaps cannot be answered with recourse to IPE at all. This, of course, is open to debate, but if we do not consider this possibility – focusing instead on what IPE 'is' – then the kind of disconnect between IR and the 'real world' that was illustrated so vividly at the end of the Cold War could also become an issue for IPE. As things stand, we are not as pessimistic as Cammack about the utility of calling one's 'home' the discipline of IPE, finding instead Germain's opening comments a good defence of the holistic potential inherent within IPE's remit. However, the recovery and forefronting of this potential *necessarily* entails the awareness that disciplinary boundaries should be viewed as fluid and not impermeable, that older works – often less marked by the specializations which are more characteristic of the contemporary era – may justify a rereading, and that our scholarship is always partial (in both senses of the word) and thus open to contestation.

Fischer and Tepe's chapter is an important contribution in this regard, for they seek both to recover for contemporary debates the importance of the Frankfurt School's writings and to highlight the need to engage much more fully with feminist scholarship. Nevertheless, and in contrast to notions of 'analytical eclecticism' that substitute pragmatism for rigorous reflection on the concepts we deploy, they do so through an acknowledgement that one cannot simply adopt a 'pick and mix' approach. Similar assertions are made by Elias, who argues for the irreducibly constitutive role of gendered hierarchies and power relations and thus the need to overcome tokenistic references to feminist scholarship, and Griffin, who reminds us that knowledge is created and reproduced through – not in isolation from – assumptions about what is 'natural' and 'universal' about human nature.

This, then, leads us to the final point. As Worth emphasizes, the notion of being critical is nothing if it does not have an emancipatory purpose at its heart. Merely destabilizing taken-for-granted ideas about the world is not enough; there must be a sense of how they could change, too, in favour of a more equitable world with human dignity, rights and possibilities at its core. This is especially important in the current climate, where the economic crisis is entrenching further the profound inequalities that characterize societies across the world (perhaps the most vivid example being the sweeping welfare cuts being proposed in Europe). While it is easy to deride these notions on the grounds of 'bias' and 'subjectivity', such criticisms are predicated on assumptions about the world that this volume has sought to problematize. Moreover, it is not just a case of competing knowledge claims, for we are inevitably part of the world that we seek to study, and surely a more holistic approach will deliver a more sophisticated and convincing account of it. As Mary Hawkesworth (2009, p. 285) puts it, 'social amnesia should not be allowed to masquerade as scientific knowledge'.

Bibliography

Abbott, J.P. and O. Worth (2002) 'The Many Worlds of Critical International Political Economy', in J.P. Abbott and O. Worth (eds), *Critical Perspectives on International Political Economy* (Basingstoke: Palgrave Macmillan), 1–13.

Abdelal, A., M. Blyth and C. Parsons (eds) (2010) *Constructing the International Economy* (New York: Cornell University Press).

Ackerley, B. and J. True (2006) 'Studying the Struggles and Wishes of the Age: Feminist Theoretical Methodology and Feminist Theoretical Methods', in B. Ackerley, M. Stern and J. True (eds), *Feminist Methodologies for International Relations* (Cambridge: Cambridge University Press), 241–60.

Adorno, T.W. (1967) Stichwort Gesellschaft, in *Hermann Kunst and Siegfried Grundmann, Evangelisches Staatslexikon* (Stuttgart: Kreuz Verlag), 636–643.

—— (1972) *Der Positivismusstreit in der deutschen Soziologie* (Neuwied und Berlin: Hermann Luchterhand Verlag).

—— (1976) *The Positivist Dispute in German Sociology* (London: Heinemann).

—— and M. Horkheimer (2002) *The Dialectic of Enlightenment* (Stanford: Stanford University Press).

Aitken, R. (2006) 'Performativity, Popular Finance and Security in the Global Political Economy', in M. de Goede (ed.), *International Political Economy and Poststructural Politics* (Basingstoke: Palgrave Macmillan), 77–96.

Allinson, J.C. and A. Anievas (2009) 'The Uses and Misuses of Uneven and Combined Development: An Anatomy of a Concept', *Cambridge Review of International Affairs*, 22:1, 47–67.

Amoore, L., R. Dodgson, R.D. Germain, B.K. Gills, P. Langley and I. Watson (2000) 'Paths to a Historicized International Political Economy', *Review of International Political Economy*, 7:1, 53–71.

Anderson, J. (2002) 'Questions of Democracy, Territoriality and Globalisation', in J. Anderson (ed.), *Transnational Democracy: Political Spaces and Border Crossings* (London: Routledge), 6–38.

Anderson, P. (1976) 'The Antinomies of Antonio Gramsci', *New Left Review*, 100, 5–78.

Angell, N. (1911) *The Great Illusion: A Study of the Relation of Military Power in Nations to their Economic and Social Advantage* (Toronto: McClelland and Goodchild).

van Apeldoorn, B. (2002) *Transnational Capitalism and the Struggle Over European Integration* (London: Routledge).

—— (2004) 'Theorizing the Transnational: A Historical Materialist Approach', *Journal of International Relations and Development*, 7:2, 142–76.

——, I. Bruff and M. Ryner (2010) 'The Richness and Diversity of Critical IPE Perspectives: Moving Beyond the Debate on the "British School"', in N. Phillips and C. Weaver (eds), *International Political Economy: Debating the Past, Present and Future* (London: Routledge), 215–22.

Arrighi, G. (2005a) 'Hegemony Unravelling – I', *New Left Review*, 32, March–April, 74–80.

—— (2005b) 'Hegemony Unravelling – 2', *New Left Review*, 33, May–June, 83–116.

Ashley, R.K. (1983) 'Three Modes of Economism', *International Studies Quarterly*, 27:4, 463–96.

Ashworth, L.M. (1999) *Creating International Studies: Angell, Mitrany and the Liberal Tradition* (Aldershot: Ashgate).

—— (2007) *International Relations and the Labour Party: Intellectuals and Policy Making 1918–1945* (London: I.B. Tauris).

—— (2009) 'Interdisciplinarity and International Relations', *European Political Science*, 8:1, 16–25.

—— (2010) 'Realism and the Spirit of 1919: Halford Mackinder, Geopolitics and the Reality of the League of Nations', *European Journal of International Relations*, forthcoming.

Auther, J. (2010) 'Living on the Edge', *Sydney Morning Herald*, 2 May, http://www.smh.com.au/business/living-on-the-edge-20100528-wldw.html, accessed May–June 2010.

Bakker, I. (2007) 'Social Reproduction and the Constitution of a Gendered Political Economy', *New Political Economy*, 12:4, 541–56.

—— and S. Gill (2003) 'Ontology, Method and Hypotheses', in I. Bakker and S. Gill (eds), *Power, Production and Social Reproduction* (Basingstoke and New York: Palgrave Macmillan), 17–41.

Bartle, P. (2009) 'The Meaning of Culture', *Community Empowerment* website, http://www.scn.org/cmp/modules/per-culm.htm, accessed September 2009.

Bates, S.R. and N.J. Smith (2008) 'Understanding Change in Political Science: On the Need to Bring Space into Theoretical Positions and Empirical Analyses', *Political Studies Review*, 6:2, 191–204.

Batliwala, S. and D. Dhanraj (2007) 'Gender Myths that Instrumentalize Women: A View from the Indian Frontlines', in A. Cornwall, E. Harrison and A. Whitehead (eds), *Feminisms in Development: Contradictions, Contestations and Challenges* (London: Zed), 21–34.

Becker-Schmidt, R. (1987) 'Die doppelte Vergesellschaftung – die doppelte Unterdrückung: Besonderheiten der Frauenforschung in den Sozialwissenschaften', in Lilo Unterkirchner and Ina Wagner (eds), *Die andere Hälfte der Gesellschaft* (Wien: Verlag des Österreichischen Gewekschaftsbundes GesmbH), 10–28.

—— (2007) '"Class", "gender", "ethnicity", "race": Logiken der Differenzsetzung, Verschränkungen von Ungleichheitslagen und gesellschaftliche Strukturierung', in Cornelia Klinger, Gudrun-Axeli Knapp and Birgit Sauer (eds), *Achsen der Ungleichheit: Zum Verhältnis von Klasse, Geschlecht und Ethnizität* (Frankfurt and New York: Campus Verlag), 56–84.

Bedford, K. (2005) 'Loving to Straighten Out Development: Sexuality and "Ethnodevelopment" in the World Bank's Ecuadorian Lending', *Feminist Legal Studies*, 13:3, 295–322.

—— (2007) 'The Imperative of Male Inclusion: How Institutional Context Influences World Bank Gender Policy', *International Feminist Journal of Politics*, 9:3, 289–311.

Beer, U. (1990) *Geschlecht, Struktur, Geschichte: Soziale Konstituierung des Geschlechterverhältnisses* (Frankfurt and New York: Campus Verlag).

Bellamy, R. (1990) 'Gramsci, Croce and the Italian Political Tradition', *History of Political Thought*, 11:2, 313–37.

—— and D. Schecter (1993) *Gramsci and the Italian State* (Manchester: Manchester University Press).

Bergeron, S. (2001) 'Political Economy Discourses of Globalization in Feminist Politics', *Signs*, 26:4, 983–1006.

Best, J. and M. Paterson (eds) (2009) *Cultural Political Economy* (London: Routledge).

Bieler, A. and Morton, A.D. (2001) 'The Gordian Knot of Agency-Structure in International Relations: A Neo-Gramscian Perspective', *European Journal of International Relations*, 7:1, 5–35.

—— (2004) 'A Critical Theory Route to Hegemony, World Order and Historical Change: Neo-Gramscian Perspectives in International Relations', *Capital & Class*, 28:1, 85–114.

—— (2008) 'The Deficits of Discourse in IPE: Turning Base Metal into Gold?', *International Studies Quarterly*, 52:1, 103–28.

Birchfield, V. (1999) 'Contesting the Hegemony of Market Ideology: Gramsci's "Good Sense" and Polanyi's "Double Movement"', *Review of International Political Economy*, 6:1, 27–54.

Blaney, D. and N. Inayatullah (2010) *Savage Economics: Wealth, Poverty and the Temporal Walls of Capitalism* (London: Routledge).

Bleiker, R. (2001) 'The Aesthetic Turn in International Political Theory', *Millennium*, 30:2, 509–33.

Blyth, M. (2002) *Great Transformations: Economic Ideas and Institutional Change in the Twentieth Century* (Cambridge: Cambridge University Press).

—— (ed.) (2009a) *Routledge Handbook of International Political Economy (IPE): IPE as a Global Conversation* (London and New York: Routledge).

—— (2009b) 'Torn between Two Lovers? Caught in the Middle of British and American IPE', *New Political Economy*, 14:3, 329–36.

Bonefeld, W. (1998) 'The New Left and the Politics of Novelty', *Economic and Political Weekly*, 33:12, 667–70.

Boothman, D. (2006–7) 'Critique and Semantic Modification in Gramsci's Approach to Paradigmatic Translation', *Italian Culture*, 24–25, 113–40.

Boraas, S. and W.M. Rodgers (2003) 'How Does Gender Play a Role in the Earnings Gap? An Update', *Monthly Labor Review*, http://www.bls.gov/opub/mlr/2003/03/art2full.pdf, accessed April 2009–June 2010.

Bowman, I. (1928) *The New World: Problems in Political Geography* (4th edn) (Yonkers-on-Hudson: World Book Company).

—— (1930) *International Relations* (Chicago: American Library Association).

Brailsford, H. (1906) *Macedonia: Its Races and their Future* (London: Methuen).

—— (1917a) *The War of Steel and Gold: A Study of the Armed Peace* (9th edn) (London: Bell).

—— (1917b) *A League of Nations* (London: Headley).

—— (1919) 'A Parliament of the League of Nations', *Labour Party Advisory Committee on International Questions*, memorandum no. 44, January. Labour Party Archives, Labour History Archive and Study Centre, Manchester, UK.

—— (1920) *After the Peace* (London: Parsons).

—— (1923) 'False Roads to Security', *New Leader*, 23 March.

—— (1924a) 'Arbitrate or Disarm. A New View of Security', *New Leader*, 12 September.

————— (1924b) 'A New Start for the League: Arbitration and the Chains of Versailles', 26 September.

————— (1928) *Olives of Endless Age: Being a Study of this Distracted World and its Need of Unity* (New York and London: Harper).

————— (1933) 'A Socialist Foreign Policy', in C. Addison et al., *Problems of a Socialist Government* (London: Victor Gollancz).

————— (1934) *Property or Peace?* (London: Gollancz).

————— (1936) *Towards a New League* (London: New Statesman and Nation).

————— (1938a) *Why Capitalism Means War* (New York: Garland).

————— (1938b) 'The Tory Policy of Peace', *The Political Quarterly*, 9, 325–33.

————— (1944) *Our Settlement with Germany* (Harmondsworth: Penguin).

————— (1948) *The Life Work of J.A. Hobson* (London: Oxford University Press).

Bratsis, P. (2006) *Everyday Life and the State* (London: Paradigm).

Brenner, N. (1998) 'Between Fixity and Motion: Accumulation, Territorial Organization and the Historical Geography of Spatial Scales', *Environment and Planning D: Society and Space*, 16:4, 459–81.

————— (2001) 'The Limits to Scale? Methodological Reflections on Scalar Structuration', *Progress in Human Geography*, 25:4, 591–614.

————— (2004) *New State Spaces: Urban Governance and the Rescaling of Statehood* (Oxford: Oxford University Press).

Brown, C. (1994) 'Turtles All the Way Down: Anti-Foundationalism, Critical Theory and International relations', *Millennium*, 23:2, 213–38.

Brown, W. (2006) 'Feminist Theory and the Frankfurt School: Introduction', *Differences: A Journal of Feminist Cultural Studies*, 17:1, 1–5.

Bruff, I. (2008) *Culture and Consensus in European Varieties of Capitalism: A 'Common Sense' Analysis* (Basingstoke: Palgrave Macmillan).

————— (2010) 'European Varieties of Capitalism and the International', *European Journal of International Relations*, 16:4, 615–38.

————— (2011a) 'The Case for a Foundational Materialism: Going Beyond Historical Materialist IPE in Order to Strengthen It', *Journal of International Relations and Development*, forthcoming.

————— (2011b) 'The Relevance of Nicos Poulantzas for Contemporary Debates on "the International"', *International Politics*, forthcoming.

Buckel, Sonja (2007) *Subjektivierung und Kohäsion. Zur Rekonstruktion einer materialistischen Theorie des Rechts* (Göttingen: Velbrück Wissenschaft).

Bull, H. (1966) 'International Theory: The Case for a Classical Approach', *World Politics*, 18:3, 361–77.

Burnham, P. (1994) 'Open Marxism and Vulgar International Political Economy', *Review of International Political Economy*, 1:2, 221–31.

Butterfield, H. (1931) *The Whig Interpretation of History* (New York: Norton).

Buvinic, M., S. Sabarwal and N. Sinha (2009) 'The Global Financial Crisis: Assessing Vulnerability for Women and Children', *Policy Brief Prepared for the World Bank*, http://www.worldbank.org/financialcrisis/pdf/Women-Children-Vulnerability-March09.pdf, accessed June 2010.

Callinicos, A. (2007) 'Does Capitalism Need the State System?', *Cambridge Review of International Affairs*, 20:4, 533–49.

Cammack, P. (1989) 'Bringing the State Back In?', *British Journal of Political Science*, 19:2, 261–90.

—— (1990) 'Statism, New Institutionalism and Marxism', in R. Miliband and L. Panitch (eds), *Socialist Register 1990: The Retreat of the Intellectuals* (London: Merlin Press), 82–104.

—— (2007) 'RIP IPE', *Papers in the Politics of Global Competitiveness*, No. 7 (Institute for Global Studies, Manchester Metropolitan University: e-space Open Access Repository).

—— (2009) 'Smart Power and U.S. Leadership: Critique of Joseph Nye', *49th Parallel*, 16, 5–20.

Caraway, T.L. (2007) *Assembling Women: The Feminization of Global Manufacturing* (Ithaca: ILR Press and Cornell University Press).

Cerny, P.G. (1990) *The Changing Architecture of Politics: Structure, Agency, and the Future of the State* (London: Sage).

—— (1997) 'Paradoxes of the Competition State: The Dynamics of Political Globalization', *Government and Opposition*, 32:2, 251–74.

—— (2010) *Rethinking World Politics: A Theory of Transnational Neopluralism* (New York: Oxford University Press).

Charnock, G. (2010) 'The Space of International Political Economy: On Scale and its Limits', *Politics*, 30:2, 79–90.

Chin, C. and J.H. Mittelman (2000) 'Conceptualizing Resistance to Globalization', in B. Gills (ed.), *Globalization and the Politics of Resistance* (Basingstoke: Palgrave Macmillan), 29–45.

Chowdhry, G. (2002) 'Postcolonial Interrogations of Child Labour: Human Rights, Carpet Trade and Rugmark in India', in G. Chowdhry and S. Nair (eds), *Power in a Postcolonial World: Race, Gender and Class in International Relations* (London: Routledge), 225–53.

Cohen, B.J. (2007) 'The Transatlantic Divide: Why are American and British IPE So Different?', *Review of International Political Economy*, 14:2, 197–219.

—— (2008a) *International Political Economy: An Intellectual History* (Princeton: Princeton University Press).

—— (2008b) 'The Transatlantic Divide: A Rejoinder', *Review of International Political Economy*, 15:1, 30–4.

—— (2009) 'The Way Forward', *New Political Economy*, 14:3, 395–400.

Cohn, T. (2010) *Global Political Economy: Theory and Practice* (4th ed.) (London: Longman).

Cole, G. (1958) *A History of Socialist Thought. Volume IV, Part I: Communism and Social Democracy, 1914–1931* (London: Macmillan).

Coleman, L. (2007) 'The Gendered Violence of Development: Imaginative Geographies of Exclusion in the Imposition of Neo-Liberal Capitalism', *British Journal of Politics & International Relations*, 9:2, 204–19.

Collingwood, R.G. (1946) *The Idea of History* (Oxford: Clarendon Press).

Collins, P.H. (1991) *Black Feminist Thought: Knowledge, Consciousness, and the Politics of Empowerment* (New York/ London: Routledge).

Connell, R.W. (1987) *Gender and Power* (Cambridge: Polity).

Cox, K. (1998) 'Spaces of Engagement, Spaces of Dependence and the Politics of Scale, or: Looking for Local Politics', *Political Geography*, 17:1, 1–23.

Cox, R.W. (1981) 'Social Forces, States and World Orders: Beyond International Relations', *Millennium*, 10:2, 126–55.

—— (1983) 'Gramsci, Hegemony and International Relations: An Essay in Method', *Millennium*, 12:2, 162–75.

—— (1987) *Production, Power and World Order: Social Forces in the Making of History* (New York: Columbia University Press).

—— (1993) 'Structural Issues of Global Governance: Implications for Europe', in S. Gill (ed.), *Gramsci, Historical Materialism and International Relations* (Cambridge: Cambridge University Press), 259–89.

—— (1995) 'Critical Political Economy', in B. Hettne (ed.), *International Political Economy: Understanding Global Disorder* (London: Zed Books), 31–45.

—— (with T.J. Sinclair) (1996) *Approaches to World Order* (Cambridge: Cambridge University Press).

—— (with M.G. Schechter) (2002) *The Political Economy of a Plural World* (London: Routledge).

—— (2006) ' "The International" in Evolution'. Presented at the 35th *Millennium Anniversary Conference*, London School of Economics and Political Science, 21–22 October.

—— (2007) ' "The International" in Evolution', *Millennium*, 35:3, 513–27.

—— (2009) 'The British School in the Global Context', *New Political Economy*, 14:3, 315–28.

Crehan, K. (2002) *Gramsci, Culture and Anthropology* (London: Pluto).

Crenshaw, K.W. (1989) 'Demarginalizing the Intersection of Race and Class: A Black Feminist critique of Antidiscrimination Doctrine', *University of Chicago Legal Forum* 139 (1989), available at http://www.heinonline.org.proxy.ub. uni-frankfurt.de/HOL/Page?handle=hein.journals/uchclf1989&id=1&size= 2&collection=journals&index=journals/uchclf#143 (accessed 6 March 2010).

—— (1994) 'Mapping the Margins: Intersectionality, Identity Politics, and Violence against Women of Color', *Stanford Law Review*, 43:6, 1241–99.

Cutler, A.C. (2003) *Private Power and Global Authority: Transnational Merchant Law in the Global Political Economy* (Cambridge: Cambridge University Press).

Dale, G. (2009) 'Karl Polanyi in Budapest: On His Political and Intellectual Formation', *European Journal of Sociology*, 50:1, 97–130.

Dalton, H. (1928) *Towards the Peace of Nations: A Study in International Politics* (London: Routledge).

Davies, M. and M. Ryner (eds) (2006) *Power and the Production of World Politics: Unprotected Workers in the Global Economy* (Basingstoke: Palgrave Macmillan).

de Goede, M. (2003) 'Beyond Economism in International Political Economy', *Review of International Studies*, 29:1, 79–97.

—— (ed.) (2006) *International Political Economy and Poststructural Politics* (Basingstoke: Palgrave Macmillan).

Dickins, A. (2006) 'The Evolution of International Political Economy', *International Affairs*, 82:3, 479–92.

Dubiel, H. (1988) *Kritische Theorie der Gesellschaft: Eine Einfuehrende Rekonstruktion von den Anfaengen im Horkheimer-Kreis bis Habermas* (Weinheim and Munich: Juventa).

Dunn, B. (2009) *Global Political Economy: A Marxist Critique* (London: Pluto).

Elias, J. (2004) *Fashioning Inequality: The Multinational Company and Gendered Employment in a Globalizing World* (Aldershot: Ashgate).

—— (2005) 'The Gendered Political Economy of Control and Resistance on the Shop Floor of the Multinational Firm: A Case-Study from Malaysia', *New Political Economy*, 10:2, 203–22.

────── (2008) 'Hegemonic Masculinities, the Multinational Corporation, and the Developmental State: Constructing Gender in "Progressive" Firms', *Men and Masculinities*, 10:4, 405–21.

────── (2009) 'Gendering Liberalisation and Labour Reform in Malaysia: Fostering "Competitiveness" in the Productive and Reproductive Economies', *Third World Quarterly*, 30:3, 469–83.

Elson, D. (1995) *Male Bias in the Development Process* (Manchester: Manchester University Press).

Enloe, C. (1989) *Bananas, Beaches and Bases: Making Feminist sense of International Politics* (London: Pandora).

Eschle, C. and B. Maiguashca (2007) 'Rethinking Globalised Resistance: Feminist Activism and Critical Theorising in International Relations', *British Journal of Politics & International Relations*, 9:2, 284–301.

Falk, R. (1997) 'The Critical Realist Tradition and the Demystification of Interstate Power: E.H. Carr, Hedley Bull and Robert W. Cox', in S. Gill and J. Mittelman (eds), *Innovation and Transformation in International Studies* (Cambridge: Cambridge University Press), 39–55.

Farrands, C. (2002) 'Critical about Being Critical', in J. Abbott and O. Worth (eds), *Critical Perspectives on International Political Economy* (Basingstoke: Palgrave Macmillan), 39–56.

────── and O. Worth (2005) 'Critical Theory in Global Political Economy: Critique? Knowledge? Emancipation?', *Capital & Class*, 29:1, 43–62.

Ferguson, L. (2010) 'Tourism Development and the Restructuring of Social Reproduction in Central America', *Review of International Political Economy*, 17:5, 860–888.

Fischer, A. (2008) 'Von gesellschaftlicher Arbeitsteilung über Geschlecht zum Staat. Eine geschlechtertheoretische Auseinandersetzung mit dem Staat bei Nicos Poulantzas', in Jens Wissel and Stefanie Wöhl (eds), *Staatstheorie vor neuen Herausforderungen: Analyse und Kritik* (Münster: Westfälisches Dampfboot), 50–70.

Foot, M. (1958) 'The Knight Errant of Socialism', *Tribune*, 28 March.

Foucault, M. (2003) ' "Society Must Be Defended": Lectures at the College de France, 1975–1976' (trs. D. Macey) (London: Picador).

────── (2010) *The Birth of Biopolitics: Lectures at the College De France, 1978–1979* (trs. G. Burchell) (Basingstoke: Palgrave Macmillan).

Fraser, N. (1985) 'What's Critical About Critical Theory? The Case of Habermas and Gender', *New German Critique*, 35, 97–131.

Gaus, G. and Benn, S.I. (1983) *Public and Private in Social Life* (New York: St. Martin's Press).

Germain, R. (2007) ' "Critical" Political Economy, Historical Materialism and Adam Morton', *Politics*, 27:2, 127–32.

────── (2009) 'The "American" School of IPE: A Dissenting View', *Review of International Political Economy*, 16:1, 95–105.

────── and M. Kenny (1998) 'Engaging Gramsci: International Relations Theory and the New Gramscians', *Review of International Studies*, 24:1, 3–21.

Gibson, K., L. Law and D. McKay (2001) 'Beyond Heroes and Victims: Filipina Contract Migrants, Economic Activism and Class Transformations', *International Feminist Journal of Politics*, 3:3, 365–86.

Gibson-Graham, J.K. (1996) *The End of Capitalism (As We Knew It): A Feminist Critique of Political Economy* (Oxford: Blackwell).

Gill, S. (ed.) (1993) *Gramsci, Historical Materialism and International Relations* (Cambridge: Cambridge University Press).

—— (1995) 'Globalisation, Market Civilization and Disciplinary Neo-liberalism', *Millennium: Journal of International Studies*, 24:3, 399–423.

—— (2000) 'Toward a Postmodern Prince? The Battle in Seattle as a Moment in the New Politics of Globalization', *Millennium: Journal of International Studies*, 29:1, 131–41.

—— (2008) *Power and Resistance in the New World Order* (2nd edn) (Basingstoke: Palgrave Macmillan).

—— and David Law (1989) 'Global Hegemony and the Structural Power of Capital', *International Studies Quarterly*, 33:4, 475–99.

Gilpin, R. (1987) *The Political Economy of International Relations* (Princeton: Princeton University Press).

—— (with J.M. Gilpin) (2001) *Global Political Economy: Understanding the International Economic Order* (Princeton: Princeton University Press).

Gough, J. (2002) 'Neoliberalism and Socialisation in the Contemporary City: Opposites, Complements and Instabilities', *Antipode*, 34:3, 405–26.

—— (2004) 'Changing Scale as Changing Class Relations: Variety and Contradiction in the Politics of Scale', *Political Geography*, 23:2, 185–211.

Gramsci, A. (1971) *Selections from the Prison Notebooks* (ed and trs. Q. Hoare and G. Nowell-Smith) (London: Lawrence and Wishart).

—— (1996) *Prison Notebooks*, vol. 2 (ed. and trs. J.A. Buttigieg) (New York: Columbia University Press).

Green, M. (2002) 'Gramsci Cannot Speak: Presentations and Interpretations of Gramsci's Concept of the Subaltern', *Rethinking Marxism*, 14:3, 1–24.

—— and P. Ives (2009) 'Subalternity and Language: Overcoming the Fragmentation of Common Sense', *Historical Materialism*, 17:1, 3–30.

Grewal, I. (2005) *Transnational America: Feminisms, Diasporas, Neoliberalisms* (Durham: Duke University Press).

Griffin, P. (2007a) 'Refashioning IPE: What and How Gender Analysis Teaches International Political Economy', *Review of International Political Economy*, 14:4, 719–36.

—— (2007b) 'Sexing the Economy in a Neoliberal World Order: Neoliberal Discourse and the (Re)Production of (Heteronormative) Heterosexuality', *British Journal of Politics & International Relations*, 9:2, 220–38.

—— (2009a) *Gendering the World Bank: Neoliberalism and the Gendered Foundations of Global Governance* (Basingstoke: Palgrave Macmillan).

—— (2009b) 'Neoliberal Globalisation and Development Institutions', in L.J. Shepherd (ed.), *Gender Matters in Global Politics* (London and New York: Routledge), 218–33.

—— (2010a) 'The Gendered Global Political Economy', in R.A. Denemark (ed.), *The International Studies Encyclopedia, Volume IV* (Oxford: Wiley-Blackwell), 2631–50.

—— (2010b) 'Why Gender Matters in/to the Global Economy', *e-IR*, 21 June, http://www.e-ir.info/?p=4454, accessed June 2010.

Guilhot, N. (2008) 'The Realist Gambit: Postwar American Political Science and the Birth of IR Theory', *International Political Sociology*, 2:4, 281–304.

Gurría, A. (2008) 'The Global Financial Crisis: Where to Next, and What Does it Mean for OECD Countries?', *Address to Victoria University and the New Zealand Institute of International Affairs*, 30 July, Wellington, New Zealand, http://www.oecd.org/document/62/0,3343,en_2649_201185_41073662_1_1_1_1,00.html, accessed April 2009.

Habermas, J. (1987) *Knowledge and Human Interests* (2nd edn) (trs. J.J. Shapiro) (Cambridge: Polity).

Hall, S. (1988) *The Hard Road to Renewal: Thatcherism and the Crisis of the Left* (London: Verso).

—— (1991) 'Gramsci and Us', in R. Simon, *Gramsci's Political Thought: An Introduction* (revised and reset edition) (London: Lawrence and Wishart), 114–30.

—— (1996a) 'On Postmodernism and Articulation' (interview by L. Grossberg), in D. Morley and K.-H. Chen (eds), *Stuart Hall: Critical Dialogues in Cultural Studies* (London: Routledge), 131–50.

—— (1996b) 'The Meaning of New Times', in D. Morley and K.-H. Chen (eds), *Stuart Hall: Critical Dialogues in Cultural Studies* (London: Routledge), 223–37.

—— (1997) 'Culture and Power' (interview by P. Osborne and L. Segal), *Radical Philosophy*, 86, 24–41.

Harding, S. (1986) *The Science Question in Feminism* (Ithaca: Cornell University Press).

Hardt, M. and A. Negri (2000) *Empire* (Cambridge: Harvard University Press).

—— (2004) *Multitude* (New York: Penguin Press).

Harvey, D. (1985) 'The Geopolitics of Capitalism', in D. Gregory and J. Urry (eds), *Social Relations and Spatial Structures* (New York: St. Martin's Press), 128–63.

—— (1990) *The Condition of Postmodernity* (Oxford: Blackwell).

—— (1996) *Justice, Nature and the Geography of Difference* (Oxford: Blackwell).

—— (2003) *The New Imperialism* (Oxford: Oxford University Press).

—— (2005) *A Brief History of Neoliberalism* (Oxford: Oxford University Press).

Haug, F. (1996) *Frauen-Politiken* (Berlin-Hamburg: Argument Verlag).

Hawkesworth, M. (2008) 'The Pragmatics of Iris Marion Young's Feminist Historical Materialism', *Politics and Gender*, 4:2, 318–26.

—— (2009) 'Policy Discourse as Sanctioned Ignorance: Theorizing the Erasure of Feminist Knowledge', *Critical Policy Studies*, 3:3–4, 268–89.

Healy, T. (2008) *Gendered Struggles Against Globalization in Mexico* (Aldershot: Ashgate).

Hewitt, A. (1992) 'A Feminine Dialectic of Enlightenment', *New German Critique*, 13 (1978), 143–70.

Higgott, R. and M. Watson (2008), 'All at Sea in a Barbed Wire Canoe: Professor Cohen's Transatlantic Voyage in IPE', *Review of International Political Economy*, 15:1, 1–17.

Hobson, J.A. (1902) *Imperialism: A Study* (London: Nisbet).

Hobson, J.M. (2007) 'Reconstructing International Relations through World History: Oriental Globalization and the Global-Dialogic Concept of Inter-civilizational Relations', *International Politics*, 44:4, 414–30.

—— and L. Seabrooke (eds) (2007) *Everyday Politics of the World Economy* (Cambridge: Cambridge University Press).

Hooper, C. (2001) *Manly States: Masculinities, International Relations, and Gender Politics* (New York: Columbia University Press).

Horkheimer, M. (1937/1972) 'Traditional and Critical Theory', in M. Horkheimer (ed.), *Critical Theory: Selected Essays* (New York: Herder and Herder), 188–243.

—— (1968) *Traditionelle und kritische Theorie: Vier Aufsaetze* (Frankfurt am Main: Fischer).

Hveem, H. (2009) 'Pluralist IPE: A View from Outside the "Schools"', *New Political Economy*, 14:3, 367–76.

International Relations (2005) 'Conversations in *International Relations*: Interview with Robert Gilpin', *International Relations*, 19:3, 361–72.

Investopedia (2009) 'Mancession', http://www.investopedia.com/terms/m/mancession.asp, accessed June 2010.

Jackson, P.T. (2008) 'Foregrounding Ontology: Dualism, Monism, and IR Theory', *Review of International Studies*, 34:1, 129–53.

—— (2010) *The Conduct of Inquiry in International Relations: Philosophy of Science and its Implications for the Study of World Politics* (New York: Routledge).

Jessop, B. (2007) *State Power: A Strategic-relational Approach* (Cambridge: Polity).

Kaplan, M. (1966) 'The New Great Debate: Traditionalism vs. Social Science in International Relations', *World Politics*, 19:1, 1–20.

Katzenstein, P.J. (1985) *Small States in World Markets: Industrial Policy in Europe* (Ithaca and London: Cornell University Press).

—— (2009) 'Mid-Atlantic: Sitting on the Knife's Edge', *Review of International Political Economy*, 16:1, 122–35.

——, R.O. Keohane and S.D. Krasner (1998) 'International Organization and the Study of World Politics', *International Organization*, 52:4, 645–85.

Keohane, R.O. (1977) *Power and Interdependence: World Politics in Transition* (Boston: Little, Brown).

—— (1988) 'International Institutions: Two Approaches', *International Studies Quarterly*, 32:4, 379–96.

—— (2009) 'The Old IPE and the New', *Review of International Political Economy*, 16:1, 34–46.

—— and Helen Milner (1996) *Internationalization and Domestic Politics* (Cambridge: Cambridge University Press).

—— and J.S. Nye (eds) (1972) *Transnational Relations and World Politics* (Cambridge: Harvard University Press).

Kerner, Ina (2009) *Differenzen und Macht. Zur Anatomie von Rassismus und Sexismus* (Frankfurt and New York: Campus).

Keynes, J.M. (1920) *The Economic Consequences of the Peace* (New York: Harcourt Brace and Howe).

King, D.K. (1988) 'Multiple Jeopardy, Multiple Consciousness: The Context of a Black Feminist Ideology', *Signs*, 14:1, 42–72.

Klinger, C. (2003) 'Ungleichheit in den Verhältnissen von Klasse, Rasse und Geschlecht', in G.A. Knapp and A. Wetterer (eds), *Achsen der Differenz: Gesellschaftstheorie und feministische Kritik*, Bd. 2. (Münster: Westfälisches Dampfboot), 14–49.

—— and G.A. Knapp (2007) 'Achsen der Ungleichheit – Achsen der Differenz: Verhältnisbestimmungen von Klasse, Geschlecht, "Rasse"/Ethnizität', in C. Klinger, G.A. Knapp and B. Sauer (eds), *Achsen der Ungleichheit: Zum Verhältnis von Klasse, Geschlecht und Ethnizität* (Frankfurt/New York: Campus Verlag), 19–42.

Knapp, G.A. (2008) 'Achsen der Differenz – Aspekte und Perspektiven feministischer Grundlagenkritik', in S.M. Witz (ed.), *Geschlechterdifferenzen – Geschlechterdifferenzierungen: Ein Überblick über gesellschaftliche Entwicklungen und theoretische Positionen* (Wiesbaden: VS-Verlag), 291–323.

—— (2010) ' "Intersectional Inviibility": Anknüpfungen und Rückfragen an ein zentrales Konzept der Intersektionalitätsforschung', Manuskript, 1–30.

Lacher, H. (1999) 'The Politics of the Market: Re-reading Karl Polanyi', *Global Society*, 13:3, 313–26.

—— (2003) 'Putting the State in its Place: The Critique of State-Centrism and its Limits', *Review of International Studies*, 29:4, 521–41.

Laffey, M. (2004) 'The Red Herring of Economism: A Reply to Marieke de Goede', *Review of International Studies*, 30:3, 459–68.

Lake, D. (2009) 'TRIPs Across the Atlantic: Theory and Epistemology in IPE', *Review of International Political Economy*, 16:1, 47–57.

Langley, P. (2008) *The Everyday Life of Global Finance: Saving and Borrowing in Anglo-America* (Oxford: Oxford University Press).

Laski, H. (1943) *Reflections on the Revolution of our Time* (London: George Allen and Unwin).

Lawson, G. (2007) 'Historical Sociology in International Relations: Open Society, Research Programme and Vocation', *International Politics*, 44:4, 343–68.

—— and R. Shilliam (2010) 'Sociology and International Relations: Legacies and Prospects', *Cambridge Review of International Affairs*, 23:1, 69–86.

Leander, A. (2009) 'Why We Need Multiple Stories about the Global Political Economy', *Review of International Political Economy*, 16:2, 321–8.

Leventhal, F. (1985) *The Last Dissenter: H.N. Brailsford and his World* (Oxford: Clarendon).

Lind, A. (2009) 'Challenging Intimacy, Struggling for Sexual Rights: Challenging Heteronormativity in the Global Development Industry', *Development*, 52:1, 34–42.

Ling, L.H.M. (2000) 'Global Passions Within Global Interests: Race, Gender, and Culture in Our Postcolonial Order', in R. Palan (ed.), *Global Political Economy: Contemporary Theories* (London and New York: Routledge), 242–55.

Mabee, B. (2007) 'Levels and Agents, States and People: Micro-historical Sociological Analysis and International Relations', *International Politics*, 44:4, 431–49.

Macartney, H. (2009) 'Variegated Neo-liberalism: Transnationally Oriented Fractions of Capital in EU Financial Market Integration', *Review of International Studies*, 35:2, 451–80.

—— (2010) *Variegated Neoliberalism: EU Varieties of Capitalism and International Political Economy* (London: Routledge).

Mackinder, H.J. (1942) *Democratic Ideals and Reality* (New York: Henry Holt).

MacKinnon, C.A. (1989) *Toward a Feminist Theory of the State* (Cambridge: Harvard University Press).

McMichael, P. (1990) 'Incorporating Comparison within a World-historical Perspective: An Alternative Comparative Method', *American Sociological Review*, 55:3, 385–97.

McNamara, K. (2009) 'Of Intellectual Monocultures and the Study of IPE', *Review of International Political Economy*, 16:1, 72–84.

Maisonville, D. (2006) 'Inter-Disciplined? Disciplinary IPE and its "Others" ', *York Centre for International and Security Studies (YCISS) Working*

Paper, No. 38, http://www.yorku.ca/yciss/publications/documents/WP38-Maisonville_000.pdf, accessed June 2010.

Maliniak, D. and M. Tierney (2009) 'The American School of IPE', *Review of International Studies*, 16:1, 6–33.

Marasco, R. (2006) ' "Already the Effect of the Whip": Critical Theory and the Feminine Ideal', *Differences: A Journal of Feminist Cultural Studies*, 17:1, 88–115.

Marcuse, H. (1974) 'Marxism and feminism', *Women's Studies*, 2:3, 279–288.

Marston, S. (2000) 'The Social Construction of Scale', *Progress in Human Geography*, 24:2, 219–42.

Martin, K. (1958) 'H.N. Brailsford', *New Statesman*, 29 March.

Marx, K. (1969) *Marx/Engels Selected Works*, vol. 1 (Moscow, USSR: Progress Publishers), 15.

——— (1973[1857]) *The Grundrisse* (Harmondsworth: Penguin).

——— (1976) *Capital: A Critique of Political Economy. Vol. I* (London: Penguin in Association with New Left Review).

——— (1977) *Selected Writings* (ed. D. McLellan) (Oxford: Oxford University Press).

——— (1979) 'The Eighteenth Brumaire of Louis Bonaparte', in K. Marx and F. Engels (eds), *Collected Works*, vol. 11 (London: Lawrence and Wishart).

Mill, J.S. (1991) *On Liberty and Other Essays* (ed. J. Gray) (Oxford: Oxford University Press).

Mills, C.W. (1956) *The Power Elite* (New York: Oxford University Press).

Mitchell, D. (2001) 'The Devil's Arm: Points of Passage, Networks of Violence and the Political Economy of Landscape', *New Formations*, 43: 44–60.

Mitrany, D. (1943) *A Working Peace System* (London: Royal Institute for International Affairs and Oxford University Press).

——— (1947) 'International Consequences of National Planning', *Yale Review*, 37, 18–31.

Mittelman, J. (1995) 'Rethinking the International Division of Labour in the Context of Globalisation', *Third World Quarterly*, 16:2, 273–95.

Morton, A.D. (2003) 'Historicizing Gramsci: Situating Ideas in and Beyond Their Context', *Review of International Political Economy*, 10:1, 118–46.

——— (2006) 'The Grimly Comic Riddle of Hegemony in IPE: Where is Class Struggle?', *Politics*, 26:1, 62–72.

——— (2007a) *Unravelling Gramsci: Hegemony and Passive Revolution in the Global Political Economy* (London: Pluto).

——— (2007b) 'Disputing the Geopolitics of the States System and Global Capitalism', *Cambridge Review of International Affairs*, 20:4, 599–617.

Moss, S. (2008) 'Does Anyone Know What Went Wrong?', *The Guardian*, 24 March, http://www.guardian.co.uk/business/2008/mar/24/creditcrunch.banking, accessed April 2009.

Muñoz, C.B. (2008) *Transnational Tortillas: Race, Gender, and Shop-Floor Politics in Mexico and the United States* (Ithaca: Cornell University Press).

Murphy, C. (2001) 'Critical Theory and the Democratic Impulse: Understanding a Century-old Tradition', in R. Wyn Jones (ed.), *Critical Theory and World Politics* (Boulder: Lynne Rienner), 61–76.

——— (2002) 'Explaining a Thriving Heterodoxy', in J. Abbott and O. Worth (eds), *Critical Perspectives on International Political Economy* (Basingstoke: Palgrave Macmillan), 178–91.

—— (2009) 'Do the Left-out Matter?', *New Political Economy*, 14:3, 357–65.

—— and D. Nelson (2001) 'International Political Economy: A Tale of Two Heterodoxies', *British Journal of Politics & International Relations*, 3:3, 393–412.

—— and R. Tooze (eds) (1991) *The New International Political Economy* (Boulder: Lynne Rienner).

Newman, S. (2005) *Power and Politics in Poststructuralist Thought: New Theories of the Political* (London and New York: Routledge).

Office for National Statistics (2008) 'Working Lives: Employment Rates Higher for Men', http://www.statistics.gov.uk/CCI/nugget.asp?ID=1654, accessed April 2009–June 2010.

Overbeek, H. (2000) 'Transnational Historical Materialism: Theories of Transnational Class Formation and World Order', in R. Palan (ed.), *Global Political Economy: Contemporary Theories* (London: Routledge), 174–91.

—— (2003) 'Transnational Political Economy and the Politics of European (Un)employment: Introducing the Themes', in H. Overbeek (ed.), *The Political Economy of European Employment: European Integration and the Transnationalization of the (Un)Employment Question* (London: Routledge), 1–10.

—— (2004) 'Transnational Class Formation and Concepts of Control: Towards a Genealogy of the Amsterdam Project in International Political Economy', *Journal of International Relations and Development*, 7:2, 113–41.

—— and K. van der Pijl (1993) 'Restructuring Capital and Restructuring Hegemony: Neo-liberalism and the Unmaking of the Post-war Order', in H. Overbeek (ed.), *Restructuring Hegemony in the Global Political Economy: The Rise of Transnational Neo-liberalism in the 1980s* (London: Routledge), 1–27.

Palan, R. (2000) 'The Constructivist Underpinnings of the New International Political Economy', in R. Palan (ed.), *Global Political Economy: Contemporary Theories* (London: Routledge), 215–28.

—— (2007) 'Transnational Theories of Order and Change: Heterodoxy in International Relations Scholarship', *Review of International Studies*, 33:S1, 47–69.

—— (2009) 'The Proof of the Pudding is in the Eating: IPE in Light of the Crisis of 2007/8', *New Political Economy*, 14:3, 385–94.

Peck, J. and A. Tickell (2002) 'Neoliberalizing Space', *Antipode*, 34:3, 380–404.

Perelman, M. (2000) *The Invention of Capitalism: Classical Political Economy and the Secret History of Primitive Accumulation* (Durham and London: Duke University Press).

—— (2007) 'Primitive Accumulation from Feudalism to Neoliberalism', *Capitalism Nature Socialism*, 18:2, 44–61.

Personnel Today (2006) 'Women in Finance Lag Behind in Pay Stakes', 20 June, http://www.personneltoday.com/articles/2006/06/20/35980/women-in-finance-lag-behind-in-pay-stakes.html, accessed April 2009–June 2010.

Peterson, V.S. (2003) *A Critical Rewriting of Global Political Economy: Integrating Reproductive, Productive and Virtual Economies* (Abingdon: Routledge).

—— (2005) 'How (The Meaning of) Gender Matters in Political Economy', *New Political Economy*, 10:4, 499–521.

—— (2008) ' "New Wars" and Gendered Economies', *Feminist Review*, 88, 7–20.

Pettman, J.J. (1996) *Worlding Women: A Feminist International Politics* (London: Routledge).

Phillips, N. (2005a) 'Whither IPE?', in N. Phillips (ed.), *Globalizing International Political Economy* (Basingstoke: Palgrave Macmillan), 246–69.

—— (ed.) (2005b) *Globalizing International Political Economy* (Basingstoke: Palgrave Macmillan).

—— (2009) 'The Slow Death of Pluralism', *Review of International Political Economy*, 16:1, 85–94.

Polanyi, K. (1944) *The Great Transformation: The Political and Economic Origins of Our Time* (Beacon Hill: Beacon Hill Press).

—— (1968) *Primitive, Archaic and Modern Economies: Essays of Karl Polanyi* (ed. G. Dalton) (New York: Anchor).

Poulantzas, N. (1978) *State, Power, Socialism* (trs. P. Camiller) (London: New Left Books).

Purcell, M. (2003) 'Islands of Practice and the Marston/Brenner debate: Toward a more Synthetic Critical Human Geography', *Progress in Human Geography*, 27:3, 317–32.

Rai, S. and G. Waylen (2008) 'Introduction: Feminist Perspectives on Analysing and Transforming Global Governance', in S. Rai and G. Waylen (eds), *Global Governance: Feminist Perspectives* (Basingstoke: Palgrave Macmillan), 1–18.

Ravenhill, J. (2008) 'In Search of the Missing Middle', *Review of International Political Economy*, 15:1, 18–29.

Riegraf, B. (2010) 'Intersektionen von Ungleicheiten und Differenzen: Kursbestimmung im Nebel zwischen Gesellschaftstheorie und politischem Gestaltungsanspruch', in K. Böllert und N. Oelkers (eds), *Frauenpolitik in Familienhand? Neue Verhältnisse in Konkurrenz, Autonomie oder Kooperation* (Wiesbaden: VS Verlag für Sozialwissenschaft), 39–57.

Robinson, A. (2006) 'Towards an Intellectual Reformation: The Critique of Common Sense and the Forgotten Revolutionary Project of Gramscian Theory', in A. Bieler and A.D. Morton (eds), *Images of Gramsci: Connections and Contentions in Political Theory and International Relations* (London: Routledge), 75–87.

Robinson, F. (1997) 'Feminist IR/IPE Theory: Fulfilling Its Radical Potential?', *Review of International Political Economy*, 4:4, 773–81.

Robinson, W.I. (2004) *A Theory of Global Capitalism* (Baltimore: Johns Hopkins University Press).

—— and J. Harris (2000) 'Towards a Global Ruling Class? Globalization and the Transnational Capitalist Class', *Science and Society*, 64:1, 11–54.

Rosenau, J.N. (1992) 'The Relocation of Authority in a Shrinking World', *Comparative Politics*, 24:3, 253–72.

—— (1995) *Along the Domestic-Foreign Frontier: Exploring Governance in a Turbulent World* (Cambridge: Cambridge University Press).

Rosenberg, J. (2000) *The Follies of Globalisation Theory: Polemical Essays* (London: Verso).

—— (2006) 'Why Is There No International Historical Sociology?', *European Journal of International Relations*, 12:3, 307–40.

Rowbotham, S., L. Segal and H. Wainwright (1979) *Beyond the Fragments: Feminism and the Making of Socialism* (London: Merlin Press).

Rupert, M. (2000) *Ideologies of Globalization: Contending Visions of New World Order* (London: Routledge).

—— (2005) 'Reflections on Some Lessons Learned from a Decade of Globalisation Studies', *New Political Economy*, 10:4, 457–78.

Sassoon, A.S. (2000) *Gramsci and Contemporary Politics: Beyond Pessimism of the Intellect* (London: Routledge).
—— (2006) 'Gramsci and the Secret of Father Brown', in A. Bieler and A.D. Morton (eds), *Images of Gramsci: Connections and Contentions in Political Theory and International Relations* (London: Routledge), 1–11.
Sauer, B. (1997) '"Die Magd der Industriegesellschaft". Anmerkungen zur Geschlechterblindheit von Staats- und Institutionentheorien', in Brigitte Kerchner und Gabriele Wilde (eds), *Staat und Privatheit: Aktuelle Studien zu einem schwierigen Verhältnis* (Opladen: Leske + Budrich), 29–55.
—— (2001) *Die Asche des Souveräns: Staat und Demokratie in der Geschlechterdebatte* (Frankfurt and New York: Campus Verlag).
Schiff, J. (2008) '"Real"? As If! Critical Reflections on State Personhood', *Review of International Studies*, 34:2, 363–77.
Schmidt, B. (1998) *The Political Discourse of Anarchy: A Disciplinary History of International Relations* (Albany: SUNY Press).
Schmidt, C. (1993) *Legalität und Legitimität* (Berlin: Dunker und Humblot).
Schwartz, H. (1994) *States versus Markets: History, Geography, and the Development of the International Political Economy* (Basingstoke: Palgrave Macmillan).
—— (2002) 'Hobson's Voice: American Internationalism, Asian Development and Global Macro-Economic Imbalances', *Journal of Post-Keynesian Economics*, 25:2, 331–51.
Seabrooke, L. (2006) *The Social Sources of Financial Power: Domestic Legitimacy and International Financial Orders* (Ithaca and London: Cornell University Press).
Sharman, J.C. (2009) 'Neither Asia nor America: IPE in Australia', in M. Blyth (ed.), *Routledge Handbook of International Political Economy* (London: Routledge), 216–28.
Shepherd, L.J. (2010) 'Locating Legitimacy: Ethics, Sovereignty and the Politics of Space', *presented at the Oceanic Conference of International Studies*, University of Auckland, 1 July.
Shields, S. (2008) 'How the East Was Won: Transnational Social Forces and the Neoliberalisation of Poland's Communist Transition', *Global Society*, 22:4, 445–68.
—— (2011) *The International Political Economy of Transition: Neoliberal Hegemony and East Central Europe's Transformation* (London: Routledge).
Simon, R. (1991) *Gramsci's Political Thought: An Introduction* (revised and reset edn) (London: Lawrence and Wishart).
Sjoberg, L. (2008) 'The Norm of Tradition: Gender Subordination and Women's Exclusion in International Relations', *Politics and Gender*, 4:2, 173–80.
Smith, N. (1984) *Uneven Development* (Oxford: Blackwell).
Smith, S. (2002) 'The United States and the Discipline of International Relations: Hegemonic Country, Hegemonic Discipline', *International Studies Review*, 4:2, 67–85.
Sparr, P. (1994) 'Feminist Critiques of Structural Adjustment', in P. Sparr (ed.), *Mortgaging Women's Lives: Feminist Critiques of Structural Adjustment* (London: Zed), 13–39.
Spykman, N. (1944) *The Geography of the Peace* (New York: Harcourt Brace).
Steans, J. (1999) 'The Private is Global: Feminist Politics and Global Political Economy', *New Political Economy*, 4:1, 113–28.

——— (2003) 'Engaging from the Margins: Feminist Encounters with the Mainstream of International Relations', *British Journal of Politics & International Relations*, 5:3, 428–54.

——— and D. Tepe (2008) 'Gender in the Theory and Practice of International Political Economy: The Promise and Limitations of Neo-Gramscian Approaches', in A. Ayers (ed.), *Gramsci, Political Economy, and International Relations Theory: Modern Princes and Naked Emperors* (New York: Palgrave Macmillan), 137–52.

Steans, J. and Tepe, D. (2010) 'Social Reproduction in International Political Economy: Theoretical Insights and International, Transnational and Local Sitings', *Review of International Political Economy*, 17:5, 807–815.

Strange, G. (2006) 'The Left Against Europe? A Critical Engagement with New Constitutionalism and Structural Dependency Theory', *Government and Opposition*, 41:2, 197–229.

Strange, S. (1970) 'International Economics and International Relations: A Case of Mutual Neglect', *International Affairs*, 46:2, 304–15.

——— (1987) 'The Persistent Myth of Lost Hegemony', *International Organization*, 41:4, 551–74.

——— (1988a) 'Review of "Power, Production and World Order"', *International Affairs*, 64:2, 269–70.

——— (1988b) *States and Markets* (London: Pinter).

——— (1996) *The Retreat of the State: The Diffusion of Power in the World Economy* (Cambridge: Cambridge University Press).

Swyngedouw, E. (2004) 'Globalisation or "Glocalisation"? Networks, Territories and Rescaling', *Cambridge Review of International Affairs*, 17:1, 25–48.

Sylvest, C. (2009) *British Liberal Internationalism 1880–1930: Making Progress?* (Manchester: Manchester University Press).

Taylor, A. (1957) *The Dissenters: Dissent over Foreign Policy, 1792–1939* (London: Hamish Hamilton).

Taylor, M. (2009) 'Who Works for Globalization? The Challenges and Possibilities of International Labour Studies', *Third World Quarterly*, 30:3, 435–52.

Thompson, E.P. (1977) *Whigs and Hunters: The Origin of the Black Act* (revised edn) (London: Penguin).

——— (1995) *The Poverty of Theory: Or an Orrery of Errors* (new edn) (London: Merlin Press).

Tickner, A.J. (1997) 'You Just Don't Understand: Troubled Engagements Between Feminists and IR Theorists', *International Studies Quarterly*, 41:4, 611–32.

True, J. (2003) 'Mainstreaming Gender in Global Public Policy', *International Feminist Journal of Politics*, 5:3, 368–96.

——— (2008) 'Global Accountability and Transnational Networks: The Women Leaders' Network and Asia Pacific Economic Cooperation', *Pacific Review*, 21:1, 1–26.

Underhill, G.R.D. (2003) 'States, Markets and Governance for Emerging Market Economies: Private Interests, the Public Good and the Legitimacy of the Development Process', *International Affairs*, 79:4, 755–81.

——— (2009) 'Political Economy, the "US School", and the Manifest Destiny of Everyone Else', *New Political Economy*, 14:3, 347–56.

Vernon, R. (1971) *Sovereignty at Bay: The Multinational Spread of U.S. Enterprises* (New York: Basic Books).

Vico, G. (1744/1970) *The New Science of Giambattista Vico* (trs. T.G. Bergin and M.H. Fisch) (Ithaca: Cornell University Press).

Watson, M. (2005) *Foundations of International Political Economy* (Basingstoke: Palgrave Macmillan).

Waylen, G. (1997) 'Gender, Feminism and Political Economy', *New Political Economy*, 2:2, 205–20.

—— (2006) 'You Still Just Don't Understand: Why Troubled Engagements Continue Between Feminists and (Critical) IPE', *Review of International Studies*, 32:1, 145–64.

Weaver, C. (2009) 'IPE's Split Brain', *New Political Economy*, 14:3, 337–46.

Weber, C. (1994) 'Good Girls, Little Girls, Bad Girls: Male Paranoia in Robert Keohane's Critique of Feminist International Relations', *Millennium*, 23:2, 337–49.

—— (2008) 'Popular Visual Language as Global Communication: The Remediation of United Airlines Flight 93', *Review of International Studies*, 34:S1, 137–53.

Weiss, L. and J.M. Hobson (1995) *States and Economic Development: A Comparative Historical Analysis* (Cambridge: Polity).

Weldes, J. (2003) *To Seek Out New Worlds: Science Fiction and World Politics* (Basingstoke: Palgrave Macmillan).

Wendt, A. (2004) 'The State as Person in International Theory', *Review of International Studies*, 30:2, 289–316.

Whitworth, S. (1989) 'Gender in the Inter-Paradigm Debate', *Millennium*, 18:2, 265–72.

—— (1994) *Feminism and International Relations: Towards a Political-Economy of Gender in Interstate and Non-Governmental Institutions* (Basingstoke: Palgrave Macmillan).

Wight, C. (2004) 'State Agency: Social Action without Human Activity?', *Review of International Studies*, 30:2, 269–80.

Wilkinson, R. (2004) 'Crisis in Cancun', *Global Governance*, 10:2, 149–55.

Williams, A. (2007) *Failed Imagination? The Anglo-American New World Order from Wilson to Bush* (2nd ed.) (Manchester: Manchester University Press).

Wilson, J. (2011) 'Colonising Space: The New Economic Geography in Theory and Practice', *New Political Economy*, forthcoming.

Winker, G. (2007) 'Traditionelle Geschlechterordnung unter neoliberalem Druck: Veränderte Verwertungs- und Reproduktionsbedingungen der Arbeitskraft', in Melanie Groß and Gabriele Winker (eds), *Queer-Feministische Kritiken neoliberaler Verhältnisse* (Münster: UNRAST-Verlag), 15–51.

Woehl, S. (2008) 'Global Governance as Neo-liberal Governmentality: Gender Mainstreaming in the European Employment Strategy', in S. Rai and G. Waylen (eds), *Global Governance: Feminist Perspectives* (Basingstoke: Palgrave Macmillan), 64–83.

Woods, N. (2008) 'International Political Economy in an Age of Globalization', in J. Baylis, S. Smith and P. Owens (eds), *The Globalization of World Politics: An Introduction to International Relations* (4th ed.) (Oxford: Oxford University Press), 242–61.

Woolf, L. (1928) *Imperialism and Civilization* (London: Hogarth).

World Bank (2003) 'Gender and Development', World Bank Operational Manual, BP 4.20, March, http://web.worldbank.org/WBSITE/EXTERNAL/PROJECTS/EXTPOLICIES/EXTOPMANUAL/0„contentMDK:20140815~menuPK:

64701637~pagePK:64709096~piPK:64709108~theSitePK:502184,00.html, accessed July 2010.

—— (2006) *Gender Equality as Smart Economics: A World Bank Group Gender Action Plan (Fiscal Years 2007–10)* (Washington: World Bank).

Worth, O. (2002) 'The Janus-like Character of Counter-Hegemony: Progressive and Nationalist Responses to Globalisation', *Global Society*, 16:3, 297–315.

Wright, M.W. (2006) *Disposable Women and other Myths of Global Capitalism* (New York and London: Routledge).

Wyn Jones, R. (2001) 'Introduction: Locating Critical International Relations Theory', in R. Wyn Jones (ed.), *Critical Theory and World Politics* (Boulder: Lynne Rienner), 1–19.

Young, B. (2003) 'Financial Crises and Social Reproduction: Asia, Argentina and Brazil', in I. Bakker and S. Gill (eds), *Power, Production and Social Reproduction* (Basingstoke: Palgrave Macmillan), 103–123.

Youngs, G. (2004) 'Feminist International Relations: A Contradiction in Terms? Or: Why Women and Gender are Essential to Understanding the World "We" Live In', *International Affairs*, 80:1, 75–87.

Zalewski, M. (2007) 'Do We Understand Each Other Yet? Troubling Feminist Encounters With(in) International Relations', *British Journal of Politics & International Relations*, 9:2, 302–12.

Index